love & logic
solutions
for kids with
special
needs

love & logic solutions for kids with special needs

David Funk

The Love and Logic
PRESS Inc.

The Love and Logic Press, Inc.
2207 Jackson Street, Golden, CO 804012300
www.loveandlogic.com

Library of Congress Cataloging-in-Publication Data
Funk, David, 1946-
  Love and logic solutions for kids with special needs / by Dave Funk.--
1st ed.
  p. cm.
Includes index.
ISBN 1-930429-35-5
1. Special education--United States. 2. Learning disabled
children--Education--United States. 3. Teacher-student
relationships--United States. I. Title.
  LC3981 .F89 2002
  371.9--dc21
  2002014473

Project Coordinator: Carol Thomas
Editing by Jason Cook, Denver, CO
Cover design by Michael Snell, Shade of the Cottonwood, Topeka, KS
Interior design by Michael Snell, Shade of the Cottonwood, Topeka, KS

Author

DAVE FUNK has been an educator since 1968 and has taught in both regular and special education classrooms. He began his career as a "core" (reading, English and social studies) teacher at Winston Park School in Palatine, Illinois. He was employed by the New Berlin (Wisconsin) Public Schools the next year to teach a class of students with academic and behavioral problems. Dave eventually served as a special education teacher for the next seventeen years. Following his tenure as a classroom teacher, Dave has worked as a diagnostic teacher and program support teacher. Dave has also been involved in university-level course instruction and administration. Dave is also a frequent presenter for parenting programs, teacher in-service sessions and conference keynote engagements. Dave has also developed and taught graduate courses through a number of colleges and universities on the topics of classroom management, effective teaching, and special education issues.

Dave received his bachelor's degree from Trinity College, Deerfield, Illinois and his master's degree in special education from the university of Wisconsin. As a result of his work with the Love and Logic Institute Dave has concentrated on applying the principles of Love and Logic to student performance in both general and special education. He is a co-author of the text *Teaching with Love and Logic* (1995), a comprehensive application of the Love and Logic philosophy to the classroom.

Dave and his wife, Diane, have been married since 1967 and have two adult children (Aleshia and Jaben) and a grandson (Edrik). In addition, Dave and Diane were foster parents to dozens of pre-adoptive infants for seventeen years.

This book is dedicated to the people who make me complete:
Diane (my beloved wife)
Edrik (our grandson)
Aleshia and Dave (our daughter and son-in-law)
Jaben and Jen (our son and daughter-in-law)

Contents

Contents

Preface

ALTHOUGH TEACHERS AND ADMINISTRATORS of special education are aware of at least the general legal mandates of their profession, their more immediate task is the instruction of children. In this respect, the goal of this book is to equip those working with special needs kids with professional information that is both legally and educationally sound. I believe that the principles of Love and Logic can be applied to accomplish this end.

This book is not intended to summarize research. As much as I respect research, I have also seen it misapplied and abused. On the other hand, I also realize that isolated examples can distort the overall reality. Characteristically, those involved with Love and Logic are storytellers.

There are dozens of stories in this book and they are told to clarify. Although some names have been changed, all of the stories are real. When dealing with kids, the hypothetical just won't work. Without the context of actual situations, it is so easy to lose the concept, and when the concept is lost, it is virtually impossible to apply the learning in other situations. Too, I readily admit, I need a story before any lesson is "locked in" for me, and I presume there are lots of other people who learn this way as well.

The following pages describe what is and what has been. There are also some descriptions of what I wish could be. And, all in all, my great hope is that the information in this book will provide some tools and insight for those involved with special needs students.

PART 1

Setting the Foundation

CHAPTER 1

Starting with Special Education

Early Experiences in Special Education

For good or ill, I have been involved with special education since even before formal legislation mandated services for disabled students. This has given me a perspective that is generally available only to us older folk. I have seen the benefits, confusions, and abuses of a system that has become extremely complicated.

I was a "regular" education teacher (which I suppose is better than being an "irregular" teacher) the first year I taught. My contract indicated I would teach reading, English, and social studies to two groups of eighth-graders. Because this was my first year, I really had no other experiences as a basis for comparison. I just presumed my job was to teach the kids I had been assigned. I found out later that the practice of the school was to take difficult seventh-grade students and assign them to the new teacher. I have taught disowned kids right from the beginning.

That year I developed a friendship with a teacher who had a class in the vast outreaches of the building—where, evidently, he and his kids could do less harm. He had nine boys and no one much paid any attention to what went on in his room. There was no name for this class. It was just "Harry's room," but there was a fascination for me. It was not a program, there were no fancy names or labels, but it was obvious that these kids did not fit into the system. In addition it pretty much seemed that they rejected educational "stuff" that didn't relate to their world outside of school.

I spent much of my available time in that class. As I look back, I think part of the draw for me was that Harry only taught things that had some practical significance in the real world. Too, he had a special relationship with these kids. There was a bond. I remember feeling somewhat cheated that I was required to teach topics like the difference between transitive and intransitive verbs and other such lessons that I hardly remember using in my adult life.

The following year I accepted a position in another district. I was assigned to a class composed of thirty-five seventh- and eighth-grade students. I was still fairly new to the teaching profession, but soon realized I was the only one in that classroom above voting age. But then the ratio was one adult to every classroom—no matter how many or what kind of kids. Furthermore, I had all of the students all day long all by myself.

The concept of "support staff" had not yet evolved. From the time the kids got off the bus to the time they got back on, they were with me. When I had to use the restroom, I took all of the boys with me—it was just part of the daily ritual. Since there were only four girls in the class, this procedure worked out fairly well.

We were housed in a not overly large room and I was responsible for everything—all curriculum, "specials," and anything else that was assigned. I learned how to do origami that year so we could have "art." Thank goodness, the middle school no longer had recess. Getting us all back from lunch was hard enough!

Although the terms did not exist then, I can look back and identify students in that class who had learning, cognitive, emotional, and health problems. One kid was even put into this room because his writing arm had been amputated. This was before the advent of any special education law, so there were no individual education plans (IEPs), no disability labels, no specialized training. The conventional wisdom of the day was to put all of the kids with learning and behavior problems together—segregate them from the "normal" kids so they could receive "special" help. Ostensibly, the reason was that instruction could be tailored for their needs. As I look back, it was really an immersion class for dysfunction.

A Temporary Break and Then Back to the Classroom

I was responsible for this class until I got drafted. Our country was well involved with the Vietnam conflict and my not-yet-extensive teaching experiences had prepared me well for a potential military experience. About the time I returned, the district was developing another program. Since there was still no formal federal or state legislation, the rules and parameters for setting up such classes were far less stringent than they would eventually become.

This third class involved twenty-three boys and was housed in a brand new building. So new, in fact, that construction wasn't finished. Bare light bulbs on precarious wires graced the halls and classrooms. The concrete had not yet been poured in some of the halls, so we all did a balancing act on boards to get from class to class.

And furniture—evidently not a necessity for my classroom. I eventually obtained a fold-down cafeteria table, and that was to suffice for the kids. As for myself, I found two large cardboard boxes and a door. Wallah! I had a teaching station. (Eventually, the carpenters repossessed the door and I made do with a piece of plywood with cement remnants on only one side.)

The criterion for "qualifying" for this particular class was unique. The kids had to have been permanently kicked out of two other classes to be eligible for mine. This was not a complicated time and the enrollment process was quick. In fact, getting into my class was essentially a schedule change done, by hand, on an index card. The whole procedure usually took less than ten minutes. No complicated evaluation procedures, no reports, no meetings.

The First Real Special Education Program

The following year I was assigned to teach a new program. I recall when the school psychologist approached me and asked if I would be willing to teach a new "SLD" class that was being developed. My response: "Yeah, that would be great! What does 'SLD' mean?"

I was to find out that the term meant "specific learning disabilities," but that didn't make a whole lot more sense to me. My degree was in English, with a minor in history and religion. I had no formal instruction in dealing with special needs kids and wasn't aware of the terminology, let alone the pending advent and expansion of special education that was coming. Although there was a position, a classroom, and a "program," there was nothing else. No curriculum, no materials, no equipment. But what the heck, I thought that was the way new programs were supposed to be—I knew nothing different from past experiences.

I was, however, told I would have the first two weeks of school to get the "program" up and running. What a luxury—two weeks to evaluate the kids, find materials (not buy, for there was no budget), and locate a place for the class, since no room had been assigned! That year I learned about evaluation, I learned how to adapt materials, and I even learned how to homestead.

To evaluate the students I made up my own tests (not knowing that there were some published tests available—but there was no money to buy them anyway). I learned how to beg, borrow, and glean. I asked other departments if I could have any money they had left (a few dollars here, a few dollars there eventually added up). I even asked for donations from other staff. I recall wanting a new board game that I thought could be used to help kids learn some reading and math skills. The deal was that donors would have their name written on the box as a major contributor. I solicited money from guidance counselors, teachers, the principal, and the special education director. I would have probably asked the superintendent, but I had enough money by then. Truly, necessity is the mother of invention!

My introduction to homesteading came about because no room had been assigned for my class. I was aware of a "conference room" that was hardly ever used. Eventually, I did come to possess a real desk, and early one morning I pushed it into the room, put a sign on the door that said "Resource Room," and smiled at everyone who looked in. To permanently secure my homestead, I bolted homemade study carrels to the wall (I still remember the principal at the door shaking his head as I drilled holes in the cement block walls). The room was small (twelve feet by fifteen feet) and sometimes I had up to nine kids at a time, but it was ours and I stayed there for fifteen years.

Benefits of My Early Experience

I had the unique and now rare situation of teaching special needs kids before having any formal training in that field. This was a great benefit to me when I finally started my graduate work to become "properly certified."

Because I had already been involved with special needs kids for a while, it was a whole lot easier to discern what would work and what would not work. In most cases the professors had limited or no experience "in the trenches" and, as many other teachers have concluded, theory and book knowledge about special needs kids is hardly sufficient preparation.

Special education was pretty primitive back then. However, I actually appreciate having started out with virtually no equipment or materials. Although I certainly appreciate the value of sophisticated technology and modern curriculum, I fear that if I'd had these resources first, I would have come to depend on them. I fear that if I'd had that dependence, I would have believed it necessary to have these things to be an effective teacher. I fear I would not have realized that teaching is more than simply disseminating information and doing research. I fear I would not have learned that the focus of teaching is kids, not curriculum. I fear I would have missed the joy of teaching.

I have been able to talk with others who started their special education careers in similar circumstances. Many taught reading, writing, and arithmetic with a curriculum that was real life. We used newspapers and job application forms from the fast food places. We analyzed the sale ads to determine if the advertised buys were really a good deal. We even had "transition services" that involved figuring out how well a person could live on minimum wage—a great motivator for finding out what was needed to get a good job.

We even taught content. I recall talking with a teacher who had taken a job in an inner-city school. She was required to teach science—with no books, no labs, no equipment. She was at her wits' end and said so to her father. He was a plumber and asked one simple question: "Does your school have flush toilets?" "Of course we do," was this young teacher's reply. "Then you have enough to keep you and your kids busy for a while," her father concluded.

And she did. She and her class studied hydraulics, leverage, gravity, and bacterial decomposition. She could even throw in some sociological issues for good measure. Necessity can force us to think "outside the box," and in today's special education climate, that is almost a criterion for survival.

The Coming of Law

In 1973 the state of Wisconsin, where I was teaching, passed special education legislation. Federal law followed two years later, in 1975. I had been teaching "special education" for a few years by this time in a locally funded program. At that time, there was no requirement to have any teaching credentials specific to special education. Because of changing funding criteria and state law, however, I had to make a major professional decision. If I were to stay in the field, I would need to be certified in special education. Eight years later I had a master's degree in special education. (And yes, it took me eight years! I still have the record in the special education department at that university for taking the longest time to complete a degree.) Three years of that time was spent writing a fascinating thesis on "errorless learning" (which I make myself review at least once every five years).

Although I was ostensibly a teacher of the learning disabled, I don't recall the students being much different than those I had the first three years I taught. Learning, behavioral, emotional, and social problems were consistent characteristics of the students assigned to me from the time I started teaching. Since there were fewer categories of handicapping conditions then, "learning disabilities" had a broad definition and basically included any student who exhibited performance or behavior problems in the classroom. Academic, emotional, and behavioral problems were all attributed to having a learning disability (an "acceptable" disability of the day). I still basically had the disowned kids.

Nagging Doubts

I worked hard and, ironically, even received a good-teaching award, which I still have on my office wall as a reminder. But in spite of all of my training and experiences, there were always some nagging doubts. Could I have learned more? Could I be more effective with my kids? Could I be a better teacher? These thoughts were no different than those of many teachers throughout history. However, with the new laws requiring additional accountability, I was even more conscious about my effectiveness.

Behavior was an especially disconcerting issue for me. I held strongly to the belief that good teachers had control of the kids in their classes, ineffective teachers didn't. My major concern was that the primary techniques I had available to me at the time involved either overpowering students through force or manipulating them with punishments and rewards (or positive and negative reinforcement, if you will). Although I had refined these two aspects for classroom management, my career "culminated" when I hit a couple of kids. In no way am I proud of those actions, and I envy anyone who has always done the right thing in stressful circumstances.

Those were some of the most painful times in my career, and the pain is still there after decades of time. However, that pain, because it resided inside, compelled me to find a better way. This quest eventually lead me to someone I had not previously heard of, Jim Fay, and to the concepts of Love and Logic.

My Introduction to Love and Logic

My initial contact with Love and Logic came when I was a teacher of learning-disabled middle school students. When I mention teaching middle school kids, many will look at me with pity or disgust, as though asking whether I couldn't do something better with my life. Although I taught for eighteen years, I went through some pretty rough spots during the first third of my classroom teaching experience. But what I did learn is that whatever works for middle school kids will probably work for just about anyone.

Although I eventually received some fairly extensive training in many aspects of special education (e.g., diagnosis), I received precious little formal instruction in dealing with the manifestations that arise from emotional and learning problems. I soon discovered that just getting a bunch of degrees doesn't always qualify a person to be effective. In a previous book *(Teaching with Love and Logic)* several incidents were mentioned of which I remain unproud. I sometimes think I should look up all the students I had for the first five years of my career and write letters of apology.

In this quest for effective classroom management strategies, I stumbled upon Love and Logic, as fate would have it, pretty much by accident. A staff development group I was associated with had invited Dr. Foster Cline to speak. After his talk, a number of us inquired about purchasing materials. Since Dr. Cline's materials from the previous day's meeting had sold out, he suggested we call his partner, Jim Fay. That was to be my initial contact with a man who would become my mentor and keep me in education.

Although an unwilling convert at first, I eventually realized that the principles of Love and Logic applicable to behavior management were also applicable to the teaching of content and skill areas. Although Love and Logic is not specifically a math or reading strategy per se, it does address the affective and motivational aspects of student performance that are of critical concern with special needs students.

My application of Love and Logic has come from within a context of special education. In the early years, the differentiation we now have as part of the law had not yet been mandated. Although I was technically a teacher of the learning disabled, just about any kid with learning, performance, or behavioral problems was fair game to become a candidate for my classroom. In addition, the sophisticated curricula, strategies, equipment, and technology that are fairly common today were not available. What I recognized, early on, was the importance of behavior. If kids weren't "behaving," there was a high likelihood they weren't learning. This is not a novel conclusion, but I thought it was a brilliant insight at the time!

Currently, Section 504 and the Individuals with Disabilities Education Act (IDEA) are the premier federal laws addressing the education of disabled students. They provide substantial protections to qualified students and in the process impose requirements on school-based teams that are sometimes difficult to resolve. In this respect, I believe Love and Logic provides a foundation for working with special needs students that is both legally and educationally sound.

Why Another Book on Special Education?

Earlier in this chapter I recounted my initial experiences with students who had special needs. Although I had an unique opportunity to teach these kids for a number of years before obtaining any formal college training in special education, an opportunity that gave me some discernment that otherwise might not have been possible, I realize that my training, in total, did not adequately prepare me to be as effective as I could have been with special needs students.

I have also had the privilege of being part of the process of special education from before its legislative beginning. I began teaching before IEPs, and because of that historical perspective I have been provided with insights that I feel obligated to pass on. At this point in my life, I have been involved with special education longer than many of my colleagues have been alive, but essential problems remain: How do we effectively work with special needs students within a legal framework that, frankly, is often confusing even to lawyers?

Beginning in the mid-1970s and accelerating ever since, teachers and parents of special needs students have been inundated with legal ramifications and esoteric instructional strategies that have altered the educational scene. Schools are often required to follow legal dictates that are confusing and even seem to be counterproductive to the long-term best interest of the student. Litigation is rampant and it can well be said there are two kinds of special education staff: those who have been involved in litigation and those who will be.

The More Things Change, the More They Stay the Same

The old problems are still so new. The year this book was started, I was in a meeting that included a first-year teacher. As I and my team members were developing a behavior plan for three of her students, the teacher removed herself from the group. I thought she had to use the restroom or make a call. However, a few minutes later, another member of the team left and then came back to the meeting together with the teacher. She was sobbing. Through her tears she said, "It's overwhelming, I don't know what to do, they never taught me about this stuff." This teacher is so good, so effective with her kids, a jewel in the crown of education. She is a wonderful teacher, and she felt terribly inadequate.

The goal of this book is to provide teachers and parents with some guidance and tools for dealing with special needs students and special education. It is intended to share an experiential base and encourage the resiliency that resides in all good teachers. It is intended to convey the hope given to me so many years ago.

CHAPTER 2

The Love and Logic Perspective

Recognizing a Better Way

Before going further, it would seem prudent to review the foundational ideas of Love and Logic. Although this book is oriented to special needs students and considers their unique characteristics, the fundamentals of Love and Logic have wide-ranging applicability. Just as there is only about a 5 percent genetic variation between apes and humans, all people are more alike than they are different. Therefore, discussion of special needs students is not isolated from consideration of kids (or other people, for that matter) in general.

My goal from the time I started teaching was to have a controlled classroom. And, as you might imagine, my great desire was to have the kids want that very same objective! I remember years ago thinking I was spending more time on the kids' behavior than I was on their academic learning. And the honest truth is that I probably was. However, it all seemed justified. After all, I had seen out-of-control classrooms (and families) where no achievement was taking place, and I didn't want to be known as being ineffective.

When I was first exposed to Love and Logic, my nagging fear that the strategies I had previously used had some fundamental flaws was confirmed. For instance, in the days when I was using pure behavior modification, I lived in fear the kids would realize what I was doing. Operant conditioning techniques are surprisingly effective—until the kids realize what you are doing! Then they feel manipulated and can sabotage the adult's best efforts.

What I eventually came to accept was that the strategies I was using were actually running in contrast to what I wanted—a classroom of disciplined kids. That was difficult to admit because I was so sincere in my efforts and working so hard. That was a tough time and I seriously considered getting out of education.

What I had thought was that to have a controlled classroom, I had to have control of the kids. The only way I knew to do this was to take all of the power away from them so they would have none to use on me. I had learned that concept growing up in rural Iowa. That's the way a lot kids were raised back then. Later in my professional training, there was nothing presented to oppose that idea. Eventually I realized that, although my goal was a worthy one (i.e., to have an orderly class), the approach I was using was counterproductive. In the very act of trying to control kids, I was setting them up for control battles. And control battles I had. Some of these incidents are related in *Teaching with Love and Logic,* and there were many more not recorded.

The ironic thing was that I knew full well, even then, that the strategies I was using on the kids would never work on me. I knew they would never work on my spouse, either. In fact, I can't think of any adult they would have worked on! Why I thought they would work on kids, I haven't quite sorted out yet.

Eventually, the clouds parted. Perhaps it was in a dream, perhaps the voice of God, or maybe just the relentless persuasion of Love and Logic: I was convinced that instead of controlling kids, I really needed to obtain their cooperation. What a revelation! A controlled classroom is attained when all members in that classroom make a decision that they want to behave! A nice thought, but there are lots of variables within our educational and societal systems that restrict this from happening naturally. Only the naive would think it an easy task.

The fact that cooperation often does not happen without substantial effort is an unfortunate circumstance for teachers and parents, but it is a circumstance we must recognize nevertheless. Too often in the heat of battle, when we adults should be doing our very best thinking, we react and emote instead. The thinking parts of our brain cramp up. We have all done this and we well may again. The point is, if we are to be constructive with kids, we need to at least recognize the effects that both the verbal and the nonverbal aspects of communication have on people.

The Importance of Interaction Dynamics

I wish I had learned the importance of interaction dynamics earlier in my life. My family, students, and coworkers would have benefited immeasurably. The whole concept is not really that novel and certainly not a new theory. It is all fairly simple. Interaction dynamics boils down to basically three factors: what we say, how we say it, and when we say it.

Virtually all of us know this. We know from early on that there is a need to "talk real nice" to those who have something we want. We also pretty much know how it feels when we have been manipulated or betrayed by someone's talk. We know how to be sincere. The trick is to use all of these skills with our kids in situations when they most need it— when they are preparing for life in the adult world.

A primary goal of Love and Logic is to understand the effects of the implied messages that result when humans communicate. How we talk with kids significantly influences how they behave. How the adults in their lives interact with them is a determining factor in a number of outcomes, including to what degree a sense of responsibility is internalized.

There is another fundamental concern when discussing interaction dynamics. Too often when dealing with kids, the adults unilaterally identify the problem, decide what consequences will accrue, and implement the interventions—all while the student sits on the sidelines and observes. This process gives kids far too much time to strategize for the next showdown. The result: the adults devise a plan that is easy to implement, involves consequences that would be effective at least for the adults, but proves eventually not to work.

Another issue of concern is that educators often don't differentiate between interactions that have short-term effectiveness and those with long-term usefulness. There are innumerable techniques that will "stop kids in their tracks" and these strategies do have a place in behavior management. However, these techniques are not effective in the long run, and overuse may even make the behavior worse. Kids can quickly become desensitized to short-term techniques. If overemployed, these strategies eventually just become annoying and open to sabotage. This observation isn't just limited to adult/kid interaction. It applies generally to all age levels.

How we interact with each other exerts reciprocal influences. This recognition is especially important when adults are working with kids, because adults have often forgotten how kids think.

Lessons from a Slot Machine

An observation of behavior in one context can often give us clues for another. Recently a casino in our area opened a brand new facility. As part of the newspaper coverage of that event, a customer was interviewed. The article indicated that she was far from wealthy, but that she would periodically "drop" a thousand dollars into the slot machines. She and her husband said they had used up their savings and were now "investing" their retirement money in the hope they would strike it big and spend the rest of their years in comfort.

Humans have lots of unique characteristics, but what about when they put money into a machine and get nothing out? I can think of only two situations where this happens on a regular basis: slot machines and broken vending machines. If you are a people watcher, you will notice that there are some significant differences in behavior.

People commonly put quarters into slot machines over huge lengths of time. In the example above, the woman said she had been working the machine for over fourteen hours and only reluctantly took bathroom breaks. Her husband even fed her and held her drink cup so she could continue gambling uninterrupted. As with so many maladaptive behaviors, addiction is a good gone bad. For some, simply having fun is no longer an issue. They have locked into artificial hope. What a sad scenario.

What a different behavior when people put money into a broken vending machine. Here is a typical script:

1. The person puts money in and pushes the selection button.
2. The person waits in anticipation, but nothing comes out. So far, the behavior is the same as with a slot machine.
3. There may be a physical response (e.g., pushing the button a few times) or some verbal comment. Again, so far, the behavior is the same as with a slot machine.
4. At this point, many people would walk away. Some will repeat

step 1. Predictably, if step 2 is repeated, step 3 will be also, although perhaps a bit more intensely.

5. The behavior—putting money into the machine and getting nothing out—ends.

I know of no one who would repeat the process a third time, let alone for fourteen hours. What is the basic difference? Essentially it comes down to just two factors: consistency and expectation. The broken vending machine is consistent, the slot machine is not. There is no further expectancy from the broken vending machine (no matter how much money is put in, nothing will come out), while there is a heightened expectancy that the slot machine will pay out.

Could there be a lesson in this story for teachers and parents when interacting with kids? What if, for instance, we were to substitute putting money into a machine with a kid's whining?

Kids, don't you love them? Any of them worth their salt are always testing limits. They are always putting their little quarters into the machine (usually an adult) and waiting with great anticipation to see what will happen. It is a way they can learn how the world works.

Have you ever seen a kid with a slot-machine parent or teacher? Kids will keep putting in their "money" (i.e., whining) for hours, won't they? Hours in the store, hours in the car, hours in the classroom. They have a stamina that would make a marathon runner blush with envy. And every time they put in their "money," they get a different response (just like the changing sequence of a slot machine). Sometimes the adults are firm (two roses and a lemon), other times they blow up (one rose and two lemons), other times they capitulate (three roses—a win for the kid).

And why do kids keep working slot-machine adults? Because of the expectation that there might just be a payoff eventually. When they believe there is a chance they will hit the jackpot, the behavior is maintained. This sense of anticipation keeps both the gambler and the whining kid going. You will never see a slot machine that doesn't give a sense of hope. You put in your money, pull the lever, and watch the pictures spin. The faster the better. And then, the "almost." "Almost" got it this time, I'll try again. "Almost" is what hooks. "Almost" is what keeps the behavior going.

Watch slot-machine adults. There is always the "almost." Some time ago I was working with some teachers and a parent to develop a behavior intervention plan for one of our more recalcitrant students. The parent was a wonderful example of slot-machining. Even when the kid's behavior was appropriate, his mom accused him of doing something wrong. When there was a correction from the parent for this "unwrong," the kid was literally enticed into the action. I couldn't help but make the analogy to the glitzy slot machine that beckons the gambler.

Soon the complaints from the parent accelerated, the kid became more excited, and he engaged in the whining syndrome. He started whining about the way he was treated, whining about wanting some new gadget, then whining about his general lot in life. The pace increased and eventually the kid and his mom were hooked into the cycle. This was pure entertainment for the kid. But sadly enough, it was an empty entertainment—nothing tangible, nothing real, nothing to build on. It was a substitution because the fundamental building blocks for relationship were being replaced by anger, retaliation, baiting, and revenge.

During that episode, the parent stated the mantra of the slot-machine adult: "I have tried everything, and nothing works." What this too often means is that the adult hasn't tried anything long enough to do any real good.

On the other hand, I have seen examples of parents who react to kids' whining like a broken vending machine. In an airport recently I was waiting for a late flight. Although I was a bit irritated because I really just wanted to get home, I realize now I would have missed a valuable opportunity to learn a bit more about adult/child relations if the plane had been on time.

A kid was standing next to his parent, who was in line to pay for some items at a gift shop. The kid was eyeball to eyeball with the candy section. Just like with a slot machine, the kid put in her quarter. "I want some candy," she said. "I'll bet you do, and you had some just a while ago," was the response of the parent. (What I noticed is that the parent stated this to the kid in the same tone of voice he used when he talked to the clerk as he made his purchase.) Since the kid evidently had at least two quarters, she decided to try again. "But I want some now," was her mournful plea. "I'll bet you do, and you had some just a while ago," was

. . . . .

the response. At that point, she stamped her foot once. And then, silence. No more whining, no more begging. Father and daughter walked to the waiting area with no further incident.

Figuratively, the kid just walked away—like from a broken vending machine—because she quickly realized that any additional effort on her part would not pay off. She was probably four years old. What a valuable lesson her dad had taught her so early in her life.

The lesson is in consistency. Every time money is put into a slot machine, a different set of pictures comes up. With a broken vending machine the response is always the same. Another question I wondered: How long would it take to know whether a slot machine is working or not? Frankly, the player may never know if the thing is broken. How do we know if the vending machine is working right? When we put in our money, push the button, and something comes out. How long does it take us to know something is amiss? Once, maybe twice, but not really that long. The feedback comes quickly. There is little wasted time.

Given an option, what would seem best for working with whining kids? Nobody has a maladaptive addiction to broken vending machines. There are no "Broken Vending Machine Anonymous" groups. Likewise, few kids continually bug a parent or teacher who demonstrates that inappropriate behavior doesn't pay off.

I remember a phrase Dr. Foster Cline mentioned when I first was involved with Love and Logic: "It takes the right technique the right amount of time." Another phrase from Jim Fay is also applicable: "There is nothing wrong with a [whining] child that a little reasoning won't make worse." The jobs of parenting and teaching are already hard enough. We don't need to create unneeded stress.

We all make choices in life. We choose where we sit in church, how fast we drive, and how we interact with our kids.

Societal Norms

The society we are in has a particular set of norms that often make teaching and parenting frustrating tasks. Frequently, these variables actually fight against the very values society ostensibly seeks to support. Although these societal variables are numerous, a few are of special significance where kids are involved:

1. **Learning should be entertaining.** Many kids, after years of watching children's television programming and playing electronic games, equate learning with amusement. The honest fact is that learning is a struggle; however, many kids have the idea, obtained from their environment, that learning should be entertaining. When learning becomes difficult (and it inevitably will), many kids simply drop out or exhibit other performance problems. The sad result is that teachers and parents often get enmeshed in this philosophy and burn themselves out trying to maintain kids' involvement by diverting their attention and trying to get them happy.

   I heard an extreme example of this in a school district that was facing budget reductions. A number of programs had to be cut. The administrator had decided that the students would determine which programs would be maintained as part of the curriculum. All of the affected teachers gave a dog-and-pony show about why their programs should be kept and others cut instead. The students then voted on what to keep and what to discard. The person telling this story said that those most in fear of losing their jobs emphasized how much fun and how little work there would be. What a sad and sick scenario.

2. **Externalized locus of control.** There is an insidious aspect of influences external to ourselves. First, it appears that, for whatever reason, there is a real aspect of our personhood that can only be validated by something or someone outside of ourselves. There are magic people in our lives whose acceptance and approval are vital to the acceptance of ourselves. Achievement is also an external aspect that contributes to our authentication. Because this phenomenon is so important to our personhood, it is relatively easy to create a distortion. Just as an external factor can validate, we can also use it to avoid being accountable for our own actions.

   Often, an externalized locus of control is simply a sophisticated way of saying, "It's not my fault." Societal norms are more and more oriented to finding reasons to reduce personal responsibility. Many social institutions, albeit inadvertently, perpetuate this concept. As a result, dealing with students who truly feel they are not responsible for their own behavior takes some very specific inter-action on the part of the adult.

The legal and helping professions in our culture have accelerated this feeling of entitlement. Just think of how our economic structure would come crashing down if everyone took responsibility for their own behavior. So, in one way, an externalized locus of control is really a full-employment provision for lots of lawyers, social workers, teachers, and others who depend on doing what others are not doing for themselves.

3. **I see, I want, I believe I deserve.** This is a sequence that is all too prevalent in our society. The advertisement, popular some time ago, that indicated we "deserve a break today" is simply represen-tative of what retailers hope we begin to believe. If we believe we deserve something, we will be discontent until we get it. However, by definition, we can never appreciate what we believe we deserve, and so a cycle begins of always wanting more with the false hope that satisfaction will eventually come from having additional "things." Using authoritarian or enabling methods with students who have this mind-set can be an exercise in futility.

4. **Ability determines worth.** Often, society places a premium on intellectual and physical attributes and ability. In turn, the valida-tion of this ability/worth connection is accentuated when the stu-dent's achievement is low. When success is attributed to ability, then failure to achieve implies low ability. To maintain their sense of self-worth, students often engage in behavior that will allow any lack of success on their part to be attributed to factors other than their innate ability. No one wants to be dumb. In fact, no one even wants to be average. Would you like to be known as an average lover, parent, or teacher? Kids don't ever want to be considered stupid and therefore engage in behavior that will allow their failures to be attributed to a number of other reasons—like school.

5. **Different is bad.** In the eighteen years I was a middle school teacher, my students taught me a lot about how sensitive people are to terms that ostensibly mean about the same thing. Just as everyone wants to be normal, hardly anyone wants to be average in aspects of life that are important to their personhood. In my

years of sitting in on meetings when parents learn that their student has an "average" IQ, there is almost always a disappointed look. It has always interested me that when "normal IQ" is substituted, there is usually a sigh of relief. Likewise, my students taught me that everyone wants to be unique, but no one wants to be different.

In the world of special needs students, this aspect is of significance. By definition, there is something about a special needs student that is significantly below average (think of the ramifications to personhood). And, of course, they are different. That's what makes them special education students.

To guide kids effectively, Love and Logic encourages teachers and parents to think deeply about how implied messages influence kids' behavior. A further question is how best to develop an atmosphere that relies less on forcing kids' compliance and more on their developing an internalized sense of responsibility.

Perception and Behavior

We all behave consistent with our perceptions. Whether we are sane or mentally unstable, whether we are honest or deceitful, our perceptions dictate what we do. Even everyday occurrences demonstrate this—like how we behave in the security of our own cars. Have you ever had the opportunity to see what people do as they are driving? People are uninhibitedly singing at the top of their lungs, putting on makeup, and picking their noses. All with the apparent perception they are invisible.

Sometimes our sacred beliefs come to a shattering halt. I recall a time I was driving back to the office from a school in the far reaches of our seven-mile-square district. I had to go to the bathroom before I left the school, but thought I had enough time before panic would set in. After all, it was just a few miles.

What I didn't remember was the road construction. A trip that should have taken ten minutes was now passing twenty-five. The pressure was tremendous. I engaged in a strategy called "jiggling," which I had learned from Junie B. Jones (a book series about a kindergarten girl). I was "jiggling" and "jiggling." I had the (false) security that I was in my car, so nobody could see me. Then I looked up through my open sunroof—into the eyes of the truck driver right next to me. I didn't even bother to make any indication of my distress—I just quit "jiggling" and waited for the light to turn green. From this experience, however, I did realize that the idea that being in my car somehow made me invisible was entirely not true. Another perception shattered!

More on Perception

Perception becomes reality and is the basis for our value systems, how we feel about our capabilities, and a number of other factors that become part of our way of performing at school, in the home, and in the community.

Perception is paradoxical. It is as strong and rigid as concrete but can so easily be influenced. Like wet pasta, it cannot be pushed, but it can be led if gently pulled. The key for teachers is that one of the most powerful tools for changing perception, with subsequent behavioral changes, is an implied message conveyed within the interaction dynamics between people. As discussed before, what we say, how we say it, and when we say it is much more effective than the finest curriculum or the most sophisticated equipment.

Our perceptions are inextricably intertwined with our "field of awareness," that is, how we interpret our environment and circumstances around us. Our perceptions filter out information that is contrary or irrelevant to the patterns we have developed to make sense of the world. Our final conclusions may be different than others', but the process by which we developed those conclusions and how we change is fairly universal.

Working from a False Premise

Differences in perception have caused innumerable confusions. A few years ago, my wife and I met a young Native American family in New Mexico. We have essentially "adopted" each other, and Diane and I have become "Grandma" and "Grandpa" to their kids. What Diane and I have come to realize, however, is that they understand the Anglo culture far better than we know theirs. They are such a gentle people and forgive our faux pas.

One summer we had their two boys (then five and three) for a couple of weeks. We noted a lack of the magic word present in every suburban society: "please." So we taught them, with some effort, to say it. What we didn't realize until later is that within their culture, asking "please" is associated with begging or pleading in the context of humiliation. In view of our friends' culture, if you respect someone, their request is sufficient—there is no reason to do more than identify a need.

In another context, we are all probably more familiar with the classic punishment of sending kids to their room—where there is a virtual entertainment empire. There is also the school version of sending kids to the office, where they can watch lots of action, be asked by the secretary to run some errands, or get a little one-on-one attention from the principal. Worse still is suspending a student for skipping school!

I was having breakfast with some educator friends of mine who were responsible for student discipline. There was mention about a student who had been truant a number of days. Comment was made that if he were truant one more time, he would be getting a "three day" (a "technical" term for a three-day suspension). I told them it looked as though the kid would simply get the equivalent of a paid vacation. He would have an "authorized" skip. However, my two friends looked at it as "doing something to show this kid we mean business." Ah, perception—it's what keeps the world turning, isn't it?

"Field of Awareness" and the Target Experience

Most of us will understand the power of perception in the abstract. What makes it real to me is an experience I had at our local Target when our grandson had just turned eight. Diane and I were taking care of Edrik for several days while his mom was away on business. This looked to Diane to be a perfect opportunity to gut Edrik's room and put it back in proper order. My wife is the world's best organizer and as part of this project, she was sorting all of Edrik's toys. She had bought a number of storage tubs for this purpose, but was running short.

So that I could feel I had some involvement, I suppose, she sent Edrik and me to get some more tubs. She was very specific: medium sized, green with red covers, in the southwest corner of the store. Off we went—it was like a hunting expedition—a wonderful opportunity for some male bonding.

We got to the store and selected the proper cart. Edrik rode on the bot-

. . . . .

tom rack, with his nose as close to the floor as possible—ah, life is good at eight years of age!

I knew exactly where to go and as we were going down the main aisle, I saw a woman coming toward us with two tubs (green with red tops) in her cart. The only other observation I made was that she had the larger size, but surely we were getting close.

I was so excited—we were on the right track. I wanted to tell Edrik about our imminent success. As the woman passed by, I spoke, in a voice loud enough to be sure Edrik would hear, "Look, Edrik, that lady has a couple of big ones!" As soon as the words left my mouth, I tried to suck them back in. Instead of excitement, I was now filled with dread. One problem was that she did have a substantial bosom. I was now thinking of harassment, of explaining my comment to the manager, or worst of all, of finding myself unintentionally behind this same woman in the check-out aisle.

We Focus on What Has Become Important to Us

Our perception dictates how we view the world, and how we view the world determines what we pay most attention to. A number of years ago I was giving a presentation to some private school staff. As the discussion was progressing (nicely, I thought), the principal raised her hand to get my attention. My presumption was that some concept needed to be repeated or clarified, and that was my mind-set as I called on her. Her response was totally unexpected on my part when she asked whether I knew that, of the last eight stories I'd told, five were about boys.

Frankly, my concern was to convey a point about Love and Logic and its relationship to student performance—gender was not a relevant issue for me. However, for this administrator, this particular matter was evidently very significant. I wondered later if she'd heard anything else in the presentation. But this experience did show me that content can become irrelevant if these perception and field-of-awareness issues are not at least acknowledged—whether dealing with adults or children.

Different Perspectives, Different Insights

Perception is also a significant influence when we are trying to develop effective interventions. I recall a situation involving a kid with some orthopedic impairments that limited his involvement in physical education. The teacher, building administrator, and parent were all at a loss about how to adapt the program so the kid could participate. Frankly, I didn't have a lot of ideas either—what with my attitude toward sports and all. Perhaps it is because I didn't like gym class when I was a kid. I am far from athletic—it is just not of too much interest to me. However, it was a problem for the others and one that needed to be addressed.

Some time later I was discussing this situation over breakfast with a friend of mine. He is an English teacher, liked sports, and had been a coach at one time. He had a different perceptual "box" and had some great insights. His suggestion was to deal with the situation as though the kid were an injured star athlete. All coaches would know what to do in that situation. The kid would study the plays, encourage the other players, and generally be part of the group.

It only took a different perspective. A view from a different perceptual set. What was an impossible situation to some was no problem at all for others.

Cookies at the Airport

Our field of awareness is that aspect of perception that gives meaning to the environment around us. It's how we interpret the direct circumstances we find ourselves in. The importance of field of awareness is that it is influenced by information, which in turn influences our perception. A good friend of mine tells this story.

Eric had just finished speaking and had arrived at the airport a bit early. Taking advantage of this time, he bought a newspaper and a bag of chocolate chip cookies—he was going to make the best of this waiting time.

After a while he glanced up from reading and, to his great surprise, saw an old acquaintance walking past him. Greatly excited, he put down his cookies and paper and hurried to catch up with his friend. They talked for just a short while and Eric went back to resume reading his paper and eating his cookies.

He couldn't believe what he returned to. An older man was sitting in his seat and, furthermore, was eating one of the cookies and giving one to each of the young girls with him. Eric was less than happy and thought to himself, "What right does that guy have to take my cookies!" To show his displeasure in a civilized way, Eric stared at the man, trying to elicit some level of guilt. But to no avail. In fact, the man seemed a bit irritated that Eric was staring.

Eventually, the man and girls left and Eric resumed his seat, picked up his newspaper, and saw *his* cookies—all of them, still in the bag! This information greatly influenced his field of awareness, his perception changed, and so did his behavior. The principle is universal and we have all had similar experiences.

Eric's field of awareness was a vital influence to his perception and subsequent behavior. Regardless of what really was happening, he saw the situation in a particular way and acted accordingly.

Teaching Style

Teaching style and interaction dynamics are inseparable. I learned this while teaching a course a number of years ago in a school district in south central Wisconsin. We had been discussing the concept of unconditional regard—the "love" in Love and Logic. We had talked about the aspect of modeling and how to interact with students who may be showing their hurt and frustration by their (inappropriate) behavior. During one of the breaks, one of the participants came up to me and said, "This stuff about respecting the kids . . . what if they call you a 'f--king a--hole'?" My response was that the very first thing I would want to make sure of was that I wasn't one. He sat back down and I don't recall any more questions from him.

Often when questions like that are asked, I stop to think and hopefully come up with a response that will at least sound enlightened. In this instance, there wasn't time to do that. I was wanting to get ready for the next part of the program and I badly had to go to the bathroom. So the response came from my subconscious. However, I would also say that this comment probably did reflect my true thoughts. Later, one of the persons who heard my comment told me that this teacher's primary technique for discipline was put-downs. He ridiculed many of the special education kids and commonly referred to them as "bottom feeders." Evidently the kids' description of him was correct. Many adults want kids to act differently, but would never think of changing themselves.

As I have contemplated this circumstance over the years, I am confirmed in my belief that kids will treat us how we treat them, disabled or not. I have worked with hundreds of kids throughout the years and, frankly, only those with severe character disorders or those who have fried their brains on drugs don't respond to being treated with dignity and respect.

Teaching style is inextricably intertwined with how teachers feel about themselves and about their students. The reciprocity of these feelings between teachers and students is often the prevailing influence in the classroom. Teachers who view students as "nasty, brutish and short" (as penned by Thomas Hobbes some centuries ago) will probably have a career of classrooms full of nasty, brutish short people, and an unhappy time will be had by all. Love and Logic advocates a "consultant" teaching style, involving students in a way that encourages a sense of dignity and worth and the development of internalized values that create a community of learners.

"Consultant" teachers demonstrate the goals and outcomes they want to see in their students. They show how well-adjusted adults handle themselves in the face of stress. They act as a guide for students in solving problems, without solving the problems for them. They encourage risk-taking in academic endeavors by providing a classroom where it is safe to make mistakes and to learn from them. They refrain from manipulation, ulterior motives, and artificial consequences to make students behave. They govern their own behavior by a set of principles that ensure that students' self-concept, autonomy issues, and need for structure are acknowledged and addressed in a positive manner. They demonstrate strength under control.

A point to emphasize is that few, if any, adults became teachers or parents with a written plan to fail and mess up their kids. However, when failure is recognized, extreme measures are sometimes taken to soothe the pain.

I have come to a conclusion that ineffective teachers and parents hurt, but don't quite have the internal strength to admit they need to change. When compensatory measures are substituted for change, an even more unhappy situation is created.

I recall talking to a student teacher who was in a classroom with a "seasoned educator" who, by all appearances, had insulated himself against the hurt of failure. When his student teacher displayed enthusiasm and overt caring for the students, his comment to her was, "I suppose you are one of those types who wants success for every student." Although these kinds of comments can initially cause an anger response on our part, upon analysis, sadness would probably be more legitimate. Think of the pain caused by the constant daily exhaustion that comes from pulling people down because it seems impossible to bring oneself up.

Systems and Principles

Many programs dealing with behavior concentrate on prescribed consequences to given infractions. Systems are popular because they are relatively easy to quantify and administer. In addition, provided all of the adults are doing the same thing, a kind of consistency and order is maintained. The problem is that kids can often use the system against the people who are using it on them. Kids are expert at creative misbehavior that takes advantage of loopholes present in any list of rules. As Jim Fay has often mentioned, kids seldom break the rules the way they are supposed to.

The Love and Logic approach defines a set of values or principles that guide the interaction between adults and kids. For instance, instead of having an extensive list of do's and don'ts (i.e., rules), we might establish a principle such as: "You can do whatever you want provided your decision doesn't interfere with or cause a problem for anyone else." Such a principle sets the standard that misbehavior will be dealt with, but in a way that will consider all of the people and circumstances involved.

Systems certainly are preferable in a number of situations when uniformity is the primary factor. When I fly in a commercial plane, my great hope is that the pilot has strictly observed the required system of checks. I don't want the captain to review only those rules that have some great personal significance. If I go to a hospital for some emergency treatment, I want a systems approach. I want everyone who works on me to be pretty thorough.

Even in some situations with people, systems are preferable. Imagine the performance of a football team for whom individual preferences about where to position themselves on the field would be the rule. Safety regulations and legal parameters may not have lots of latitude, either. There are times we need to follow a regimen regardless of our own personal feelings or values.

However, using a set of principles seems best in most situations that require people to learn from their mistakes, develop a sense of responsibility for their own behavior, or determine what is the most workable of several options. Whereas systems give parameters, they often do not allow for unforeseen variables or individual circumstances. Utilizing principles allows one to identify the parameters while still being able to absorb the variables that invariably come when working with people.

Love and Logic "Rules"

I have only one poster in my office—"How I Run My Love and Logic Classroom." Even though I no longer have my own classroom, it reminds me how I should treat people:

1. I will treat you with respect so you will know how to treat me.
2. Feel free to do anything that doesn't cause a problem for anyone else.
3. If you cause a problem, I will ask you to solve it.
4. If you can't solve the problem or choose not to, I will do something.
5. What I do will depend on the special person and the special circumstance.
6. If you feel something is unfair, whisper to me, "I don't think that's fair," and we will talk.

Establishing a principled approach is especially important when we are looking at the development of long-term goals like guiding values or character development. These are aspects of human personality that must be deeply established so unanticipated circumstances can be dealt with rather than capitulated to.

Four Key Principles

The intent of Love and Logic is to address the above-mentioned issues as they relate to teaching and parenting. Through the work of Jim Fay and Dr. Foster Cline, a program built on "Four Key Principles" has been developed. From these principles, applications can be made to achievement, behavior, and other aspects important to raising and teaching kids. The following is a brief description of these principles:

. . . . .

Self-concept. Self-concept is a building block for behavior. Those with a healthy self-concept tend to have fewer discipline problems and achieve more. But there is a paradox: There appears to be little "self" in "self-concept." Much of what we feel about ourselves comes from what we think the magic people (significant others) in our lives think about us. Additionally, what we think other people think comes from the implied, or covert, messages we receive far more than from what is actually said. Teachers need to know this when instructing and realize that their nonverbal interaction will affect students to a greater extent than just the words spoken. Within the framework of Love and Logic, teaching should be a building-up process, not a stripping of dignity and worth.

Shared control. Many teachers have the feeling that to control students, all of the power must be taken from the kids so they cannot fight back. However, when this is done, the scenario is set for very sophisticated power struggles that, in all probability, the student will eventually win. Students will often do an "end run" and, rather than engaging in a direct confrontation, will create "new and improved" ways of sabotaging the teacher. In one extreme case, a student accused a teacher of behaving inappropriately toward her in a private, school-related situation. The student's story was false, but she did "get back" at the teacher in a way that eventually destroyed his career. I have also heard of kids calling social services to turn their parents in—even when no wrongdoings had taken place. Most of the time, kids' undermining behavior is not so dramatic, but the everyday chipping away at the adult's authority (and eventual sanity) takes the fun out of teaching and parenting. Love and Logic addresses this issue with the technique of shared control, which teaches how to give away the control you never had or didn't need in the first place in return for getting control of the really important factors in the classroom.

Empathy with consequence. People often must hurt before they are willing to change their behavior. However, we need to differentiate two kinds of pain: from the outside in, and from the inside out. The first comes from punishment and can consist of hitting, yelling, grounding, reducing grades, giving extra work, and the like. In essence, pain is inflicted from an outside source. The normal human reaction is to avoid pain, and kids often become quite sophisticated at not getting caught (the "flight principle"). Likewise, we try to avoid the other kind of pain, that which is caused from experiencing the consequences of our own behavior. However, because this pain is "inside," we cannot avoid it by running away or fighting. In fact, there are only two primary ways that this kind of pain is normally dealt with: wait until it goes away, or make a decision to change our behavior. The combination of consequences with an equal balance of empathy is the key. Empathy locks in the learning much more than moralizing, criticizing, or lecturing.

Shared thinking. When dealing with students, we can usually get a lot more accomplished if they are in the thinking, rather than the emotional, state. Orienting people to this frame of mind is much easier with a skillful use of questions. A phenomenon that has been observed is that, although the human mind is extremely complicated, it only does one cognitive function at a time. People can argue or they can solve problems, but not both at the same time. When teachers interact with students in such a way that thinking rather than reacting is taking place, constructive communication is much more easily accomplished. Love and Logic teaches that the skillful use of questions asked with a "calm alert" is a powerful combination in dealing with issues of student performance.

The Joy of Whining

When our grandson, Edrik, was seven years old, I took him to the local Wal-Mart. Buying a toy was not part of the agenda that particular day. Have you ever noticed how a seven-year-old, without any formal instruction, can become expert at whining? Edrik is no exception. Since kids are going to whine, the question that adults must answer is: How will these opportunities be used? Will the kids learn to be more efficient whiners, or will they learn that whining isn't worth their effort?

When Edrik and I got back into the car, the conversation went as follows:

EDRIK: Grandpa, I wanted a toy!

GRANDPA: I know, and toy buying will be for another day.

EDRIK: Wwwhhhyyy? (This is the word "why" as best I can
            describe how Edrik pronounced it. The spelling is
            difficult to portray, but every adult with children
            knows exactly how it sounds!)

At this point there is a temptation to tell him that he already has so many toys that he can hardly fit them all into his room. And there is the morality issue as well. Think of all the children in the world who don't have any toys. However, these reasons would better be left to a time they could be effective. The conversation went on:

GRANDPA: Well, Edrik, I have three reasons that I can think of.
            Would you like to hear any of them?

EDRIK: Nnnooo.

GRANDPA: Well, if you change your mind, just ask.

A few minutes passed and then, from the back of the car, came these words:

EDRIK: Grandpa, I will ask when you least expect it (giggle).

Frankly, I would rather deal with seven-year-old humor than with the whining.

The Misaligned Lenses

Rick, a friend of mine who is the principal of a middle school, had gone to a week-long conference and was sick the whole time. He suspected it might be because of the new glasses he had taken up wearing just prior to the conference. There had been some slight changes in his vision and he thought he might just be having a hard time getting used to the new prescription.

When he returned he went to his eye doctor to see if anything could be done. What he found out was both a relief and an annoyance. The eye doctor told him that the new prescription had been incorporated into his new glasses; however, there were some problems. First, the right lens had been placed in the left frame, and vice versa. Second, the bifocal partition was reversed: the part for closeup viewing was at the top of the frame, and the part for faraway viewing was at the bottom. Everything was right, just in the wrong order.

When I heard this story, it seemed to approximate what goes on in schools and homes. Often, all the right elements are present, but sometimes they are in the wrong order. There is opportunity to learn content and to build skills. There is also the opportunity for kids to learn how to live in the real world and develop healthy relationships with people. The key is to get all of this into the right sequence so that kids are a finished product by the time they reach adulthood.

CHAPTER 3

Establishing a Viewpoint of Special Education

Times Change Easier Than People Do

Although there have always been special needs students, they have not always been accommodated within the prevailing social and educational systems. Throughout history some people with disabilities have been revered, but mostly they have been mocked, shunned, destroyed, or given attributes that stem from a terrible misunderstanding. Unfortunately, even today our society has not completely escaped this cruelty.

For a presentation some time ago, I did some brief research about how "special education" students have been treated historically within the educational system. Some examples indicate how special needs students have been considered. In 1893 the Massachusetts Supreme Court upheld the expulsion of a student who was "weak of mind." Several years later, in 1919, the Wisconsin Supreme Court approved exclusion of a student who drooled and had a speech impediment and facial contortion. In 1958 the Illinois Supreme Court upheld exclusion of a student with mental impairment. Prior to 1975, a student could be excluded if school officials deemed that he or she could not benefit from school or would be disruptive to other students. There was a view that exclusion was an appropriate option.

The disabled student's legal protection to be allowed to attend a regular school with regular kids is a relatively new phenomenon. I recall the scene in *Forrest Gump* when Forrest's mother wanted him to attend his local school. The extreme measures she went to reflected a prevailing view of the times! Special needs kids were simply not considered as belonging in a regular school.

These attitudes are still not entirely of the past. Neither does a level of discrimination against disabled students only appear in the movies. Handicapped students give ample opportunity to exercise unconditional regard that is the "love" in Love and Logic.

Even by Those Who Should Know Better

Just three years before this book was being developed, I was speaking with a staff member about a couple of our district's special needs students who had fairly significant cognitive problems. Her comment was that she didn't see why "those kind" were even at this school, "what with sucking up valuable resources that could go to kids who could get some good out of education." "Those kind"—sounds strangely like a different species, doesn't it? It brings back very bad memories from years ago of ethnic groups being called derogatory terms as though dehumanizing certain people made them a bit more dispensable. Maybe it's a way of objectivizing these students so less guilt sets in for those who want to set them aside.

And this "discrimination" doesn't only happen by those outside the ranks of special education. Only a few years ago we were trying to rectify a mistake in our district. One of our special education students had extremely low skills, but the teachers, not wanting to engage in a conflict with the parent, agreed to "grade" the student in such a way to keep the parent at bay. The student received A's and B's on her report card based on her effort and completion of her modified work. Her actual level of skill mastery was in no way indicated.

Eventually, the teachers realized the long-term consequences if this practice were to continue. In essence, they were engaged in institutionalized lying and eventually there would be serious ramifications for the student in any post–high school activity she might pursue. The justification that being on the honor roll made this girl feel good (and her parents as well) was a false encouragement. Both the student and her mother were getting a distorted view of her accomplishments and level of skill. Placating parents may have a place in education, but the price is often very expensive for the kids.

The teachers eventually made a decision that the student would benefit from a current events class conducted within the special education department. In actuality, this would have been academically appropriate for this young lady. The big problem, however, was that a couple of students in that class had Down's syndrome and some others were in wheelchairs. The parent became incensed when she heard this and stated, in no uncertain terms, that her daughter would not be attending class with "those kids." And besides, she argued, with her daughter's grade point average as high as it was, why should she be in a class like that anyway?

As a matter of fact, some of "those kids" had higher skills than the girl in question, but that was of no consequence to the parent. They "looked different," she explained, and would make her daughter "feel funny." She fought up the administrative ranks to keep her daughter out of that class. Eventually, there was a win/lose situation. The parent won, the daughter lost.

There Ought to Be a Law

Through legislative mandates, beginning in the mid-1970s, special needs students have been given federal and state statutory rights to educational services. These laws, prompted by civil rights legislation, afforded special needs students protection against discrimination based on specified handicapping conditions. It is sad that we must make laws for any group of people to be treated right. It is sadder still to know that even making a law doesn't do it for some.

The laws that currently govern special education have their genesis in statutes created two centuries ago. The first was passed by the Fifth Congress and addressed medical needs of sick and disabled seamen. Until the 1960s, the few other laws addressing disabilities were focused on the needs of war veterans with disabilities connected to military service. Since the 1960s, there have been a number of federal and state laws as well as significant court cases that concentrated on the legal framework relative to education of the disabled.

Although states may have their own laws and regulations, all special education legislation must conform to the basic tenants of federal statute. The point is that students determined to be educationally disabled have a massive resource in federal (and subsequent state) legislation. These laws are increasingly used to compel districts to provide resources and programming for special needs students.

To a large degree, these laws were promulgated because of inadequacies of the educational system as established at the time the legislation was initiated. However, whether because of national guilt, or because these laws are not always adequately understood by those implementing them (i.e., educators), the good intentions have sometimes gone awry.

A National Epidemic?

The advent of laws and changing views of special needs individuals have altered the social and educational landscape. There is certainly more that can be done to equalize the rights and opportunities afforded to disabled people. However, there are also some cautions to be exercised.

To a very large degree, special education has become more extensive (and more expensive) than ever intended or envisioned. "Hidden handicaps" have swelled the ranks. Interpretations of disability definitions have become broad to the point that some sincerely believe that disability simply means a student is working below potential or having trouble in school.

This is exacerbated even by language in the federal regulations (the "interpretation" of the actual law). For instance, part of the definition of a learning disability is an "imperfect ability" in reading, writing, or mathematics. Think of that: an "imperfect ability." Although "imperfect ability" is not defined, it would seem to be a fairly high standard. The whole idea of what special needs even means gets easily distorted.

A Changing View of Disabilities?

The public relations and media people have done a terrific job in changing the image of disabilities available to the public. However, this perception may be somewhat sugar-coated. Whereas it is commendable that disabled persons are no longer thought of as "defective," truly having a disability is seldom fun, comforting, or exotic.

I thoroughly enjoyed Dustin Hoffman's portrayal of a person with autism in *Rain Man*. We hear of the Thomas Edisons of the world making it big while not being able to read. I have also read that Albert Einstein was educationally disabled and flunked French. The list of disabled people who have excelled in life is extensive and my wish is that their stories are an encouragement for special needs kids, their parents, and their teachers. But I have a concern. Although laudable and maybe even necessary, good-feeling images can simply be a diversion. We must never neglect the fact that truly disabled students need intensive special instruction to attain a reasonable level of independence as adults. There is also the obligation of orienting students within the limitations innate to their disabilities.

I am familiar with a student who insists he has the ability to become a doctor, and if not a doctor, then an astronaut. His parents have made public statements that they never want any teachers mentioning his limitations. This young man has traumatic brain injury, is virtually wheelchair bound, and, even as a high school student, struggles with academic material beyond a midelementary level. Being realistic does not mean crushing a student's aspirations. Rather, being realistic puts a firm foundation under a legitimate hope.

Another distortion that has become appealing to some is to believe that having a disability has some distinct advantages (in addition to getting the best parking spaces). The perception of being declared handicapped has so turned in our society that students who do not actually qualify under the law are recommended to programs for special needs students because of the perceived benefit they will receive. A few years ago I learned of a situation where a parent, with the full support of the teacher, wanted to keep a student in special education because this was the only way she could maintain her "A" grade point average. This is, by far, not the purpose of special education.

Others view being in special education as their "ace in the hole." There is a perception (often false) on the part of many, that being in a special education program will give students an advantage in getting social services, assistance in college, or deference when taking standardized or placement tests. These perceptions get even worse. Some years ago I was told of a parent who wanted "papers" to apply for SSI (supplemental security income). She explained that since her other three children were "special ed," she just knew the other one (still, by the way, in utero) would be as well. She wanted to get a head start so there would be no down time. The person telling me this story also indicated there was a suspicion that the parent had "made" her other children eligible for special education. She evidently looked at having disabled children as a steady source of income.

The Problem and the Cure Start at the Same Point

Special education law mandates a team approach to determining eligibility and programming for disabled students. The team approach is a strength of the special education process. At the same time, it is a weak link. Certainly, the expertise and perspective of several individuals can give a needed balance. However, some students are identified as disabled because the evaluation team has an inadequate understanding of the process or legal definitions. Even more unfortunately, some students are declared disabled because of pressure from parents or the administration. How many times have kids with discipline problems been slated for special education to get them out of the school's proverbial hair or to avoid lengthy and expensive litigation?

In addition, the advent of special education law has created a situation ripe for the development of educational materials and strategies. Whole industries have evolved around special education. Educational technologies have been created out of very thin air. Experts have magically appeared. Specialty schools, nutrition programs, and esoteric theories have emerged from the woodwork to promote their products to an audience who are desperately searching for a magic cure.

The Creepy-Crawly Method

Early in my teaching career, I recall a technique eventually referred to as the "creepy-crawly method." This was during the infancy of learning disabilities, when nobody—and I do mean nobody—really knew what to do. This method seemed as good as any of the others being bantered about, based on the nascent research base available in the field. Besides, the term "neurological reorganization" (the term preferred by the program developers) sounded like it could be the key to unlocking the mystery of learning disabilities.

This method was developed on the presuppositional base that if a student walked before he or she crawled, the neurological pathways were screwed up and that is why the student couldn't learn to read, write, or do arithmetic. The obvious answer was to replicate the "normal" neurological pattern and get the student to crawl. It didn't matter if the kid was a teenager. He or she had to start over to get those neurological pathways in order!

. . . . .

I remember the first time I heard about this technique. A student of mine (a fourteen-year-old eighth-grader at the time) had been enrolled in the program by his parents. Although he was reading far below his grade level (according to both tests and classroom performance), he one day proudly announced that he was reading at the "senior" level. The parent confidently reaffirmed to me her son was now reading at a "senior " level as a result of this program. In addition to her delight about the fact that her son was achieving so well, she was equally disgruntled with me for not being able to produce the same results.

To be very honest, I wanted this method to work. Being castigated by this parent was more than unpleasant. To find out if I, too, could work this magic, I contacted the agency to learn about its technique. What I found out would have been amusing had it not been so irritating. This agency liberally used a kind of educational slight of hand. Among its repertoire was the time-honored practice of twisting the meaning of a common term.

My first discovery was that the kid couldn't read any better with the creepy-crawly program than he could with me. The agency just had different nomenclature. What I called third- to fourth-grade reading level, it called "Senior I." This program did have a strength in making kids feel better about themselves, but it was based on a false premise. I was angered by the pretentiousness of the program, and also annoyed that the parent used this "progress" to put me down.

However, there was some satisfaction to be had, eventually. Since the technique was so popular, it was only a short time before it was subjected to external verification studies. It was essentially quashed by peer review and a simple experiment. In this experiment, one group of students was processed through the complete program. Another group was talked with and given ice cream. In the end, both groups gained a similar increase in reading level. No one thought the ice cream did it. Rather, the experiment concluded that the individual attention and resultant increase in sense of capability and expectation were the important variables. When the students' sense of worth increased, so did their academic skills. In essence, this was another verification of the Pygmalion effect.

I reflect on this situation often. Certainly, just feeling good about themselves didn't make these students smarter, but it did influence their motivation and task engagement. There are no quick fixes when it comes to people, especially for students who truly have special needs. However, the development of positive relationships between the kids and adults does have a beneficial effect and is especially important for special needs kids.

Frankly, I don't want Love and Logic to be considered some type of mysterious magical cure, because it is not. Effective use of Love and Logic with special needs kids takes thought, caring, and application of common sense. People problems, whether involving learning or interaction dynamics, require thoughtful interaction and time. Quick fixes are simply not sustainable and have limited benefit for special needs kids in the long term.

Responsibility—Is It an Endangered Species?

Special education has created a problem perhaps never envisioned by the legislative authors. I am certainly sensitive to the fact that special needs kids must grapple with the academic, emotional, and social ramifications of their disabilities. However, my greater concern is that those adults working with them will interact in such a way that the students will use their disabilities to avoid personal responsibility for their own behavior.

In any discussion about working with kids within a Love and Logic framework, the concept of personal accountability is nearly always part of the context. An unfortunate phenomenon that has occurred within special education is the focus on an externalized locus of control. This is an insidious mind-set, and unless we have an adequate understanding of the dynamics of this factor, we, as teachers, parents, and others working with special needs kids, will actually contribute to the problem.

Many special needs students have heard often and learned effectively that their disability is not their fault. This is generally true unless the disability is the result of some unwise decisions (e.g., brain damage because of drugs). What is dangerous, however, is to allow students to become active victims or passive recipients of resources.

As mentioned in Chapter 2, validation of our personhood is significantly influenced by factors external to ourselves. Approval, attention, and achievement all fall into this category. However, to take these positives and use them to encourage maladaptive behavior is not in the long-term best interest of anyone. Disabled students are just as capable of sucking adults dry as nondisabled kids are. Within Love and Logic, we certainly view an internalized sense of responsibility as being essential to independence and employability, the stated goal of special education law.

What Those Working with Special Needs Kids Face

Those involved with special needs kids constantly face the unanticipated. Few parents of special needs children planned on dealing with the learning, emotional, and physical needs that accompany these kids. One parent told me that when his son was born with fairly significant handicaps, the family's life was turned upside down. Instead of planning for college and grandchildren, the parents were focused on who would care for their child when they were gone.

Special education teachers themselves face many variables that are often not part of their formal training. Even excellent teachers who are immersed in special education have often expressed to me their lack of confidence in understanding the complexities of diagnosis, instruction, the IEP process, and even how special needs kids think. In addition, the special education process is confronted with legal restrictions, controversial teaching strategies, restrictive funding, pressures from advocacy groups, and students with extreme needs.

Because of these and other factors, effectively raising and teaching special needs children can be extremely difficult. Whereas most children will develop and succeed, sometimes even in the face of adversity, special needs children often require a structure and consistency that is exhausting.

In Special Education, a Rose by Any
Other Name May Not Even Be a Plant

To complicate matters further, the people of special education use seemingly limitless abbreviations, acronyms, and esoteric vocabulary. Terms come, lose favor, and then go. It's as though changing the name of a condition somehow explains it better. More often, the new terms are simply euphemisms that in turn develop negative connotations. Perhaps it's a way of reducing the pain when adults feel helpless to change the kid.

I once saw a list of over two hundred terms for learning disabilities, many of which I had not even seen in the three decades I have been in the special education field. We tend to communicate through cryptic messages and I suspect that the people of special education could construct a paragraph that would challenge the Navajo Code Talkers of World War II. If we are not careful, this practice will isolate those who have not been initiated into the club.

The fact that special education has so many obscure terms represented by initials often takes a humorous turn. I remember a situation I encountered a number of years ago at a national legal conference on special education. The speaker was quite interesting, but mentioned a category of kids a number of times. Although I was familiar with lots of special education terms, I could not figure out what the speaker met by "M.A.H." kids. Since this speaker was from another state, I concluded that the terminology used there must have been different from that used in Wisconsin. However, since there are a finite number of impairment conditions, this term had to fit somewhere. I just knew the "M" must have stood for "mental" and the "H" must have stood for "handicapped," but I could not figure out what the "A" represented.

Evidently, a number of other people in the audience had the same confusion and we were all glad when one brave soul raised his hand and asked, "What does 'M.A.H.' mean?" The speaker looked a bit bemused and said, "It stands for 'Mean As Hell' kids." Although there is no such impairment condition, of course, we all knew what he meant. What it does point out in retrospect, however, is that we educators had been given just a little taste of the confusion that parents and classroom teachers must face constantly.

This issue is exacerbated by the fact that terms used in special education were largely established by those in the field of law and interpreted and implemented by those in the field of education. In no other part of education is the legal aspect so intimately woven. School districts spend huge sums of money consulting with attorneys to determine operational definitions for even common terms. I have seen the entire special education process stymied because of disagreement about what "benefit from" means in an individual context. Pity the poor IEP team members who simply want what they think will be appropriate for the kid.

. . . . .

What Is the Next Step?

My previous book, *Teaching with Love and Logic,* took a generalist view of the application of Love and Logic to the classroom. For the most part, nondisabled kids need some fine-tuning. Their learning systems are intact and they pick up reading, writing, and arithmetic from regular exposure and instruction. They learn how to get along with others by observation. They get from place to place pretty much on their own. Given the guidance of Love and Logic principles, they pretty much figure out how to live in the world.

Whereas the concepts of Love and Logic are effective when working with regular education kids, I am convinced that for disabled kids their use is essential. By definition, special needs students have performance problems because they have not followed a normal developmental route. They need specially designed instruction (part and parcel of the definition of "special education") in order to be prepared for a satisfying adulthood. They need a consistency and intensity that takes special thought and consideration on the part of the adult.

PART 2

Applying Love and Logic

CHAPTER 4

The Role of
Love and Logic
in Special Education

Searching for the Universal

Like many other teachers, from early on I desperately searched for the universal reinforcer to keep kids involved in the learning process. I tried every tangible reward I could think of and probably spent more time, effort, and money on gum, candy bars, and trips to McDonald's than I did on curriculum and instructional strategies. For a while, I concentrated on intangible reinforcers even to the point of trying to memorize a list of "107 Ways to Say 'Good Job.'" That was hard, because I have trouble remembering a seven-digit phone number.

When I became involved with Love and Logic, there was a fundamental shift of thinking. I had been sincere, to be sure, but the reinforcers had actually become the goal. What I understand now is that a different orientation could have better benefited the kids and a joy of teaching would have been easier to maintain. Acting on a philosophy emphasizing short-term fixes may get us through the hour, day, week, or even year, but may not at all prepare the kid for life.

What Could Be More Important Than External Reinforcers?

Teaching both skills and content is obviously important. This is a fundamental purpose of having schools in the first place. However, it doesn't take any great insight to understand that kids must be engaged in the process to learn and apply that learning. To accomplish this engagement, more than kids' bodies must be involved. And more than externalized rewards and punishments need to be used. There are affective aspects of learning that require attention as well.

By definition, students with special needs have some level of adverse performance in school. Not only are the academic aspects of school hard for special needs kids, but they face negative social and emotional experiences as well. The question is: What can keep these kids invested in school?

For a long time, education has relied on external reinforcers to keep kids involved (and in line). Too, it seems, the more problems a kid has, the more intense the reinforcement regimen. However, heavy doses of external reinforcement can have some unanticipated backlash. Students can satiate themselves on rewards and become desensitized to punishments. Students may come to feel manipulated or come to the conclusion that if what is taught is so important, why must they be "paid off" to learn it? Students can turn the tables on the adults and make behavior changes contingent upon getting the reinforcer—a form of behavioral blackmail.

At any rate, dependence upon external reinforcement may not at all be the answer to students being invested in their own learning. Too often, the value of the reinforcers becomes the focus rather than the learning or behavioral changes. If it is agreed that engagement in the educational process is a goal, a sense of belonging may well be the prerequisite.

A Testimonial

Throughout the years, there have been many opportunities to substantiate Love and Logic. It's refreshing to meet teachers and parents who have regained a sense of satisfaction, effectiveness, and empowerment. But the highest validation for me came from an unexpected source.

Some time ago I had the unique opportunity to befriend a friend of our son. Kevin had ended his schooling before graduating and eventually acquired his family's landscape business. Because of our work schedules and a penchant for starting the day early, he and I would often eat breakfast together at a local restaurant. Our conversations often centered around our backgrounds, which were distinctly different, especially regarding education. I had spent all but the first five years of my life in school. He had stopped attending at age sixteen.

. . . . .

Most of the writing I did for *Teaching with Love and Logic* was done in those early morning hours and Kevin had ample opportunity to see the work in progress. When the book was published, he asked to borrow a copy. Some weeks later when he had finished reading it, he made a statement I hope never to forget: "If my teachers would have treated me like the book says, I would have stayed in school."

He went on to say that even though school was hard and there were lots of things he was required to learn that he didn't think were all that important, he would have been willing to keep up the struggle if he had felt that he "belonged there." That comment gave me cause to reflect, because I couldn't even remember whether the word "belong" was actually used in the book. That was one of those teachable moments—but it was for the teacher.

As I have contemplated this conversation, I have realized how significant, even fearsome, is the adult influence over how kids feel about themselves and how this single factor affects performance. In all probability, Kevin's teachers made no direct statements about his not being wanted. However, he received that message nevertheless. What he told me that day was pure and honest—there was no one to impress or attack. He wasn't bitter. Rather, there seemed more a sense of loss.

In that comment, he was validating one of the primary presuppositions of Love and Logic: Student performance involves far more than updated curricula, sophisticated techniques, or "best-practice" strategies. As important as these are, the most significant aspect of school, especially for students who find learning and behaving difficult, may well be a relationship with a teacher who provides opportunity for the student to feel accepted.

This sense of belonging is not limited to students with learning, cognitive, or emotional limitations. A number of years ago I was asked to consult on the behavior of a middle school student with a measured IQ of 146. In addition to having some conduct problems, he was especially annoying to his teachers because he never came to class or did homework, yet he aced all of the tests! In one of our initial conversations, he stated knowing that no one wanted him at school, so why not fulfill their expectations.

My Maiden(form) Voyage into the Unknown

Have you ever been in a situation where you knew you didn't belong? Maybe you have gone to a gathering where you didn't know anyone. Maybe you have attended a service with unfamiliar rituals. It could have been at the very first meeting with the family of your significant other. At any rate, remember how uncomfortable you felt, how slowly time went by, and how you felt like running away?

A number of years ago my wife, Diane, was asked to be the matron of honor for a friend we had known since she was a teenager. In preparation for the event, Diane said she would have to do some shopping and wanted me to go along. One of the items she said she needed was a "foundation garment." Since the only thing I associated with "foundation" was the concrete you build a house on, I was initially confused, but went anyway.

The first place we went to was Victoria's Secret. This was awkward for me, because I was brought up being told it was not at all appropriate for a boy even to look at the women's underwear section of a retail catalog. Feeling as though I was in a virtual den of iniquity, I experienced a mild panic. Even though I was with my wife, there was some sort of strange feeling that someone would "catch" me in there and I would be in some sort of trouble!

Then, to my great chagrin, Diane thought I should be able to differentiate a lined bra from a padded bra. Believe me, I have no need for such knowledge and as I was "testing" each sample, I prayed the ordeal would be over soon.

It was, but what came next was not any better. Evidently, Victoria's Secret did not have the right "foundation garment" (I still did not have a good concept of what this actually was), so we went across the mall to Fredericks of Hollywood. At this point, the phrase "out of the frying pan and into the fire" kept coming to mind.

While Diane went to the dressing room, I desperately tried to find the men's section. And when I found it an even greater sense of panic set in. It consisted of the skimpiest of thongs on a rack over in a corner. At that point, I prayed again, this time even harder—that Diane would not see that rack, lest she want me to . . . well, you can probably imagine my fear!

After wandering aimlessly for a while, I eventually found myself in front of an entire wall of bras. I was amazed at the names of the different options. Admittedly, I did ponder the difference between "wonder," "majestic," and "serenity" bras.

Actually, I wanted just to wait out in the mall. And then a serious thought hit me. The reason I was so uncomfortable was that I didn't feel I belonged there. It didn't really matter why—I just knew I would have rather been in the power tool section of a hardware store.

Then I had an even more serious thought. Lots of kids probably feel this way every day they go to school. They know they don't belong there. They know people have described them as round pegs in square holes. They know they would rather be somewhere else and suspect others have the same thought.

I recalled the phrase "emotion precedes logic." I remembered that brain/learning research states that sensory information is processed through the emotional centers of the brain before getting to the "thinking" part. What triggers these emotional memories is quite individual, but the principle holds that our feelings influence nearly every experience.

Admittedly, some of the unique problems special needs students encounter come from the very structure of our educational systems. Schools are institutions, and somewhat artificial at that. For many of these kids, school is a daily reminder of what they are not good at and never will be good at. However, for the foreseeable future, special needs kids must continue to cope with academic, social, and emotional demands. Whether or not these kids are ready for the real world after school will largely depend on what they learn from adult interactions as they are growing up.

The "Love" in Love and Logic

The "love" in Love and Logic translates into unconditional regard for the student. This implies an acceptance that is neither contingent nor dependent on reciprocity. In a way, this flies in the face of a societal norm that says, "I will be nice to you if you will be nice back." This is certainly not to say that inappropriate behavior should in any way be overlooked, but there is an awesome power in validating the student's personhood with no strings attached.

This sense of belonging is imparted to students through natural every-day interactions. Students, even those with special needs, are not fooled by words that are inconsistent with actions. Any attempt to formalize this sense of acceptance only through some commercialized curricula or "made-up" lessons will fail in the long run because these are artificial ways to interact with people. Whether parents or teachers, we mostly influence how kids feel about themselves through the covert messages embedded in our communications.

A number of years ago, Jim Fay developed the idea of a "three-legged table" to help visualize the components of self-concept. The first leg of this table states, "I am loved by the magic people in my life" and involves this concept of unconditional acceptance. Certainly, we could talk about the highly sophisticated psychological theories and applications that this statement represents, but it really boils down to the fact that nurturers and teachers significantly influence how kids feel about themselves. Since behavior is consistent with perception of self, these natural interactions are of significant concern, especially when dealing with students with performance problems.

The issue can also be described as sincere caring. Above the cash register at the place where I get the oil changed in my car, there is a sign that says, "Nobody cares how much you know until they know you care." This message is evidently important enough to be seen by the employees every time money is taken from a customer. The idea might be of value to teachers and parents of special needs kids as well.

Teacher training so often emphasizes new instructional strategies and technology. Sadly, given the history of education, much of this knowledge will probably be determined obsolete within a few years of its introduction. What would schools be like if as many resources were allocated to ensure children have a sense of belonging as are now given to addressing their deficits?

Our Feelings Are Important Because Our Past Learning Stays with Us

In a way, the emotional part of our brain is more influential than the thinking part. Although we may not recall specific details of situations, the feelings associated with those experiences influence our behavior. What we learn early on stays with us. We all have individual experiences to verify this. For instance, what has stayed with me for decades is how I felt about shopping for clothes.

. . . . .

Perhaps some will remember, as I do, the ordeal of buying clothes as a seven-year-old youngster. I can look back now and realize that, for my mother, saving time was as important a factor as saving money. Too, shopping with four little kids and another on the way would put a strain on anyone. But regardless of all the reasons, I fully realize now as a parent myself that these time-saving strategies still had an early impact on my perception of this particular activity.

Like other moms of the time, mine thought fitting rooms (and the privacy they could afford) were unnecessary luxuries. In addition, my mother had no sense of being able to determine by visual estimation whether clothes would fit. Oh, no, every item had to be tried on. Off with the old, on with the new—right there in the middle of the store. I still recall Mom saying, "Oh, don't worry, nobody will see you." Oh, sure! Seven-year-old boys in their underwear become invisible in stores. The worst fear was that somehow, some girl classmate would accidentally wander out of her own appointed section of the store and see me. Ah, the fears of childhood! Even now my preference would be to have all of my clothes bought by remote. For me, whether they fit or not is purely secondary.

Periodically, Diane, my beloved wife, will trick me into buying something new to wear. She knows my aversion to this activity and I am usually enticed by words like, "Let's just see if they have a pair of jeans in your size." Since "my size" has not changed for years, it would seem that this would be a quick and easy task. Why my presence is even required to get a thirty-six-inch waist, thirty-two-inch inseam, I'm not entirely sure.

Once we are at the store, when I least expect it, Diane starts holding clothes up to me. At first, I accept the reason: she just wants to see how the color goes with my graying hair. Then, it's "just try on just one pair of slacks" (at least I am allowed to go to the dressing room now). Then I have to come out so she can see how the slacks look. Just like Mom, Diane cannot visually estimate.

Then, when I come out for inspection, there is no Diane. She's taking advantage of this rare opportunity and is looking for other items that will go with what I now have on. I realize I am now at the point of no return. There I wait in that nether land between the dressing room and the rest of the world. I'm dressed in pants with legs too long, tags hanging all over, and no shoes. I try to engage in an awkward casual conversation with people I hope don't know me.

When Diane returns, she scans me with an intensity usually reserved for a museum specimen. Then she says, "Turn around so I can see how the seat fits." I hoist my shirt and twirl slowly like some disoriented ballet dancer. I am now back to being seven years old, hoping no girls I know walk by.

When I think of how I feel about buying clothes, I can only imagine the ramifications for kids when school consists of years of consistently negative experiences. I often wonder whether these kids can hardly wait to be voters at their school districts' annual meetings.

Ignoring the Role of Perception Is Risky Business

Regardless of the sophistication of any teaching strategy, there will be no learning if the student is not engaged in the instructional process. Nearly any kid will disassociate because of boredom, laziness, dislike for the teacher, or not seeing the relevance of content to a personal goal. For kids with disability-related performance needs, there is an additional, even more significant, factor. For these students, their very personhood is at stake. Since our society has a tendency to associate worth with achievement (i.e., high achievement equals high worth), failure in school for special needs kids carries a very high price tag.

The key to engagement lies in developing instructional strategies that consider the essential factors governing volitional behavior. However, to write a comprehensive book of strategies for even the limited number of conditions identified in IDEA would be an exhaustive if not impossible task—certainly one beyond my own capabilities. Granted, having an extensive list of instructional strategies may be helpful. But more important may well be knowing how to create interventions that will be effective with individual kids under unique circumstances.

There are so many variables to consider when working with special needs kids. During the course of my career, I have known students whose IQ scores were double my own, but who were so impaired in body or mind that they could never live independently. Some kids were only semi-aware there was a world outside of their own mind. Others were dynamite on the football field, but couldn't read a stitch. Still others had socialization skills that may have been humorous as a plot in a Three

Stooges movie, but in actual life were quite tragic.

For those qualifying for special education services, there is a mandate to individualize. In addition, there is an immutable fact that interventions must be determined "on the spot." When kids break rules, they seldom do so in a prescribed fashion. Likewise, students with learning problems need encouragement that is often quite situation-specific.

To develop interventions, it would seem more than helpful to have a paradigm that allows for this diversity. To be effective, interventions should consider individualized characteristics of the student coupled with the unique aspects of the circumstances. A main focus of Love and Logic is a concentration on understanding the qualities that characterize effective strategies. Once these characteristics are understood, constructive interventions, based on need and situation, are significantly easier to devise.

Even before confirmed by brain research, Love and Logic recognized perception as the primary determiner of behavior. Built on this fundamental concept are the Four Key Principles, which allow an analysis of influences on peoples' actions. The goal of Love and Logic is to equip parents and teachers to develop interventions that avoid preconceptions that may actually hinder effective interaction with kids. The following story was given to me a number of years ago and demonstrates this point.

The Darter

The school psychologist received a call from a relatively inexperienced and obviously frustrated elementary school principal. A student had several times darted from the classroom and this time had bastioned himself in stall number one of the boys' restroom. The administrator, acting on the theory that darters must be caught, started the chase.

He had followed the student into the restroom and was now evidently engaged in what he thought should be the first level of intervention: telling the kid what to do. However, none of the principal's orders were being followed. He upped the ante and brought out his heaviest verbal artillery, telling the student to come out under threat of "really being in trouble this time."

Perhaps largely because of the entertainment value of this whole situation or perhaps because of a deep experiential base developed from being chased and threatened many times before, the student refused to comply with the principal's order. Evidently perceiving there was no other alternative, the principal decided to crawl under the (locked) stall door, grab the kid, and bodily pull him out. (That the principal even considered crawling on the floor in a boys' restroom indicates the high level of anxiety he must have been experiencing. This is proof positive that extreme stress can cause a virtual inability to use the frontal cortex—the thinking part of the brain.)

At any rate, the student was somewhat more nimble than the principal (who was a tad out of shape and a bit overweight). By the time the principal had made his way into stall number one, the kid had leapt the wall and was now standing on the toilet in stall number two.

Realizing that he had to apprehend this kid just to save face, the principal crawled under the wall between stall number one and stall number two. What he had not anticipated was that the partition between the stalls was somewhat closer to the floor than was the door. This resulted in the principal getting stuck between the two stalls. Imagine, if you will, an overweight adult male in a suit crawling on the floor of a boys' restroom, stuck between two toilet stalls.

The principal, still locked into the concept that darters had to be caught, made a desperate lunge, catching the boy's pant leg. The boy, because of his distinct positional advantage, had no trouble kicking his way free. In the ensuing fray, the principal hit his head on the toilet, leaving a nasty bump.

By the time the principal was fully inside stall number two, the kid had bivouacked in to stall number three. Realizing the fruitlessness of trying to be in the same stall at the same time, the principal crawled back under the partition and exited to the hall. (Why the principal crawled back under the partition rather than just unlocking the door and exiting upright is anybody's guess.)

Not willing to continue the chase, yet knowing "something" had to be done, the principal called the psychologist assigned to his school. Depending on the developmental phenomenon that most kids that age are afraid of the dark, the psychologist suggested that the lights be turned off and they wait to see what would happen. The strategy worked. The student came out of the restroom within a very short time . . . and darted down the hall!

. . . . .

Eventually, the student's instructional team, with the participation of the psychologist, analyzed this whole situation. During that meeting, a number of important variables were identified. First, the darting only took place in the early morning. Second, math was the first subject taught each day. Third, the kid hated math and was very poorly skilled in the subject. Fourth, the student did not have high-level communication skills—he acted out his feelings rather than talk them out. Fifth, the kid was seated in the back of the room—right next to the door.

Does a pattern seem to be emerging? With just some simple information, the adults were able to change their perception of this whole situation. In essence, the team conducted a functional behavioral assessment and were then able to identify characteristics of an effective intervention for this student.

Living in Two Worlds

If I were king, I would decree that special needs students be treated in a way to allow them to develop a sense (i.e., perception) of belonging. The difficulty in having this wish granted is that the most visible indicators of belonging in school are often inaccessible to kids with learning and behavioral problems. Being part of popular groups or excelling in academics and athletics often elude these students. They are seldom recipients of high-status rewards.

I recall a comment a teacher once related to me. She was sitting with her cognitively disabled students during an academic awards presentation. As the awards were being very publicly distributed, one of her students said, "Yeah, sure, I don't think any of us will ever be up there." In essence, this was another opportunity for public humiliation. It's hard to feel that you belong in an organization that constantly reminds you of your failures and defects.

I recall a conversation with Andrew, a high school special education student with some significant behavior issues. The conversation was non-confrontational, almost casual, but nonetheless important. I was asked to talk with him to gain some insight into why he was behaving in a manner that was getting him into trouble and generally annoying the adults. As we talked, he started to cry. The kid was seventeen years old, six feet tall, and crying. What he most hated, he said, was being thought of as bad when he didn't think he was being bad at all—he was just being himself. Even my conversation with him contributed to his pain. He almost seemed resigned to the fact that he could never conform to what others wanted him to be.

I have been privileged in my life to have very close friends of different ethnic backgrounds. I also have deaf acquaintances who live in a hearing world. These people live in two worlds and have stated that they don't feel they belong in either one. I imagine that special needs kids take this as an inevitable fact of life. How difficult it is for them to develop a positive attitude toward school.

The Source of Information

Another role of Love and Logic is to offer reminders that the best source of information about kids is from kids. Those who make decisions about individuals from esoteric research more often than not will miss the mark. Research is wonderful for coming up with generalities, but given the nature of research studies, they often have little value for dealing with specific kids.

Some years ago in my undergraduate work I was studying a bit of medieval history. The discussion was about the scholars of that day and how they went to great lengths to apply pure logic to answer questions with very little practical application. How many angels can dance on the head of a pin, and whether God can create a stone so heavy He can't lift it were issues debated endlessly.

In that context, I remember reading a story that involved a number of clerics arguing about how many teeth a particular horse had. Their arguments were complicated and, I suppose, used an elevated logic. In the middle of their discussion, as the story goes, a stable boy walked by. Wondering how there could be such an extended discussion about a mundane question, he simply asked, "Why don't you just open the horse's mouth and count them?" The story ended by stating that the academicians beat the boy soundly for his irreverence.

The phenomenon of not going directly to the source still exists. The experience of students is often discounted as being immature or irrelevant. However, kids can be one of our most valuable sources of information about kids.

. . . . .

I recall a particular lesson from our grandson, Edrik, when he was six years old. That year, Tuesday afternoon/evening was set aside for our "special time." One spring day I came home at the appointed time and was told by Edrik that he would like to play with the neighbor kids up the street. This was somewhat disconcerting and my initial reaction was to emphasize to him that this was Tuesday, it was our special day, and by golly we were going to spend time together and have fun!

Without too much thought, anyone could predict that under those circumstances, there would be very little fun. Fortunately, the technique of putting statements into questions prevailed and the interaction went something like this:

GRANDPA: Well, Edrik, sounds like you would like to play with the Crawford kids. Is that what I'm hearing?

EDRIK: Yeah.

GRANDPA: Right now, I think there is a problem. If I would have known you would rather play with your friends, I would probably have stayed at school and done some more work. I'm wondering, do you have any idea about how we can solve this?

Edrik started to think and literally within seconds came up with a solution:

EDRIK: Well, Grandpa, I could go to Crawford's for twelve minutes and then come back and play with you.

It was a perfect solution. How Edrik came up with twelve minutes, I don't know, but it was just the right amount of time to change clothes and talk a bit with Diane. I don't know how he did it, but twelve minutes later Edrik was back. We had a wonderful time together.

What I learned from that experience only reinforced what I should have learned long before. A six-year-old is really good at solving six-year-old problems. Teenagers are really good at solving teenager problems. Provided they are given the opportunity. As an older adult, frankly, I can no longer think like a kid; however, I can interact with kids in such a way that they can exercise their own insight and developing wisdom.

. . . . .

I learned most of my lessons about teaching and parenting from kids and wish it had not taken me so long to come to this understanding. I hope to maintain a missionary zeal in encouraging others not to make this same error.

Fire, Ready, Aim

When working with special needs kids, another role of Love and Logic is to maintain a balanced perspective guided by thoughtful common sense. The learning and conduct problems of special education students are on the extreme end of the continuum. Because typical strategies are often less than effective, educators and parents often grab at whatever vendor touts the promise of success. Tabloid "snake oil" peddlers will always have an audience for new products or promises of financial gain, and education, unfortunately, is not exempted.

Even in the News

One aspect of news reporting that can simultaneously annoy and amuse is the emotional language that is often used to get people's attention. I have lived in Wisconsin for a number of years and winter weather is seemingly what our local forecasters live for. If there is even a potential for especially bad weather, the TV stations can devote hours to reporting it.

I recall a few years ago that there was prediction of well over a foot of snow, bad winds, and just about everything else that could accompany such a storm. Speculations were that schools would close, that highways would be impassable, and, in brief, that the world would shut down for a while.

I recall watching TV periodically through that night and early morning the next day. With increasing excitement, weather people warned, like meteorological prophets of doom, that the storm to end all storms was coming. Each local station seemed to be trying to outdo the others with claims of accurately predicting this immanent disaster—it was as entertaining as it was "informative." Like some high-tech Chicken Little, announcements kept predicting that the sky would surely fall (or at least a lot of snow). It was as though the weather forecasters were desperately hoping that their all-night ritual, complete with litany, would somehow make the bad-weather gods perform.

. . . . .

It never happened. By morning, there was a little snow, a little wind, but no disaster. However, there were lots of upset people: parents who had made daycare preparations for their kids because of anticipated school closings, the kids who now had to go to school instead of play all day, and those who had already called in sick in anticipation of using the day for snow sports!

Many years before, a similar phenomenon happened with the close of the Vietnam War. I recall night after night on the evening news being told that tomorrow would be the day the conflict would end. Tomorrow would be the day soldiers would be coming home. This "tomorrow" was repeated for weeks and weeks. Eventually, when the war was really over, there was no sense of relief, no celebration.

Two reasons were primarily responsible for this lack of closure. First, no one could really be confident that each "tomorrow" was anymore certain than those of the previous announcements. Second, even if the date were sure, people were generally so desensitized or angry with the whole morality of what was happening in Vietnam that there was no longer an orientation toward "victory." The perceptions of the entire nation were affected.

Not Even Schools Are Exempt

This phenomenon of creating news by prostituting words happens all the time, and education is certainly not exempt. Violence in schools is a prime example. "Epidemic" is the term often used as newscasters report the subject. "Epidemic"—what an emotionally laden word. It conjures up all sorts of visions of uncontrollable and widespread pestilence.

Often when "epidemic of violence" is mentioned, the incident at Columbine and other high-profile school shootings are focal points. These tragic incidents have certainly prompted schools to action. Metal detectors, closed circuit TV, and memorials are now relatively common in schools. However, if the reactions of the schools deal only with the overt manifestations, the problem can hardly be expected to go away.

Just as enough pain reliever may somewhat alleviate the aching of a brain tumor, attacking only the symptoms will make the problem worse in the long run. If there is an emphasis only on the symptoms of the problem, those entrusted with developing solutions may well have their attention diverted away from the primary causes and, therefore, effective intervention.

Emphasis on the Long-Term Solution

As discussed previously in this book, and more extensively in *Teaching with Love and Logic,* perceptions are the driving force of overt behavior. Unless the behavior and learning problems are addressed at the source, long-term solutions may be evasive at best, and never attained at worst.

A number of years ago I read about a large urban school district that had made a decision to address the issue of teen pregnancy. The premise of those designing this program was that teens apparently lacked knowledge about how to prevent pregnancy. A significant amount of money (more than the entire budgets of some smaller school districts) was spent on programs to inform students about the biological process and to provide contraceptives.

The naiveté and/or ignorance of the program developers was fairly obvious. Of course, the students involved already knew about how pregnancy occurred and, indeed, how to prevent it. In actuality, having a child was the intent and goal of these teens. Having a child represented a sense of affinity and achievement. Having a child actually raised the (perceived) status of the students. For the boys, they could thus demonstrate their "manhood." For the girls, they now had some tangible achievement and someone who would love them.

Those designing the program were operating under the perception that teen pregnancy was negative. The group they were trying to influence was not. The program was basically a failure. In spite of the huge outlay of money, the teen pregnancy rate actually rose. There was no absence of sincerity, organization, or strategy. The plain issue was a clash of perception.

Violence and Schools

The rate of people in the United States trying to do away with each other has risen dramatically. In the four decades following the mid-1950s, when the FBI started keeping statistics, the aggravated assault rate went from about 60 per 100,000 to over seven times that amount. The statistic may have been even worse were it not for the fact there was increased imprisonment of violent offenders (the prison population in the United

States nearly quadrupled in the twenty years after 1975, and this country's incarceration rate is the highest of any industrialized nation).

Whereas the imprisoning of violent offenders may have some dampening effect on the murder rate, another, less obvious phenomenon has had even more ramifications. While it may seem encouraging that the murder rate in the United States has declined, that fact can be attributed in large part to medical technology, not to a decrease in violent acts. Wounds that would have been fatal 90 percent of the time in the World War II era are now treatable. The point is that statistics may lead readers to inaccurate conclusions.

Violence in our schools certainly is somewhat a reflection of society in general. Violence probably has some positive orientation for those engaging in it. Perhaps it relieves some stress or gives some artificial sense of control or power. Or it may be an outlet for students who have experienced pain in school and want to hurt others in retaliation.

In a quest for "realism," video games that involve killing the opponent (originating from the desensitization of soldiers to overcome their innate reluctance to kill) are now considered a sophisticated form of entertainment. Children have ample opportunities for such exposure to the culture of "violence as fun."

These influences have become hot topics and ensuing high stakes lawsuits have caused video-game manufactures to declare that no link has been established between aggressive behavior and prior exposure to brutal media. Conversely, groups opposed to such games identify research that does establish a link and rally with the admonition that it is a sad situation when winning is based on how many people can be killed or how many places can be destroyed.

There may be additional ramifications as a result of this advanced technology. Whereas violence on TV is received passively, sophisticated video games require the player to be directly involved. This interactive capacity increases the chances the player will identify with or even identify as the aggressor.

Other groups are as concerned about how gender roles are portrayed. Media messages are powerful in our society and act as teachers of values, ideologies, and beliefs. In general, video games present an overwhelmingly traditional and negative portrayal of women. Girls may expect that they will continue to be victims and dependent. Boys may determine that their role is to be possessive of girls even through the use of violence. Although such studies may not be the final word relative to violence in our schools, there are certainly some ramifications to consider.

Focus on the Real Epidemic

There may well be an epidemic in schools, but it is not glamorous enough to make headlines. A consistent finding of those students committing these extremely violent acts was that they were "getting back," avenging the pain they had experienced in school. A sense of alienation is a consistent theme.

What is the appeal of violent video games? Maybe it's the sense of power and control over others as well as a sense of being better than everyone else. These traits are all highly valued in our society and are at least temporarily available to the players. There is little in the general cultural environment that will inspire children away from adopting these values.

Special needs kids are especially susceptible. Because of their experiences, environment, and even neurology, they have self-worth and control issues. As a result of a different perspective on reality, these kids are often extremely vulnerable to substitute satisfactions.

I think about students for whom school is a not at all a fun place. I recall a conversation with my supervisor about a school story from her own past. A new girl had moved into the community and entered school midway into the year. Although this was a fine, church-related school, there was lots of unpious activity. The established group of girls made a pact to systematically exclude this new student—and they did. In a historical perspective, the group's actions were a mean-spirited characteristic of kids' immaturity, but cruel nonetheless.

And these painful experiences are not limited to just kid-on-kid. So often I hear teachers talk openly about their students, often within earshot of the kid—as though the kid does not exist or is incapable of understanding. Maybe they don't realize they are contributing to the kid's pain, but can this really be an excuse? The teachers are at least getting a paycheck; the kids are getting their personhood devalued.

I once read a newspaper article about a girl who committed suicide by jumping from a parking structure after a teacher read a confiscated note in front of the whole class. I don't know all of the details, but it would seem reasonable there was more than just one note—a history of rejection for which this was simply the culminating episode.

The Influence of a Special Adult

So, what about the role of Love and Logic? Fundamentally, it is to convince those working with kids that interaction is the vehicle for determining a sense of belonging and the accompanying attribute of hope. A number of years ago I first heard Jim Fay say that the business of being a kid is learning how to be big. Part of this process is learning how the big people make the little people feel.

We will not soon be rid of the parts of school that make kids feel bad. Activities that emphasize being the best will long be part of what is associated with school. It appears there will be an increased pressure to achieve, as reflected by the emphasis on high stakes testing. Society-wise, we will not be rid of guns, video games, violent media, or destructive music. However, individuals can make a difference in families and classrooms, and with individual kids.

Making Our Words Gold

Over the years, Love and Logic has emphasized the need for consistency between what we say and what we do. Jim Fay repeatedly cautions his audiences to make sure their words are gold, not garbage. Words are so easy to spew forth. For instance, how many of us have heard people say they will think about or pray for us, knowing this is essentially an attempt to be polite. What a comfort when there is a demonstration that verifies their words.

Diane and I once attended a concert of a Native American musical artist. During that performance he related a tradition of his people that can have great value as we work with kids. The tradition, originating when warriors went to battle, was that the prayers and thoughts on their behalf were memorialized with a prayer stone. These individual stones were piled atop one another and when the warrior returned, he had tangible evidence of the people's words.

The tradition has expanded today to include times when individuals are away from their families. As those behind pray and remember, their thoughts are represented by another stone added to the pile. This entertainer told his audience how comforting it is when he sees these piles of stones in his yard and knows that each represents a promise fulfilled.

One standard assignment I give to graduate students is to present a strategy ("Trick of the Trade") that will contribute to the professional knowledge base for other class members. One of the most moving stories was from a young high school teacher. Although most participants made oral presentations, she had hers all written out. She knew she would need to read her presentation, because she was certain she would "break down." She did, and a fellow student finished reading her story. Following is what she wrote as submitted in its entirety:

Throughout this course I have reflected a lot about myself as a teacher. In the past, some teachers have asked me, "How or **why** do you get along with certain students?" I honestly didn't know until now. I never really thought about it. All I know is that I give every student the same respect as I would my mother or best friend. I don't belittle the student that isn't the brightest bear in the woods—for they might have the biggest heart imaginable. I don't stereotype against students who have body piercings, blue hair and buy their clothes at Goodwill—for they sometimes are the most creative and energetic. I don't assume low achievements from my diverse population in class, because studies display this evidence. If anything, I push them harder to prove those stats untrue.

My personal contribution to education probably begins when I was in high school. I was a med bio monitor during my study hall and lunch hour. My teacher had me tutor other students who were struggling, along with other things, such as washing and preparing fetal pigs for dissection and feeding milliworms to the newts. When I tutored, it gave me a sense of accomplishment because I was helping someone. I would make students feel comfortable, not stupid or dumb. I was their equal. Soon, I was not only tutoring, but I was listening to life's problems, daily tribulations and high school hardships. I never had solutions to these situations, for I had no concept of such things—poverty, drug abuse, gang activity, violence, broken homes, neglect, the list goes on. Even though I had no answers, I listened.

. . . . .

Since then, I have gone through many hardships myself. I was in a serious car accident which spiraled into many health problems, including three spinal fusions, a crushed tailbone, staff infections, grafted hipbones and scarlet fever. On the personal side of the coin, I had a born-smart brother who not only made me feel inferior, but also diminished my self-worth at a young age as he shined during his academic career. I struggled compared to him. I've had to work very hard to accomplish my goals.

I personally believe that these misfortunes have made me a stronger person and a better teacher. I really try to understand students who are having a bad day. I listen to them when they are upset, fearful or discouraged. I also celebrate with them when they've just passed their driver's test, or have just been asked to prom.

I have somehow bonded with many students who maybe have never had a positive adult in their lives who listens. Just listens. I feel it is important that students realize their potential and acknowledge their own self-worth. My trick of the trade would be an annual senior letter that I send out to all the seniors that I have had in class. I write down each student's name and describe them by using three adjectives. Then, I write a personal letter to each acknowledging these qualities, their contributions to class, and events that will never be forgotten.

I never thought of the impact until I received a response in the mail two years later from a former student:

Ms. J—

What's up? Not much happening around here. Bad stuff mostly. I miss you Miss J—. We all miss you. Me, D—, and S— want to come visit you one day. Man, Miss J—, you need to come back [here]. You were the only teacher whoever gave me a chance. You let me talk when we walked. You never told me to shut up. You told me you believed in me. No one ever said something like that before.

You know that letter you wrote me? I still keep it in my wallet. When I'm about to do something bad, I pull it out and read it. It's hard not to do bad stuff around here. Maybe, I could come to [your] school, so I won't get into no more trouble. I need to get out of here. My life is messed

*up and it keeps getting worse. Maybe if I could get out of this neighborhood
I could be somebody someday.*

*Well, that's all for now. If I don't hear from you, just remember that
I'll never forget you. I'll never forget that you think I am good, when
everyone thinks I am bad. And your blue eyes, smile, and shortness.
I promise [to] stay out of trouble if you could be my teacher again.*

Your favorite student ever,
C—

This student died from gunshot wounds only a few weeks after his
letter was written. What might have happened if he'd had other teachers
like Miss J?

CHAPTER 5

Love and Logic's Four Key Principles

The Four Key Principles express the foundational ideas of Love and Logic and have been used as a format for developing and implementing strategies to address student performance. These principles are described in Chapter 2 of this book and have been identified as Self-Concept, Shared Control, Empathy with Consequence, and Shared Thinking. The intent of Chapters 5–7 is to provide background information about their development, application, and implementation. For a more thorough discussion of the concepts represented, the reader is referred to appropriate chapters in Teaching with Love and Logic.

Developing a Common Understanding

Our brains perform a marvelous function to keep us from going nuts. That function is to establish patterns allowing us to make sense of the world. Subsequently, our brains then filter out information that doesn't fit. If we had to equally consider all possible options when making choices, the time and effort expended would be exhaustive. Most of us would be paralyzed from making any decisions at all. Instead, when we are confronted with such situations, we tend to screen out entire categories of alternatives that don't fit our intended purpose.

These mental filters become the basis for the principles or values that influence our subconscious thought process. Having a set of principles provides a sense of security and stability and, in large part, actually predetermines what our decisions will be.

For instance, I have a personal set of principles about what I prefer to eat. I really only like meat that oinks, moos, clucks, or gobbles. I don't like food that ferments or reproduces by spore. So beef and turkey are in; beer and mushrooms are out. For me, it provides a fairly stable culinary existence. Since I have no need for adventure in food and am somewhat taste-blind, I am very satisfied with these simple boundaries. Also, I am not intimidated by exotic menus.

Depending on the individual and circumstance, specific principles may vary. However, the process of applying these principles remains fixed. For instance, when looking for a car, considerations may include how much I can afford or what the vehicle will be used for. If the primary purpose is for transporting kids, groceries, and pets, the field is significantly narrowed. I don't have to consider all automobile options, only the ones that have made the initial "cut."

People also use principles when making decisions about their own conduct. Although temperament, experience, and circumstances provide individual nuances, everyone has some basic human needs. A strength of Love and Logic lies in the way it understands those needs relative to volitional behavior.

For a number of years, Love and Logic has summarized this understanding as the "Four Key Principles." As is the case with other concepts, these principles have a story.

The Four Key Principles—A Historical Perspective

I first started using Love and Logic in the recommended way: select one idea that seems workable, practice it, and then check how it turns out. Even though those early efforts were fairly amateurish and segmented, the students responded surprisingly well. After a few successful ventures, however, a nagging caution started to creep in. Although interactions were going well, I wasn't at all sure why. My fear was that what was making all of this a success might eventually fail.

What I did know was that just about any technique can be successful during the proverbial honeymoon period. Kids will often act better just because their attention has been diverted to analyzing the new system and how they might turn it to their advantage. At one point, I wondered if a person would have to be a Jim Fay clone to have long-term success. In my own best interest, it seemed pertinent to learn why Love and

Logic worked—mostly to see if I had the wherewithal to maintain the needed effort.

Although my research skills were limited, some comparisons with what I had been doing were relatively easy to make. First, although I had refined operant conditioning methods (behavior modification) into a fairly workable system, there was the full recognition I would not want done to me what I was doing to my students. I would not want to be manipulated or bought off into being good.

On a more practical basis, I also recognized that these strategies would very quickly cease to be effective if the kids knew what I was doing to them. Can you imagine telling any kid, "Young lady, your behavior is less than acceptable and we (the adults) will be systematically shaping new conduct through a system of reinforcement schedules." Most of the kids I worked with would respond with, "Oh, yeah? Just watch and see how your 'system of reinforcement schedules' will work on me!" It was like being involved in some CIA covert operation. If my cover were blown, it would all end.

With Love and Logic, secrecy was not an issue. A basic tenet was that kids should be treated with dignity and respect and that they could actually be told what was happening. They could not only be informed of the goal, but be involved in the process as well. In fact, the kids were an integral part in making decisions. There was no need for me to constantly be on guard of being blackmailed over something I was trying to hide. I remember thinking that even if Love and Logic was no more effective than behavior modification, it sure was a lot less stress on me!

Another factor was the "delivery model." Before Love and Logic, I was so intent on adhering to strict regimens, reinforcement schedules, and extrinsic rewards. Now I found myself much more interested in understanding what the kids were thinking and, aghast, what they were feeling. Often just asking them what they thought should happen if their behavior continued was the only "intervention" needed. I started to realize that kids often capitulate to some plan or work for external rewards because that's all the adults offer them.

Love and Logic had a structure, to be sure, but it did not lock the adults into an untenable system. There was no artificial sequence. Problem situations could be dealt with in a way that fit the circumstances and considered the needs of everyone involved. The focus was on the internal changes in kids' thinking rather than worrying if a strong enough tangible reward could be provided. Kids could be treated individually and win/lose situations did not have to be the inevitable result when disciplining.

Further, there was, for lack of a better term, a different "attitude" with Love and Logic. Every concept was rooted in real-life experiences. Even mistakes had a different connotation. Since errors are inevitable in the human experience, teachers and parents were encouraged to use such incidents to help kids build wisdom.

As I listened to Jim's tapes (there wasn't a lot of print material back then) and thought about my students, it locked in that Love and Logic worked because basic human needs were met rather than diverted. The trick seemed to be that these needs were met in a way that absorbed the inevitable variables encountered when people are involved.

There were, however, a number of constants intertwined in Jim's stories. Kids were to be treated with unconditional regard, even if they were in trouble. Jim also emphasized that destructive power struggles should be avoided (primarily because it was usually the adult who lost). Another repeating theme was that when kids made mistakes, lessons would be learned best if they believed that what happened to them was directly connected to their decisions. Finally, throughout Jim's stories and interactions there was the definite understanding that whoever created a problem should exert the most mental effort in creating the solution.

To be sure, everyone has different perceptions about life, but what seemed universal was that, given these ideas Jim taught, the outcome of a disciplinary intervention could be fairly well predicted. Why Love and Logic worked was starting to take shape.

Confirming the Hypothesis

These observation were made in relative isolation. I was a middle school special education teacher and didn't know anyone else who had much heard of Love and Logic. I wanted to talk with Jim—basically to check out if my thinking was on the right track.

The opportunity came when he had a speaking engagement in Milwaukee and one in Madison the following day. I offered to drive Jim,

. . . . .

thinking this would be an hour and a half to have a private consulting session. As we drove (in my own mind I consider that stretch of Interstate 94 as the "Love and Logic Highway"), the essential concepts of Love and Logic were brought into focus. Not so much a revelation as an understanding. By the end of that drive the concepts were gelled. I related to a phrase the television series *A-Team* made famous: "I love it when a plan comes together."

As we talked, observations were put into some basic categories:

1. Kids behave consistent with the view they have of themselves. When kids are put in a position of having to defend their worth, they engage in all sorts of behavior to either hide a weakness or hurt others in retaliation. What people feel about themselves is often contrary to the evidence. Some kids consider themselves dumb even when confronted with test scores that indicate the very opposite. Some wonderfully skilled athletes consider themselves inadequate because there is someone better. Many kids go ballistic when they are teased; others go to illogical lengths to avoid blame for their mistakes. On the other hand, people who accept responsibility for their actions seem to be the stronger for it. Well-adjusted people seem to make changes when they make mistakes; maladjusted people seem to make excuses. When people feel good about themselves, behavior is usually not a problem. These observations are summarized in the term **self-concept.**

2. People don't like to be made to do things even if what is being required is in their own best interest. People tend to resist compliance requests either openly or in some hidden form. The desire to have some power and control seems to be universal, and when people perceive that power is being taken away from them, they will fight to the end to get some back, and try to control others in the process. When people have legitimate options they are much less likely to resist. From these ideas comes the term **shared control.**

3. When a person feels bad after making a mistake, there is a strong tendency to want to alleviate the pain by putting the blame on someone or something else. However, it is nearly impossible to do this when the person feels understood and makes a logical connection

between the inappropriate decision and what happens as a result. Without these two factors of understanding and logical connection, people are much less accepting of the cause/effect relationship between what they did and what happened to them. Where there is an unwise decision, the result is almost always some kind of pain. When this pain comes from the outside (e.g., punishment), the tendency is to become resistive or try running away. However, when the pain comes from inside (e.g., remorse), there is a completely different response. When people feel understood and make the connection that what they do influences what happens to them, they seem more motivated to make changes. These two concepts, **empathy** and **consequence,** when combined, are more powerful than the sum of their parts.

4. People seem to figure things out better when they are not being yelled at. Stress cramps up the thinking part of our brains and we can do little more than react. Sometimes these reactions take place on a pretty primitive level, in survival mode. Also, the solutions people come up with for their own problems are usually much more effective than solutions someone else creates for them. Thinking through a problem is an investment in the solution. When kids can practice solving their own problems, they are making deposits in their own wisdom account. The term coined to explain this phenomena is **shared thinking.**

The Four Key Principles, Found Through Discovery

A validating characteristic about these principles is that they were discovered, not contrived. Although the tenets of Love and Logic can be supported by research and sound psychological theories, they were developed from commonsense conclusions from working with actual people in real environments. There was no need to extrapolate from animal studies or translate from esoteric theory to reality.

I am reminded that in the days prior to global exploration there were some who sat down with preconceived ideas about the world and determined that the earth was flat. Those who advocated this position had little trouble finding sufficient "evidence" to support their ideas. After all, they reasoned, if the earth was round, those on the bottom would fall off!

During that same time, there were others who decided to "try and see" what would happen if someone sailed west and just kept going. What these explorers found is that they eventually got back to where they started. Since there was no falling off the edge, they concluded that the earth must be round.

When educational institutions are isolated, they are vulnerable to esoteric learning theories. Special education is certainly not immune. Sophisticated-sounding concepts like "psycholinguistic programming," "neurological reorganization," and "right-brain/left-brain learning," not to mention obscure nutritional diets, dominate for a while and then are discounted and replaced. Sometimes the constructs forming the basis of these methodologies have been determined not even to exist. Even then, to a degree, such theories can be made to work. Just like the flat-earth theory works if you aren't planning to travel very far!

Perhaps education (and special education in particular) is vulnerable because of pervasive insecurities on the part of teachers and parents. Being effective with kids is hard; being effective with special needs kids is even harder. Self-doubt seems to be a built-in part of the job.

The overall effect, however, is that many educators and parents are kept in a perpetual state of uncertainty. In their desperation to be effective, teachers and parents are driven to find better ways to help kids learn and behave. In the process, the adults wear themselves out and lessen their productiveness. They have tremendous faith that there is "something else" that could be done for or with a kid.

I imagine that the early explorers who surmised the world was round had more than occasional anxiety. What made the difference for them was their observations and the tools they had available. They observed that when a ship sailed away from land, it was gradually lost to sight. First the decks, then the sails, then the mast. They also had faith in the tools that demonstrated to them that the world was round.

At the risk of being melodramatic, Love and Logic likewise provides observations and tools to work with kids who are in the process of learning how to get along in the world. Love and Logic is little interested in strategies and theories that are difficult to understand or require a clinical setting to implement. The Four Key Principles were developed not only to provide a paradigm for understanding the attribution of behavior, but also as a format for developing interventions.

The Purpose of Pattern

Life is hard. To ease the inherent anxieties that come with living, we develop patterns to make sense of the world. Language is perhaps the best example. Certain sounds and combinations come to have meaning and become part of our normal repertoire. Other sounds have no meaning and are essentially filtered out. Those of us who have tried to learn a foreign language late in life are acutely aware of this phenomenon.

The patterns we develop for other aspects of life (e.g., values) are created by a similar process. What we come to believe as good, bad, or indifferent is used to determine how we cope and react to the situations we find ourselves in. Without some sort of filter or pattern, we would pretty much live in chaos. Making decisions would be inefficient at best and a sense of satisfaction would certainly elude us.

There is little difference when devising instructional or behavioral interventions. Think of it. No one we can foresee every eventuality that can occur. Kids seldom misbehave on cue or with prescheduled regularity. There is no historical record of any kid telling the teacher, "Next Tuesday at about 10:15, I will be engaging in some misconduct. I'm telling you now so you have time to research an effective intervention."

A benefit of the Four Key Principles is that they can serve as a format for deciding what to do regardless of the variations that are part of daily interactions. Adults can have the confidence they need to influence kids without fear of damaging them.

The Four Key Principles: A Reflection of Intrapersonal Needs

Humans have a hierarchy of needs that range from basic survival to having fun. Reduced to the simplest terms, behavior, whether appropriate or not, is for the purpose of either obtaining or avoiding "something." Although this "something" may involve survival for some children, generally the issue stems from some basic affective need. An additional factor is that the acceptability of any particular action is most often judged within a social context. As a simple example, yelling would not be acceptable in a quiet study hall, but would be expected at a football rally. Even extremes, like infliction of pain, are condoned in contact sports, body piercing, and medical treatments.

. . . . .

What has interested me for some time is how people can interpret the same actions so differently. For instance, when I engage in a behavior that others might consider negative, I have little trouble giving that action some positive attribution. I have a somewhat offbeat sense of humor and what I consider witty and funny, much of the rest of the world would consider immature and annoying. What I might consider leadership qualities, others might consider manipulative.

What I have also "discovered" is that just about everyone thinks the same way I do. That is, everyone can justify their own behavior (at least at the time it occurs) and criticize others for doing virtually the same thing. It is a convincing argument that, from the perspective of the person behaving, virtually all conduct has some positive twist.

Some March to a Different Drummer,
Others Aren't Even in the Same Parade
The effective use of the Four Key Principles is increased once the behavior is understood from the perspective of the "behavee." Whether the subject is simple or complex, we all have our own way of understanding (i.e., perceiving) the proper order of things.

For instance, my wife, Diane, and I have completely different viewpoints about turning on the car heater when the weather is cold. Frankly, I must admit that I don't know if I can even comprehend her position on this matter, and it has been a source of no small contention between us.

My method is to turn the fan on full blast right away. That way, my theory goes, every ounce of heat will be captured. Diane has a very different approach. She waits, and waits, and waits. Even after the temperature indicator shows the engine is as hot as it's going to get, she waits. Then, after what seems an interminable amount of time, she turns the fan to the first click. Then the second click, and so on. Sometimes we are at our destination before the heater is blowing at maximum capacity.

I have stopped asking her why she uses this method because the answer has always been, "It's my car and that's the way I want to do it." To fill in what seems, to me, a reasoning gap, I have a theory. Diane has an almost pathological aversion to cold and I suspect she doesn't want frigid air circulating around the car. This doesn't make sense to me, but on the other hand, my practice doesn't make sense to her either. (I once did share this explanation with Diane. Her response was, again, "It's my car and that's the way I want to do it.")

Life is replete with examples of how people understand the world in very different ways. When working with special needs kids these discrepancies in perception are even more pronounced. The special needs kids have the factors of learning, emotional, physical, and/or social characteristics that, by definition, are outside normal parameters—otherwise, these kids wouldn't have special needs! When we interpret another's behavior through our own perception, there is a good chance wrong conclusions will result (except, of course, with car heater behavior).

Misbehavior: A Way to Meet Intrapersonal Needs
Schools place heavy emphasis on student actions considered incompatible with acceptable school performance. Regardless of how these actions are labeled, the listing is nearly always from the perspective of the adult. Perhaps the adult is inconvenienced or annoyed. Or maybe there is a violation of some established value. Regardless, the kid's behavior is given a negative attribution and is slated to be reduced or eliminated.

Upon reflection, however, this orientation may have some fundamental drawbacks that greatly restrict effectively working with kids. If, for instance, inappropriate behavior were to be viewed as a maladaptive or inefficient way to meet a basic intrapersonal need, we may well approach the disciplinary action very differently. Certainly, there is little rationale for condoning misbehavior and it is fully recognized that some conduct is innately wrong or destructive. However, most behavior is for the express purpose of meeting some affective need. Unless interventions are developed to address these needs, an essential key for orchestrating effective strategies will have been missed.

We all have physical, cognitive, and affective facets of our being that influence how we express intrapersonal needs. Love and Logic recognizes that the primary business of life is to obtain a feeling of well-being. Not having basic human needs met over the long term can result in a whole lot of hurt, and trouble usually emerges when these needs are met in ways that cause a problem for others.

Although people may have the same few basic psychological needs, the triggers that prompt discontent are highly individual. What results in a defensive posture in one person may not even be noticed by another. These idiosyncrasies combine to create unique perspectives (perceptions) and, subsequently, reactions in an effort to regain homeostasis.

Given this premise, there are two critical prerequisites to the development of effective interventions. The first involves expectations of the adults. So often the adults presume that when a behavioral plan is in effect, the kid should be good immediately—as if by magic. This has been a confusion to me, because there would be no such expectation for other school-related skills. If a plan were devised for a reading-disabled student with the promise the learning problem would be resolved within a year, that strategy would be exalted as a miracle.

The expectation for behavior change is different. When a behavior plan is drawn up, the expectation is often that the kid will be good, not just better, by the next day. Actually, if change came that quickly there would be concern about the kid's mental stability. Quick changes don't usually result in any kind of permanency. Just like cramming for a test, the results will be temporary.

The second important prerequisite is knowing what need the kid is trying to meet with the maladaptive behavior. As mentioned previously, there are relatively few human needs; however, the triggers for these needs are infinite. Therefore, it is absolutely necessary to know how the kid is perceiving the situation. Not what is the norm. Not what the adults think. If the purpose (function) of the maladaptive behavior is not understood, interventions developed will be hit-or-miss. And, unfortunately, that is what happens all too often in our schools.

Behavior plans often focus on what reward or punishment the kid will receive. In fact, these would be better termed as "behavior consequence" plans because there is so much emphasis on reward and punishment. I have seen instructional teams struggle to find an external repercussion strong enough to have the desired effect while still being possible to implement. I have seen other situations where kids are bargaining for rewards like they are negotiating a benefits package. Usually, the "implementability factor" takes precedence, even if the adults know the reinforcer probably won't work. The time and energy spent are essentially dissipated when the plan fails.

· · · · ·

What is not often realized is that the most appropriate "reward" is right in front of our proverbial eyes. To paraphrase an old campaign slogan, "It's the needs, stupid." If we identify what need the kid was hoping to meet from the inappropriate behavior, we have the ultimate reward for that individual kid. The key is that the replacement behavior must allow the kid to obtain what he/she was hoping to get in the first place. And that is what takes insight and expertise.

If a kid is seeking to regain a sense of self-worth, then a few minutes of free time will not do the trick. If the student is working for a sense of control, giving a few stickers will hardly be enough. Unless we understand this perspective, we will be quite prone to developing interventions that will have limited, if any, long-term success.

Brandy's Experience

The Four Key Principles assimilate primary affective needs people seek to satisfy. In addition, these principles give parameters for instruction. When self-concept is maintained or strengthened, defense mechanisms are reduced. When the adults demonstrate that they are interested only in controlling themselves and their part of the circumstances, kids are less prone to engaging in power struggles to satisfy a need for control.

The learning value of logical consequences is accentuated when a student's feelings are first validated with an empathetic response. When this sequence is maintained, kids tend to focus on the need for internalized change rather than blaming others for their mistakes. And finally, the more practice kids have in heavy thinking, the greater their potential for becoming better problem solvers.

Brandy was a fifth-grade student. Although very bright, she did not like being with other kids and had developed exceptionally effective ways of getting sent to the office, put in the hall, or otherwise being removed from her classmates. At one point, she had threatened another student with the point of a compass and the school was forced into taking some action.

An IEP meeting was called to develop a behavior intervention plan. The staff had created a very detailed protocol and it was evident they had put much effort into researching techniques. The plan was an impressive three pages with dozens of steps. It was so thorough that the question was whether it could actually be implemented.

. . . . .

In situations like this, there is a fine balance between staff training and making people feel defensive in front of parents and colleagues. The staff who had done the actual writing were asked (tactfully) if they could recall any specifics of the plan without first looking at it. Even though the plan had been composed just the previous day, all but a few items had been forgotten. This was one clue the plan may have been too complicated to be workable.

Another observation was made. The plan essentially detailed what the teachers would do—it was in actuality a behavior management plan for the staff. The primary references to Brandy involved rewards if she conformed to the stated expectations and penalties for continued infractions.

After talking with the staff, a decision was made to revise the plan, this time with Brandy's participation. That subsequent meeting opened as follows:

FACILITATOR: Brandy, do you know what this meeting is about?

BRANDY: About how I am acting in class.

FACILITATOR: That's right, and what behavior do you suppose concerns your mom and teachers?

BRANDY: Well, when I get mad, I yell, throw things, run out of the classroom, and slam the door.

Amazing! Although there were some additional behaviors of concern, Brandy's list was consistent with the adults' inventory. So far, everyone is pretty much on the same page. Further in the discussion, Brandy also identified the triggering (antecedent) events to her behavior. There were two: when kids teased her, and when things didn't go right.

The next step was to determine whether previous interventions were working. The adults knew they weren't—that was the reason for the meeting. The key, however, was whether Brandy had the same opinion:

FACILITATOR: What usually happens when you yell, throw things, run out of the classroom, and slam the door?

BRANDY: Usually, I get sent down to the office.

FACILITATOR: How many times have you been sent to the office, say in a week?

BRANDY: Lots.

FACILITATOR: How many is "lots"?

BRANDY: Oh, about eight.

FACILITATOR: How many times do other kids get sent to the office?

BRANDY: One girl was sent down three times this year and a couple others were sent down once.

FACILITATOR: That was for this whole year, so far?

BRANDY: Yeah, the whole year.

FACILITATOR: So, it sounds like you about hold the record for your class. And how do you think being sent down to the office is working with the four things we are talking about? Good, or not good?

BRANDY: Not good, because I am still doing that stuff.

The group decided to concentrate on Brandy's reaction to the two triggers she had mentioned. The next step was to identify viable replacement behaviors. Although it would be fairly easy for the adults to make the selection, there is a higher probably of success if the kid is involved with the decision. To be satisfactory, replacement behavior needs to meet two criteria: it must be acceptable to everyone on the team, and it must satisfy the same need as the offending behavior. The meeting continued:

FACILITATOR: Brandy, do you have any idea about what you could be doing instead?

BRANDY: Don't know. (And she probably didn't. This is where instruction comes in.)

FACILITATOR: What you told us is that when you are teased or things don't go perfectly, you start feeling mad inside. Then, you . . . ?

BRANDY: You mean . . . yell, throw things, run out of the room, and slam the door . . . ?

FACILITATOR: That's right. And you can't think of anything right now to do instead. Do you think other kids and adults ever get mad when they are teased or upset when things don't go as planned?

BRANDY: Yeah.

FACILITATOR: You're right. Would you like some ideas about what they do?

Predictably, Brandy said she would be interested. At this point, we did a round robin and the adult members of the team offered their ideas:

1. Ignore the teasing.
2. Have a piece of banana cream pie and a cup of coffee.
3. Start a fight.
4. Walk away.
5. Use an "I message" to tell how you feel.
6. Write your feelings on a piece of paper.

Brandy was also part of the brainstorming, and contributed an idea of her own:

7. Draw a picture and then scribble it out.

The conversation continued:

FACILITATOR: Are there any ideas on that list that you think would work for you?

BRANDY: Well, if I ate pie, I would get fat like Mr. H— (the teacher), and if I hit the kids, I would get into more trouble. I'd pick drawing and writing what I was thinking on a piece of paper.

Other components of this plan were finalized. The meeting was on a Wednesday and Brandy said she would start the following Monday. This would give her and her mom a chance to get a special tablet for writing her feelings and drawing the pictures.

We also discussed how the team would know whether the plan was working or needed to be revised. Brandy's suggestion was that if she were sent to the office less than twice per month, that would show the plan was working.

The next issue was when this replacement behavior should kick in. Since it would probably be too late once Brandy was having a fit, we talked about how it would be better if she could prevent the outbursts rather than deal with the aftermath. Brandy was asked if she knew how she felt inside after being teased or when realizing that things weren't going well, but before she decided to yell, throw things, run out of the room, and slam the door. After some thought, she said, "Yeah, I feel tense." It is of great benefit if the kids do know these antecedent feelings and can give a name to them. At this point, we are ahead of the game for Brandy.

We talked some about the benefit of engaging the replacement behavior when she felt tense, because once she was angry, it would be too hard to remember what to do. Then we talked about record keeping. What data would be collected, by what method, and by whom:

FACILITATOR: The last thing to talk about is who will keep track of how you are doing. Who do you think should do that?

BRANDY: The teachers and my mom?

FACILITATOR: That's one possibility, but could I ask a couple of questions? (Brandy consented.) First, is this a plan for the teachers or for you?

BRANDY: For me, I guess.

FACILITATOR: That's right. You see, your mom and teachers are already behaving okay, so they don't need a plan. And they are already working pretty hard, so if they had to keep track, it would be kind of like extra work for them. Would you be willing to pay them if they did this for you?

After Brandy found out what the cocurricular hourly pay was (and that her mom would work for the same rate), she was more than willing to keep track of her own data. As the meeting progressed, she also identified what information should be kept, the format (she devised a chart), and who should be informed. This whole process lasted less than twenty minutes. To be sure, the adults had some responsibility to guide and encourage, but Brandy was the majority stockholder.

It is important to point out another factor. You may notice that there is a conspicuous absence of punishment or reward. There are no threats of suspensions, take-backs, or giveaways. The consequence of the plan working was to be a feeling of success and control. The consequence of failure (determined by Brandy herself) would be to revamp the plan.

. . . . .

Brandy's behavior was her attempt to control her environment. She was not one to be gregarious or overly social—and probably never would be. Although her previous methodology for obtaining her own space was efficient, it was maladaptive. Eventually, she developed alternative behavior to get her needs met in a way that was not so conspicuous.

In a conversation with her teacher, he related one of those workable solutions. As in many classrooms, the teacher had students place their desks in clusters with several desks butted up against each other. This, of course, was not the configuration preferred by Brandy and she started feeling "tense." Rather than engaging in her former technique, however, she and the teacher negotiated her space and they agreed she could place her desk up to three inches from any other (a moat, if you will). Not only was this a workable solution, but Brandy also received practice in precise measurement. Brandy was happy, the teacher was happy, and I presume the rest of the kids were happy. And all for the sake of a three-inch strip of air.

It's the Law: A Wake-up Call That
Special Needs Kids Need to Be Ready for Life

One of the first overheads I remember seeing from Love and Logic materials was a picture of a youngster walking through a doorway with the caption: "I recognize this world, I practiced for it at home." The question arises, "What is necessary to be successful in life?" The answer lies in large part with having a **self-concept** that provides a foundation for a feeling of worth; the willingness to **share control** so productive relationships can be developed; an understanding of cause-and-effect relationships that come from the **consequences** of behavior; and the ability, engendered through **shared thinking,** to solve intra- and interpersonal problems for the common good.

The framers of federal law were cognizant that in the first two decades of special education legislation, many injustices had been corrected. Disabled students were no longer systematically denied access to school and parents had increased participation in their student's program development. Great strides were made in other areas to address the educational and discrimination issues of students with disabilities.

However, in spite of these commendable improvements, dropout rates for special education students remained unacceptably high. In addition, even when disabled students graduated, indicators such as high unemployment demonstrated that shortcomings still remained. As a result, the 1997 revision of the law placed an emphasis on planning for disabled students once public school services ended. The sad fact is, however, that when the kid's educational program does not focus on skills for success in adulthood, the school becomes a primary source of a problem it is mandated to address.

Few would argue the value of such long-term planning (referred to as "transition"). However, immediate concerns like just getting students through some current crisis or onto the next grade are so often underscored that what the student will be doing as an adult is little considered. When there is such an imbalance and the "future is being sacrificed on the altar of the immediate," the kid and parents must deal with the consequences at a time when school no longer can be involved in any part of the solution.

To repeat, one of the primary goals of special education law is for disabled students to be independent and employable. This is a very practical aspiration and, although in schools there is often a heavy emphasis on academic skill development, the honest fact remains that affective behavior is even more important.

There was also a recognition of the obvious: school will end sometime for every disabled student. At some point, the security of the institution of education ends. To many kids and parents, this is an unpleasant surprise. The legislature recognized that this lack of preparedness had to change, and to change it, someone had to be responsible. That someone was the public school system.

What Are We Doing in Our Schools?

A number of years ago a fellow special education teacher confided that she had a serious concern. Her conflict was about getting her students ready to reintegrate into the regular education classroom. Although this was an explicit part of her "job description," she was sincerely wondering if this goal was worth her time and effort.

It appeared, she said, that the purpose of any given grade was to get kids ready for the next. Further, it seemed that the purpose of elementary school seemed largely to get kids ready for middle school and, in turn, the purpose of middle school seemed largely to get kids ready for high school. Continuing with the theme, it often appeared that the purpose of high school was to get kids ready for college.

This teacher had a gift for grasping the obvious. From that conversation, I realized that even my own graduate-program specifics were largely determined by a decision whether or not to pursue a doctorate. On the surface, at least, it would be quite easy to conclude that the purpose of school is more schooling. An inherent problem is that entitlement to public education ends someday.

Our educational systems certainly have faults and drawbacks; however, school can be a place for kids to get ready for life. In addition to being a place where academics can be developed, school is a place where the affective skills can be learned and practiced. Learning to be responsible, how to work cooperatively, and how to accept limitations are essential skills for kids to be successful as adults. The first priority may be simply getting kids ready to be ready.

A question faced by those working with special needs kids is how to teach these necessary skills. Special education has a number of variables to consider. These kids may not perform well in traditional settings or respond to common methodologies. Politics of education also enter in. Parents are uniquely involved in special education and often have a different orientation than school staff.

Certainly, formal instruction and curricula are keys to some of this necessary learning. There is an obligation to have kids acquire academic skill development. Reading, writing, and arithmetic should not be underestimated. For kids to acquire affective skills, however, necessitates a different kind of instruction and teacher preparation.

There are some lessons that can be best learned in the context of natural interactions. The problem is that these opportunities are usually not predictable. They take us by surprise. If we don't have some internalized process to take advantage of these teachable moments, we can lose some valuable opportunities. However, this degree of unpredictability is precisely what makes these moments so powerful in learning. Being able to take advantage of these incidental opportunities may be what separates professional educators from "classroom managers."

A number of times I have heard that ministers must always be ready to "preach, pray, or die." Teachers have a similar obligation always to be at the ready to guide kids toward the goal of being ready for life.

Getting Zeke Ready for the Real World

In schools and homes there is an entrenched mind-set that infractions need to be taken care of immediately. I have often wondered why this is. Immediacy doesn't seem so vital in other circumstances. For instance, when we call a high-powered therapist or counselor regarding behavior of a student, it means the school is at its wits' end—every idea has been used up. What we hear from the therapist is, "I have some time two weeks from Wednesday." Even though our call to an outside agency is indicative of how serious we consider the situation, the person we are calling usually does not share any sense of urgency.

At first this irritated me. But then, things seemed to turn out all right in the long run. I now understand that immediate closure is not always best. Time is needed to calm and think. It takes a strong person to use this process in disciplinary situations.

Zeke was a middle school student who had been in special education for the vast majority of his school career. Although rather unsophisticated, he could use defiance and aggression fairly effectively to get what he wanted. Zeke had long since lost any apprehension of adults. He had years of practice developing and refining his modus operandi. And what did these actions get him? Mostly what he wanted. At least in the short term.

Zeke was disabled, to be sure. His anger and control issues were significant. If he did not change, it was very predictable that his behavior would have serious ramifications to himself and others. He had a unique take on reality, to be sure; however, the process for change is the same for him as for anyone else. Long-term change must come from inside. The professional skill is to interact in a way that change is effected by the student's own volitional choice.

Before any behavior plan will work, the kid must first believe that the problem that has been created may tangibly affect him. Zeke, as many other kids, had not quite mastered this concept. However, it was not for lack of trying on the part of the adults in his life. All manner of punishments and rewards had been implemented without much success. By seventh grade, Zeke was expert at sabotaging any plans the adults could devise.

The premise of Love and Logic is that behavior change starts with a change in perception. The role of the adult is basically to provide information in such a way that perceptual change can be initiated. A quick start to this process is for the "instruction" to begin at a point of mutual agreement. That is, if there is a point at which both the kid and the adult have the same understanding, the roadblocks to the change process are reduced. Mutual agreement reduces opposition, avoidance, and a number of other factors that result in resistance to change. The trick is to make sure the agreement facilitates the goal.

Enter the real world. Kids from a fairly early age understand that, although school is an entitlement, a job is not. Since Zeke was in middle school at this time, he was old enough to grasp this fundamental concept.

As we go through the sequence of owning and solving problems, the first step is for the kid to recognize that there is a problem. To simply tell Zeke he had a problem would have violated the principle of mutual agreement and would only have started an endless debate. With different interaction, there is a different result.

Zeke often used his talents to get himself removed from classes he didn't like. One of his most memorable incidents involved him telling a teacher to perform an act that, frankly, would be physically impossible to do given the fact that she did not have dual-gender characteristics. On cue, the teacher told Zeke to leave her class, with no other direction or details.

Given no other specific destination, Zeke exercised the "option" of coming to my office. After a few minutes of letting off steam, the following dialogue took place:

ADULT: Zeke, we've had some time to talk and it seems that we both pretty much agree on what went on in Mrs. W—'s class. Is that correct?

ZEKE: Yeah.

ADULT: Since we agree on the facts, the next step would be to see who will eventually have the biggest problem if this kind of behavior keeps up? Does that seem reasonable?

ZEKE: That bitch never leaves me alone, she's always checking up on me. I act the way I do to get her off my back.

What Zeke just did is referred to as a "bird walk." That is, he answered a question that was not asked. Kids are so expert at this that they can usually divert the adult. And that is precisely the goal. Whenever the questions are "too close to home," we would all rather talk about something else. The adults need to recognize when this strategy is being employed, and get back to topic. The encouraging thing is that when kids go on bird walks, it confirms that the adult is on the right track:

ADULT: I'm pretty sure that's how you feel, and what was the question?

ZEKE: I don't know, say it again.

ADULT: I pretty much limit myself to repeating only one question per conversation. Do you want this to be that one question? There might be others that are more important, so do you still want this to be the one?

ZEKE: Yeah.

ADULT: Since I'm pretty much into efficiency, would it be okay if I repeated the question and asked the next one I was going to?

ZEKE: I guess.

ADULT: The first question was who will eventually have the biggest problem if this behavior keeps up? The next question was, if you acted like this at a job, what would happen?

ZEKE: I guess I would have the problem, and if I did this on a job, I'd get fired. My dad said he fires lots of people for doing stuff like that. He even said he would like to fire me from the house sometimes.

ADULT: Sometimes I wish we could fire kids from school, but have you ever heard of that being done?

ZEKE: No, that would be stupid.

ADULT: Well, stupid or not, it probably won't happen. And, in this district, it's really hard to even keep a kid back a grade. So, given those facts, Zeke, with any luck at all, how long will you be in seventh grade?

ZEKE: What do you mean?

ADULT: Well, barring anything like some kind of disaster, how long do you think you will be in seventh grade?

ZEKE: You mean . . . like a year?

ADULT: Yeah, that's what I mean. I've talked to your folks a lot so
           I know it's their great hope that you will go to high
           school after next year. By the way, how long do you plan
           to be in high school?

ZEKE: Four years . . . ?

ADULT: We all hope it doesn't take any longer than that. How
           long do you plan to have a job when you are a man?

ZEKE: What? What do you mean?

ADULT: I was thinking that unless something tragic happens,
           you will be a student for a little over five more years
           and have a job until you retire—so, what would that
           be, maybe forty or fifty years? Since you can't get fired
           from school, I'm wondering if this would be a good
           place to practice.

           You said you wanted the teacher off your back. I'm
           thinking you are telling her you want to be more inde-
           pendent. Would I be reading that right?

ZEKE: Yeah. I hate it when she's on my ass all of the time.

ADULT: So, it sounds like you would like to be more independent,
           would that be another way of saying how you feel?

ZEKE: Yeah.

ADULT: Would you like some ideas that would make you feel
           more independent and not get you into trouble?

ZEKE: You mean like tricking her?

ADULT: I'm not much into tricking people, but I think you and
           I could come up with some ideas that would work. I have
           a meeting to get to pretty soon, but what about coming
           in early tomorrow? Would that work out for you?

Zeke came in and we talked. First about wrestling (his preoccupation
at the time) and then about what he could do to feel independent and
not get into trouble. Change was not immediate, but within a few weeks,
he was no longer getting kicked out of classes and he had even curtailed
his foul language and fighting in the lunchroom. His parents, who had
just about given up on him, contacted me a few weeks later and said Zeke

was acting out less at home. The vicious fighting with his sister had even diminished.

The involvement with Zeke was incidental. There was no formal plan—just an interactional relationship facilitated by the Four Key Principles. These interactions were focused on encouraging Zeke to evaluate how his behavior would affect him. Forcing him to behave had not worked in the past, and there was no reason to believe forcing him would work in the future.

Zeke often came around to buy a soda from my private stock and tell me how things were going. He changed, but not immediately. Zeke got a late start and his progress took a lot of effort on his part. Life is hard, and getting ready for it takes time.

CHAPTER 6

More About Using the Four Key Principles

More Than Behavior

For the first few years after my introduction to Love and Logic, I thought the principles applied only to discipline. It took some time for me to recognize that this knowledge could be used for other aspects of teaching. There was a "paradigm paralysis" on my part that kids had to behave before they could be taught academic skills. The problem was that sometimes I didn't quite get past trying deal with behavior. A fundamental shift in thinking occurred when I realized that achievement and conduct were not isolated entities. One did not of necessity precede the other, nor did either have a differential status. Rather, if anything, there was an interdependence.

Sad to say, I don't know if I would have ever understood this if not for some of my students who had no discipline problems. These kids behaved just fine, but the intense labor necessary for them to learn reading, writing, and arithmetic was painful to watch. I spent hours honing discipline strategies, and then additional hours refining techniques to teach academic skills. Had I been a quicker thinker, I would have been able to concentrate on one set of skills rather than two.

In my own defense, I had simply accepted one of the most powerful presuppositions that has influenced education throughout history. That is, discipline and achievement are separate and isolated from each other. The logical extension is that these two entities are often addressed individually, and while one is being worked on, the other is sequestered. In fact, one of the most common discipline strategies is to remove students from the classroom setting altogether (i.e., suspension) or segregate them in a room where they do little or nothing (i.e., detention). Typically, when a kid is being disciplined, other learning is put on hold.

Like railroad tracks, behavior and academics are too often treated as parallel entities. They may seem to converge on the horizon, but really never come together. In fact, often the only time behavior management and academics merge is when schoolwork is prescribed as a punishment. One wonders why there seems to be so little understanding of what happens when kids are made to do extra work after class is over. It is an interesting observation that prisons and schools are the only two institutions where if you're bad, you stay longer.

What would happen if recalcitrant teachers were treated this way? If a teacher disrupted an important faculty meeting, I highly doubt that he or she would be made to write "I will not disrupt meetings" five hundred times or be made to sit for a Saturday morning motionless at a desk. Such a penalty would be considered demeaning and irrelevant to the infraction, and plainly just wouldn't work. Why such strategies are applied to children remains a mystery. The only plausible explanation is that such strategies have a short-term effect on enough kids to keep the adults locked in. And what the heck, since most teachers will have kids for only a year or so, someone else can experience the long-term fallout.

There is an additional irony. The oft-used punishment of suspension is the escape many kids hope for. Suspension is looked upon as a well-deserved reprieve from the daily reminder that school is a place where achievement is elusive at best. The bad part is that this removal separates the most disadvantaged kids from the instruction they so desperately need. Contrary to appearances, isolation and removal are not very good strategies. When the punishment reinforces the very behavior it is intended to eliminate and further isolates the student from the benefit of appropriate intervention, there should be a review of the procedures.

I often wonder what other profession would tolerate such action. Imagine going to a physician with a serious illness and being told that because you were sick you had to sit in the waiting room or go home until you were better. Or, worse still, to be denied treatment until you "decided" to contract a disease the doctor already knew how to cure. Such incompetence would hardly be tolerated. There is little excuse for condoning similar ineptness in education.

Solutions to problems of student performance are elusive because the perspectives of the adults and the students often clash. When each side becomes increasingly entrenched in their stance, deterioration of both student performance and teacher effectiveness is an inevitable result. Someone must make a conscious decision to break the cycle. Waiting for change to happen through some natural process might exceed the time left in our careers.

We often miss the obvious, and the relationship between discipline and achievement falls into that category. What is clear is that when kids are satisfied with their progress, conduct problems significantly lessen. In the 1970s, research from Precision Teaching established that curricular adaptations were the most effective behavior modifiers. That is, when kids feel good about their learning, there are precious few reasons for them to disrupt it. If it weren't so sad a commentary, it would be amusing that research had to confirm what everybody has pretty much known for most of human history.

A First Look at Achievement

Achievement and self-worth are inextricably connected. A job well done gives us a sense of satisfaction. Achievement is a way to validate ourselves. To achieve is an innate desire, but what happens far too often is that conditions are imposed on some students that make accomplishing the normal requirements of school a painful task. For some students, the demands of school deteriorate their sense of worth to the point that they have little alternative but to protect themselves by engaging in behavior ranging from apathy to aggression.

Fundamentally, achievement requires a determination to start a task and remain engaged to completion. Whether learning a replacement behavior, social skill, or academic competency, the student must first be willing to participate. There must also be a willingness to take some risk. For kids with disabilities, new learning often attacks their own sense of worth. Taking risks for these students has an added dimension that goes to the heart of their very personhood. The question is, given the circumstances within the school environment, how can kids be encouraged to venture into new learning? The answer lies in understanding the dynamics of achievement.

Although there are all sorts of achievement present in our educational and social systems, all basically fall into one of two general categories: comparative and individual.

Comparative Achievement

Comparative achievement occurs when a student's performance is rated against others or an external standard based on expectations of someone other than the kid. Schools are replete with contests where there is a best, first, or other differentiation of winners and losers. To depend on competition to motivate students to expend the effort necessary to acquire or maintain new skills may be acceptable for those on top, but questionable for all of the rest.

Most kids know how they compare with others in their group. Knowing where one ranks has become an integral part of the school experience. When our grandson, Edrik, was in third grade, he matter-of-factly mentioned his relative status in reading and math. He knew that his rank for writing was further down the list and he even had a position for his running speed. I would bet that the results of a sophisticated testing system would end up with a very similar finding.

Fortunately, Edrik did not connect his sense of self-worth to his relative status in the classroom—to him, self-worth and status were different things. Far too often kids equate their worth with their position in the queue. Some have even come to believe that they are good only if they are better than everyone else.

I recall a number of years ago watching Olympic women's gymnastics. I am fascinated by this sport mostly because I cannot even contemplate my body bending, twirling, and landing upright. It's in the same category as real magic for me.

As one contestant completed her run, she started to cry, and by the time she got to the pit areas she was openly weeping. Given my awe of what she had done, I presumed that these were tears of joy. How wonderful to be able to do what she did. How marvelous to have so much coordination and control over mind and body. But my perception was way off. Although her voice could not be heard, anyone could clearly see she was repeatedly saying to her coach, "I am so sorry."

The announcer made some commentary about this young woman eliminating herself from first place. The honest fact was that she was among the most skilled gymnasts in the world. And as my departed father would have pointed out, "For Pete's sake, she was good enough to be at the Olympics!" But in the face of being second, the satisfaction of that accomplishment was lost. Interestingly enough, the announcer also mentioned that a few years previous, a gymnastic coach in an Eastern European country had committed suicide because her team had not done well enough. That's a pretty drastic reaction—a permanent solution to a temporary situation. However, whenever there are few winners and lots of losers, most are left in the wake with a conspicuous absence of the rewards that symbolize success.

I recall a message on a T-shirt that stated: "Second place is first loser." I imagine that the creator of this phrase was intending to express some witticism; however, for many special needs kids, being at the top of any hierarchy is important because it so seldom happens to them. Even the most difficult of students, in situations where they feel safe to take risks, will confide that they would like to be good at school. When this is impossible for them, they will substitute being skilled at something else. How many students are essentially forced to brag about their maladaptive behavior because that's the only thing they feel good at? And how many students "level the playing field" in their own way by sabotaging the success of others?

Taking the Spirit Out of Spirit Week

Some years ago, the school where I was teaching celebrated "Spirit Week." Basically, this activity was the middle school version of homecoming. Part of the doings was to have a door decorating contest. Each of the home rooms entered the fray with gusto to win the prize. And it was a fairly substantial prize. The winning class would get to go to Great America. The rest had a regular day at school. The fanfare started and the race was on.

One of my students, a fairly scrawny seventh-grade kid named Jeff, put his heart and soul into this project. He couldn't read, write, or do arithmetic very well, but from the depth of his very being he energized his class and organized them far beyond what anyone thought he was capable. He rallied the troops, supervised the door decorating, and rested firmly in the thought that his efforts would result in glory and honor. The day of judgment came and Jeff was full of anticipation. He knew that his class would win and was already mentally preparing for the victory speech and the trip.

But his class didn't win. They didn't even come in second (but there was no big prize for second, anyway). When Jeff came into my room after the announcement, his animation had left. He sat in a corner study carrel and didn't interact with anyone that day. He tried valiantly to hide his tears.

The next year Spirit Week rolled around again. Jeff seemed to have a very different view than the previous year. Not only did he not support the door decorating contest, he openly mocked the whole activity. That year, several of the doors were vandalized. Although we could never catch the kid, Jeff was among the suspects. I found out long after that it was him. He had a whole year to plan his perfect crime and he pulled it off (literally) without a hitch.

Individual Achievement

There is another kind of achievement—one on which any other kind depends. For convenience of reference, this will be labeled as "individual achievement." This is learning that is based on accomplishments toward a goal or purpose without regard for what achievement might be set for others. Regardless of the content or methodology being used, the indispensable component for students to achieve is a personal willingness to initiate and remain engaged in a task until it is completed.

This has tremendous relevance to the instructional planning and behavioral interventions for special needs students. Whereas students without disabilities may gain innate satisfaction from just learning new information or skills, handicapped students, by definition, have adverse educational performance. For them to maintain engagement in the educational process carries a cost and can be quite threatening.

If the disabled kid views some aspect of learning be overwhelming, even getting started will take extraordinary effort. However, since individual initiative is just as important for special needs kids as anyone else, extra considerations are to be made because of disability-related issues.

. . . . .

This concept of individual achievement as a prerequisite to acquiring skills does not represent great intellectual insight. Likewise, it is no great revelation that kids need to be engaged in any given experience to learn from it. The question is, how do we encourage kids to stay involved in the process long enough to derive benefit? Many adults, apparently, rely on luck and false hope. Others try to fool kids into working or go overboard in their manipulation of every variable imaginable. Some just cut to the chase and go right for direct control.

The Life Plan

Several years ago a graduate student related a story about his brother-in-law. The student said he could tolerate being in this relative's presence for about three minutes at a time. As he told the story, the reason was apparent.

When the brother-in-law married, he determined that his wife would conceive a son first, and then a daughter. When his wife became pregnant, the brother-in-law sat at the dining room table and developed a written outline for his yet-to-be-born child's life. Details of this plan included position on the football team, college that would be attended, and career that would be pursued. Prior to the birth of the second child, determined to be a girl, he did likewise. That second plan even detailed the profession of the man the daughter would marry and how many children they would have.

The first child was born—a boy. The initial step was successfully completed. The next child was a girl. The plan was pretty much working so far. As the years passed, whenever either of the kids would get a bit off track, the father would sit them at the table, review their plan, and get them back on schedule. According to the story as told, through high school, the kids appeared to be very compliant with this whole program.

Eventually, however, the father's plan went somewhat awry. The daughter did follow through with every detail—right down to the profession of the man she married and the number of children she had. Then her marriage went down the tubes and she moved back home—this time with three grandkids.

The son went a different route. He dropped out of society and became heavily involved with drugs. At the time his uncle was relating the story, the son was among the street people of a city fairly distant from where his father lived.

This story, of course, is an extreme. But it does point out a number of factors that have fairly universal application when discussing achievement. The first, certainly not to be overlooked, is that adults want their kids to "do good." The second is that adults do what they think is needed in order for their kids to "do good." The third is that if the kid is not invested in the plan, there may be unintended outcomes.

Components of Achievement

The parents and teachers of special needs students want them, often desperately, to achieve. Because these kids have so much difficulty learning under traditional conditions, esoteric strategies have been developed in the hope of making a difference. Actually, some of these efforts are commendable, but unless they consider a full range of needs, including the affective, their success will be limited in the long term.

Since learning seems to be an innate drive, it is probably a misconception that recalcitrant students do not achieve anything. What is more accurate is that students with "performance problems" are not attaining what is intended by the adults. However, when students believe the task is beyond reach or irrelevant to them personally, there is a tendency to focus energies on what can be accomplished or does have some purpose. Whether maladaptive or appropriate, the process of achievement is pretty much the same and the dynamics involved can give clues for instruction.

Whether learning addresses academic, social, emotional, or behavioral skills is irrelevant. Acquiring new learning involves factors that are always present. Some of these factors can be controlled, some can be influenced, and some can only be accepted as is.

Innate ability, task difficulty, luck, and effort constitute four omnipresent components of achievement. These factors intermingle and certainly their emphasis varies with the individual and task. Understanding these factors is important because they significantly influence the level of investment students are willing to make in their own performance.

Innate Ability

Innate ability is a factor of achievement that, try as we may, probably won't change. We all have inherent intellectual, physical, and even emotional limitations. Unless we are somewhat delusional, we believe this and adjust our lives accordingly. Having limitations is part of being human and necessary for diversity. Imagine a world where everyone is good at everything. In a sense, if even two people are exactly alike, one of them probably isn't needed.

Most of us can work around our limitations, and by the time we acclimate to adult life, we simply avoid what we are not good at. For special needs kids, life is a bit different. Just as we may stand in awe of extraordinary talent, disabled kids wonder what it's like to be normal. The dyslexic kid looks at reading the same way I look at banjo picking. I watch people play what seems to be a thousand notes at the same time. I don't get it and doubt that I ever could.

The issue of innate ability is especially relevant for those with special needs. The limitations most people experience still allow them a usual range of options. On the other hand, the limitations experienced by special needs kids prevent them from doing what society considers necessary just to be normal. The restrictions disabled students experience prevent them from accessing aspects of life that most take for granted.

Whether it be a physical, learning, or emotional impairment, special needs kids face real-world consequences without reprieve. Those without disabilities may certainly have a degree of empathy; however, there is no way to simulate living with a handicap. The reality for these kids is that there will be some things they won't ever be able to do. Some things will take longer or require significantly more effort.

The amount of courage needed on their part is often phenomenal. I think of Chrissy, who can only view the world from within a body she cannot control. Or Mike, who graduated from college with honors but can't obtain a job because he can't feed himself, use the toilet without help, or even wipe his own nose. He has a brilliant mind. He might even be able to figure out the cure for his condition, but we will probably never know.

Given our long-standing cultural norm that puts a high value on ability and physical perfection, the trick is for kids to maintain a sense of personal value while accepting how the world views their innate limitations. It is hardly enough to keep telling kids that everyone is different, or that God made them special. Such reasoning, in my opinion, ranges from illogical to blasphemous. Having a true disability (not some watered-down version that has crept into our institutional thinking) is serious business and is not fun. It is far better to be up front with students so they can develop necessary skills from a foundation of honesty. In the absence of such a foundation, the disabled kid may not learn how to solve problems without causing a problem for someone else.

The Task Itself

Another variable that determines levels of achievement is the task itself. Special education is replete with sorting tasks by relative difficulty. Items on standardized tests, benchmarks for IEP goals, and anything else that is task-analyzed is organized in some type of hierarchy. Those in special education have been thoroughly acclimated to working from easy to difficult as a presumed sequence for teaching.

A problem arises because those who must follow the sequence have little input into its development. Because difficulty of task and innate ability are somewhat mutually dependent, what some do with ease may be nearly impossible for others to do at all.

I remember speaking with a well-meaning curriculum and instruction director who stated that all students, including the disabled, should be involved in higher-level math and language arts. She did concede that the "really, really, really disabled" might not benefit, however, and could be exempted. Her reasoning was that advanced course work was exciting, intellectually challenging, and a necessary component in the district's quest for academic excellence.

It was pointed out to her that some of our disabled students were almost ready to age out of special education and needed to know how to complete job application forms, read well enough to get information from a newspaper, and have sufficient math skills to not get ripped off by some financial charlatan. Of what value would calculus and Shakespeare be to them when they enter their real world? When asked how much of this high-level academic learning even she used outside the school setting, she had no answer. (The answer is "just about never.") We need to be governed by common sense and the impending pressure of getting these kids ready for the circumstances they will, in all likelihood, live in for decades after school.

Although task difficulty can correlate with innate ability (like me playing a banjo), we have all been presented with a difficult task wherein we knew, given time and study, we could achieve. I have watched our son, Jaben, make several of his own guitars. His first was made with the hand and power tools in my workshop—none of which were designed or intended for fine craftsmanship. He has shown developing insight and skill at this endeavor. He spends hours making up jigs and figuring out how to make all the parts right. He has researched and found just the right esoteric tool for some particular facet of his project. The task is intricate and hard, and, with a combination of trial and error coupled with heavy-duty thinking, he has been increasingly successful.

However, there is more to attempting what is difficult than just needing to "try harder." Sometimes the challenge of the task is fairly subjective and the difficulty factor can even be transient. I have a teacher friend who remembers "freezing" as a child every time there was a math test. Regardless of how much she studied, when the test paper was set before her she could hardly remember single-digit addition facts. To make her anxiety worse, she knew that after the test was handed back, her math-skills repertoire would reappear as if by magic.

An age-old strategy used to address task difficulty has been to make the task easier. On one level, this makes lots of sense; however, there is also a drawback. You see, if someone tells me a task is easy and I still can't accomplish it, I have a tendency to conclude that whereas before I thought I was dumb, now it is confirmed. On the other hand, if I actually can do the task, what satisfaction comes from completing something easy? In either case, there is a high likelihood that the student's motivation to expend the necessary energy is remote.

And what may be easy for most kids may be unimaginably beyond the reach of those with special needs. Even when students complete work commensurate with their skill level, they often translate their efforts as proof they are stupid. To exacerbate the problem, teachers sometimes believe so strongly that they have created appropriate tasks, their response is to become angry at the kid for not working. It is not a rare occurrence for the victim to be blamed for not learning. I have seen disabled students admonished to "look harder" at their work. Since I don't know what that means, I doubt that the kids did either. But I do know that when my best effort is not good enough, I engage in all sorts of alternative behavior to avoid a feeling of discouragement and despair.

Luck

A third factor that affects achievement is luck, just plain ol' blind luck. The reason luck is such a factor is largely because of some very established aspects of our educational system. The way we assess kids is but one of those covert contributions that teach kids the opposite of what is intended. How many of us have just happened to mark the right bubble on a test scan sheet? Or, just by chance, who hasn't remembered an isolated fact that resulted in a passing grade? It's happened to all of us. As a student I remember being relieved when the test format was true/false or multiple choice. I at least knew what the odds were of getting a right answer.

But luck is a two-edged sword. Just as the right answer might be obtained by chance, so can the wrong one. Whether the response is right or wrong, either way, we don't have a clue about how to replicate the success or avoid the failure. Dependence on luck is extremely common, but may not be a good way of getting ready for the real world.

The destructive aspect of luck is when it becomes a sorry substitution for faith. Faith is defined in the New Testament book of Hebrews as the "assurance of things hoped for, the evidence of things not seen," and no one needs this kind of encouragement more than special needs kids. Sadly, many confuse the two concepts and justify buying lottery tickets or otherwise gambling their lives away. Faith is not nebulous—it is based on substance and evidence. Faith allows the belief that my actions affect my outcomes. Luck is simply random and not built on anything solid—there is no foundation on which to establish perseverance.

But let us not ignore the fact that luck can have some heavy benefits. Many have locked onto luck with the strength of an addiction. Most people recognize that when luck is the reason for their success, there may not be much personal satisfaction when "things go right." There may be some momentary exhilaration, but because there is no cause/effect relationship, the pleasure is quickly dissipated.

. . . . .

However, the real hook is that luck is viewed as a protection. If luck is the reason for my failure, my sense of personal responsibility is minimal to none. And given the choice, I will avoid feeling responsible for my failures, even though the cost is high. And why? For starters, it's less threatening to personhood, and for special needs kids, their sense of self-worth is on the auction block at all times.

Effort—The Vital Factor

The final consideration is effort. Although I may try hard and fail, it is a surety that if I don't try at all the job will never get done. Effort is more than just working hard. Effort, in terms of achievement factors, means a willingness to start a task and stick with it until it is done. The fact that effort is required reflects no great breakthrough in learning theory. It's one of those commonsense concepts that is often glossed over because it lacks a certain sophistication.

A long-established principle in human volitional behavior is that failure after high effort is one of the most destructive forces to motivation. In fact, this phenomenon has its own special term: "discouragement." When we prioritize all of the negative feelings common to us humans, discouragement makes the top ten. Whereas sadness, anger, and other emotions take their toll, many of those feelings result from outside influences. Discouragement, however, is solidly based on the fact that life is going down the tubes and I don't have the wherewithal to do anything about it. In actuality, discouragement incorporates all of the achievement factors we have discussed. I can't do something because of innate limitations, the job is too hard, luck is against me, and no matter how hard I try, things go bad.

There is also the aspect of "learned helplessness." Since its coining, this concept has been used so long in education that its meaning has somewhat changed. Now the term often is equated with dependency or even laziness. However, the initial research findings were somewhat more ominous.

Picture, if you will, a laboratory doghouse with two rooms. One of those rooms has an electrical grid on the floor that can issue a nasty shock. Now picture a dog in that room and the researcher throwing a switch. Not a big problem, because the dog can move to the adjoining room through a door and settle down in comfort. Very quickly the dog realizes that room number one is not a fun place to be and stays in the room where the floor doesn't hurt.

Now picture the same dog and the same two-chambered house. The unsuspecting canine is placed in the "shock room" and the juice is turned on. There is one change nobody told the dog. The door to the other room is still there, but is now covered by Plexiglas. The dog can see where he would rather be, but can't get there. What happens is sad for the dog, and the applications to people are even sadder. You see, the dog eventually gives up trying to solve the problem. Even when the Plexiglas is removed, the dog does not seek reprieve. He just lays down and takes increasingly high voltage. In such experiments, some of these dogs became so dysfunctional that they had to be destroyed.

Learned helplessness, in its originally intended sense, is not laziness or wanting others to cater to whims. Learned helplessness is the conclusion that the solution to a problem cannot be accessed, even when it is readily available. This is much more the picture of truly discouraged kids.

Maybe this is all part of the human condition, and those who have not experienced despair and discouragement will have great difficulty understanding when it occurs in others. However, it is an extremely important factor to consider when working with special needs kids. It is the rare disabled kid who will not eventually give up. By the time they are in secondary school, many have gained reputations of being lazy or troublemakers. Unknown to the adults doing the categorizing, these kids would much rather have these labels than one of "dumb." These kids have given up.

Additional Considerations for Achievement

A goal of instruction is for kids to apply what they have learned. For this to happen, knowledge must be brought to working memory. If a letter sequence is not remembered, accurate reading or spelling will be sporadic at best. If a more adaptive replacement behavior is forgotten, there will be a tendency to revert back to previous conduct. In brief, if new learning is insufficiently established, the problem at hand will not be solved.

To a large degree, we remember events and circumstances that are associated with three factors: emotion, novelty, and previous learning. This simplistic analysis is certainly not to discount the complex neurology of our memory systems, but does well serve those of us who work with kids.

Learning and Emotion

Sensory information is routed through the brain's emotional centers first. The reason this happens is essentially for survival. If our ancestors didn't have this characteristic, humankind might have gone extinct some time ago. If our ancient forbearers had contemplated the beauty and grace of the saber-toothed tiger chasing them, they would have been removed from the gene pool. Likewise, if I analyze the characteristics of the car coming toward me at a high rate of speed, instead of reacting immediately, literally without thinking, and jumping out of the way, I may not live to influence others.

This emotional connection with learning is powerful and we all recall events that are associated with strong feelings. Those events stay with us so vividly that we can recall minute details years later. Many remember the exhilaration of a situation of imminent danger or their first kiss (mine was with a girl named Fay, in the Floyd [Iowa] cemetery, on an old cast iron bench, in June of my twelfth year).

We have all had situations in our careers that come vividly to mind because of the emotions they created. One such time for me was when I allowed kids in my class to watch a movie I had not previewed. It was the day before winter break and the kids had earned some time off. We decided to watch a movie, eat popcorn, and just in general, mentally prepare for the vacation ahead.

In a moment of naiveté, I let a kid bring a film that had just been released on video. Since I was not much into going to movies, I had a significant lack of awareness of the content. There were no vulgar or sexual terms in the title, so it passed my cursory censorship. We started the video and I thought all was well. It was a rather good feeling. Just me and the kids watching a video together eating popcorn. What a warm, relaxing, bonding experience. Who said a special education classroom was only drill and practice?

Then it happened. As one scene faded, another opened to a roomful of unclad women. I was only five feet from the video machine, but everything was in slow motion as I lunged to the machine and pushed the

. . . . .

"off" button. My head reeled as the boys in the class cheered and I thought to myself, "Depending on who finds out about this, I may pretty much have my professional future freed up real quick." Fortunately for me, there was no negative fallout, but I did remember always, and I mean always, to preview any program I showed the kids.

Learning and Novelty

We can all recall facts that have some twist of the unexpected. That's what made Robert Ripley famous. Anomalies of nature, distortions of facts, and historical oddities are often locked into our memory. Often these facts constitute useless information, but we remember it nevertheless.

Novelty especially strengthens initial learning. When I was about six years old, our family got its first phone. We lived in rural Iowa and when there was a phone right in our own house—well, it was like a miracle. Compared with today's standards, our first number was rather strange-sounding: "1-5-2-F-2-1" is as easy for me to recall fifty years later as it was then. We were on a "party line" (eight phones were connected to the same line) and each household had a special "ring." I can still remember that "ring" as well: short, long, and two shorts.

Emotion and novelty are certainly relevant to at least some learning. The question, however, is their practicality as primary techniques for teaching special needs kids. Could anyone sustain novelty and emotion as the primary connectors for new learning? Does our brain even have the capacity to retain so much information received as relatively isolated bits of data? Unless the specific lesson learned can be applied in other situations, the practical ongoing value of most information gained on this basis is somewhat limited.

Pity the poor teacher or parent who overuses the hooks of emotion and novelty. Most will burn out before their time. Or worse, kids will come to expect they are the passive recipients and need to be entertained to learn.

Learning New by Building on the Old

The third way people remember is by having new information connected with learning that has already been established. Upon analysis, this is the kind of learning that is most practical, because it has a contextual base (i.e., what has been learned before). Skills achieved in this manner have more meaning and are easier to apply to subsequent learning. It may very well be the model of choice for teaching in general and special education teaching in particular.

Some years ago an administrator I worked with related the following story. He was a building principal at the time and had scheduled an assembly program that dealt with drug and alcohol issues. The opportunity for having this group present came because of an unexpected cancellation and there was not a lot of lead time to inform staff. The program was scheduled for third hour on Friday. An announcement was placed in the teachers' mailboxes on Tuesday of that same week.

Seemingly just moments after the last announcement was distributed, the math department chairman came storming into the principal's office. He was red hot and looked as though he would explode through the hair flap used to cover his mostly bald head. His anger was apparent, but the principal didn't at all know why.

"How can you do this?!" the teacher shouted.

"Do what?" was the principal's sincere question.

Still in a very agitated state, the teacher yelled, "Have this assembly during one of my math classes! How can you do that?! You know I always test the kids every Friday!"

The principal somewhat remembered that Friday testing was routine for this teacher, but didn't realize the importance of this regimen until the conversation progressed.

"How about just giving the test on Monday?" the principal asked.

This apparently viable solution just infuriated the teacher more and he literally screamed, "I can't do that! If I don't test the kids right after I teach them, they forget everything!"

Had the teacher been in more of a thinking state, he might have realized the implications of what he was saying. If his kids couldn't remember the material over a weekend, the question of the day was whether they ever really learned the material in the first place.

But the expectation that kids will forget most of what they are exposed to in school has become an unfortunate assumption. However, this may be another phenomenon that is a result of presuppositions rather than a necessary part of education. The concern is especially relevant when dealing with special needs kids. Linda Hammond, in a conference presentation some years ago, made the following statement:

> There has been an enormous conceptual change in our understanding of human learning during this past half century. We once thought of children as empty vessels and teaching as the pouring of little pieces of information into their little heads, preferably in small bits that could be organized in a predetermined sequence and drilled until they were memorized for later retrieval.
>
> We got this idea from studies of rats and pigeons in the 1940s and 1950s when they were asked to do things they would never do in their natural habitat. . . . We thought this would add up ultimately to proficiency. . . . We now know this doesn't add up—that decontextualized information is quickly forgotten, often misunderstood, and rarely applied. About 90 percent of what is learned as isolated facts in a disconnected manner is forgotten within six months.

If this conclusion about what is forgotten is correct for kids in general, what about the disabled? In this author's view, an overriding consideration in special education is establishing a foundation paradigm, a theoretical base as it were, for student learning that first considers the affective aspects of achievement, and second, uses what has been previously mastered as a primary basis for new learning.

Sustained Continuous Learning

Decades ago Ferdinand Hoppe described "sustained continuous achievement" as performance that is beyond current levels, yet obtainable through practice and effort. Hoppe also concluded that motivation to achieve remained persistent when progress was contingent on effort and practice. That is, when the variables for performance are directly under the influence of the individual, achievement is significantly increased because of the factors of motivation and engagement in the task.

Anyone involved with a hobby completely understands this. When the choice of activity and pace of learning is under individual control, skills increase from a basis of established mastery. This pretty much explains why people are often more expert at their hobby than they are at their job. It also explains why some kids can tell you everything there is to know about their favorite sport, but can't answer enough questions to pass a test.

Through his research, Hoppe found that for students to remain engaged in the learning process, they had to have a feeling of success, irrespective of the performance of others. That is, when students felt a sense of personal satisfaction with their accomplishment, they had a higher level of willingness to maintain involvement in the task or activity. As a result, they increased skill mastery because they stayed the course longer. The innate value of the activity was secondary to the subjective satisfaction that came from completion. Isn't it interesting how research often identifies what is right before us and confirms what we already know? In addition, isn't it interesting how we disregard this research?

Hoppe recognized the very commonsense conclusion that a willingness to engage in, not just be exposed to, the learning process is critical. He also recognized that this engagement is conditioned by the affective aspects that accrue to the student as a result of performance. In plain words, if the student feels satisfied with present success, goals will be set that are in advance of current mastery. The critical factor Hoppe established was this sense of satisfaction that occurs when progress is relative to a person's own past performance rather than in comparison with what someone else has accomplished or attaining a standard set by others.

Although there is an exhilaration for the winner when the competitor has been beaten, that satisfaction is in a sense external and there is always the nagging fear, the next time around, that the current winner will be the future loser. However, when people accomplish their own goal, they experience an innate satisfaction that can never be taken away. It is this inherent gratification that propels people to make stable improvement.

The plain fact is that when people are able to participate in setting their own goals, they will inevitably set the mark between what is too easy to be satisfying and too hard to be accomplished. This point is subjective—that is why it is so vitally important for the individual to be directly involved. When individuals set their own goals, there is an extremely high potential for achievement.

And there is nothing like the feeling of success and satisfaction that comes from accomplishment. From a framework of the Four Key

. . . . .

Principles of Love and Logic, achievement validates our sense of worth (self-concept), satisfies our need for autonomy (shared control), confirms cause/effect relationships (i.e., consequences), and encourages higher thought processes (i.e., shared thinking). Because of these characteristics, it is of utmost importance that teachers and parents influence the learning environment to ensure that kids can obtain this sense of achievement.

I remember when Edrik was a toddler and just learning to stack blocks. When he stacked four without them tumbling down, he took such glee in his accomplishments. He felt good about his achievement because before he could only stack three. He never looked at his stack of four and thought it was not good enough because, after all, his mother could make a stack many times higher. He was well pleased with his success and, as a result, was encouraged to work on increasing his skill.

We have probably all seen this phenomenon in children and, frankly, we have probably all experienced it ourselves. I remember one instance in the early days I was learning to use a computer. The tech guy, Jon, was working on a computer in an adjacent office at the time I figured out, all by myself, how to change fonts. Not your high-level computer skill to be sure, but a brand new one for me at the time. I actually went into the next office to get Jon and show him what I could do. I wanted to share the joy of my feeling of success with him. I was virtually bursting with the satisfaction of my accomplishment.

Now keep in mind that Jon knew how computers work (most of us simply know how to work computers) and what I had just learned was less than elemental for him. But he reinforced my excitement with his encouragement. My enthusiasm to learn more was not abated because I didn't know as much as Jon. I wasn't comparing myself with him. I set my goals higher because I had success relative to my own performance, irrespective of the performance of anyone else. An additional aspect was that I was so pleased with myself that I harbored no resentment toward Jon for knowing more than I did. I had no desire at all to sabotage his work—it didn't even come to mind.

The Role of Love and Logic

In our educational system, having a difficult student is very often like a bad pregnancy. It's rough for nine months, but there is an end. As a result, there is a tendency for some teachers to tolerate kids for the duration rather than expending the effort necessary to resolve interpersonal problems. An interesting fact is that in most industrialized countries, teachers stay with their students at least two years and often many more. The rationale is that individual characteristics of students must be known before the students can be effectively taught. A specified purpose of special education law is for eligible kids to be provided services sufficient to ensure their progress in the general curriculum and to meet other educational needs resulting from their disability. This is a highly individualistic standard and very much requires teachers to know the kids before instruction can be truly effective.

The BASF Corporation has a slogan that conceptualizes the role of Love and Logic: "We don't make a lot of the things you use. We make a lot of the things you use better." Curriculum, strategies, and methodologies are all acknowledged aspects of achievement. However, in the words of the writer of Ecclesiastes: "There is nothing new under the sun." The goal of special education is to develop independence and employability. Translated, this basically means getting kids ready for the real world. To do so, students need to believe in themselves, work collaboratively with others, understand causal relationships, and use their intellect to solve problems. In brief, these are precisely the factors embedded in the Four Key Principles of Love and Logic.

CHAPTER 7

Using the Four Key Principles in the Trenches

Lessons from the Dinosaurs

Dinosaurs dominated the earth when their world had a very specific and stable climate. They were masters of the planet. Some of them grew to huge proportions and for a very long time, all seemed well for them. However, when the environment drastically altered, the dinosaurs were virtually wiped out. Efficient as they were, absorbing the variables of climate was not their forte. Mammals, on the other hand, were adaptable. Not so big, perhaps, but they were equipped to survive in the face of change.

The basic reason people have survived and flourished is because we have a brain that is more adaptable than efficient. The mass of neurons that sits on our neck constitutes about 2 percent of our body weight but represents 20 percent of our energy use. As complicated and mysterious as our brains are, a primary function of our minds, secondary only to survival, is to establish patterns to allow us to make sense of the world.

The easiest example for me to understand is language. Language is a pattern of sounds that represent actions, things, or other forms of ideas. Within given groups, these configurations of sounds are processed by the brain and meaning is conveyed. Any number of other paradigms are developed that determine moral, aesthetic, societal, and other values. Once these patterns become established, other patterns become incomprehensible (e.g., a "foreign" language). The paradigms we establish serve as filters to contrary beliefs. One has only to read the opinion page of a newspaper to realize that the same objective fact can be understood very differently, given the perspective of the individual.

These patterns are based on an innumerable number of variables including gender, culture, sensory acuteness, and experiences. As a result, we all have a slightly different take on life. However, the basic goals of volitional behavior are universal and include protecting our sense of self-worth, exercising autonomy, and figuring out how one event affects another. Given these goals, our thought processes are focused on how to best meet the affective needs that result.

Efficiency is always preferred when possible, and in a number of situations is the key to success. The problem is that efficiency works best only when the problems don't vary and the answers are the same. In such situations, a system of predetermined sequences saves time and effort. Even in education there are instances when efficiency is in order. Ensuring the validity of a standardized test or getting students out of the building for a fire drill would be two common examples that require an efficient system.

However, if there are variables, adaptability is the key. Being adaptable does not imply lack of structure. Without a structure, there tends to be lots of chaos. However, the structure for adaptability is different than the structure for efficiency. To be sure, trouble will be brewing when efficient strategies are applied to variable problems.

The Four Key Principles give form to dealing with kids while allowing for the absorption of the unexpected events that are innate when dealing with people. Although lockstepping into a routine behavior management system may have some administrative convenience and a type of consistency, not a lot of higher-level thinking is required.

This discussion of efficiency versus adaptability is important to the topic of having kids invested in their own learning and behavior. As emphasized previously, developing responsibility requires students to be engaged for the long term. We can get kids ready for life either on purpose or by accident, and on purpose will probably be in everyone's long-term best interest. Although the limitations of some disabled kids will preclude their living and working independently, the fact is that most will assume adult legal obligations at the age of majority. In preparation for this inevitable prospect, a primary focus of Love and Logic is for kids to develop a sense of accountability for their own decisions.

The Mechanism of Influence

When all of the glitter is stripped from teaching, what is left is an intent to exert influence. This is not mind control and should not even be put in that category. However, there is an element of wanting the kids to do what is in their own best interest and the best interest of others as well.

A number of years ago I consulted with an advertising professional to design a Love and Logic brochure. She said the message of any promotional material needed to convey the essential message upon first impression. If people must study, or even read the ad twice to figure out its meaning, the impact will be lost. Confusion is not a desired element when trying to get a new idea across to people.

As I explained the philosophy of Love and Logic she said, "Oh, so instead of making kids behave you want them to decide to." That was it! This was the first time she had heard of Love and Logic and so she didn't have any preconceptions to work through (like I did when I first heard about it). This was her first impression and she had precisely identified the essence of Love and Logic. Only when kids "decide to" is there any real long-term change. And long-term change is the only sure proof that teaching has occurred. The problem occurs when, in the attempt to establish long-term change, we interact with kids in a way that actually inhibits attainment of the desired goal.

An Unfortunate Mind-Set

A "motel mentality" too often describes kids' mind-set toward their own performance. Most of us who have used such temporary lodging view our responsibility to keep things in order there far differently than we do at home. During stays at a motel, seldom, if ever, do we hang the towels neatly back on the rack, make the bed, and ask housekeeping for a vacuum so we can tidy up a bit. Rather, common practice is to leave used towels on the floor. If they get kicked behind the toilet, few of us would get churned up much. The bed remains unmade and if there is popcorn all over the floor, hey, what the heck.

We have this attitude because cleaning up the room is somebody else's job. Of course, there is no justification for trashing the place, but after all, good money was paid to basically sleep, watch TV, and take a shower. Since the bill will be the same whether I straighten up the room or not, why do any work? If something is spilled, it's somebody else's job to clean it up. I can sit back and complain if things aren't done correctly, and I don't have to expend much effort making things right.

There is a kind of comfort in expecting somebody else to be accountable when I make a mess. However, that comfort is fairly short term. Eventually, we must leave that relatively protected environment and go back home. Having someone else responsible for cleaning up, fixing what's broken, and waiting on us may be a viable option at a motel, but that same attitude at home would only delay the inevitable. And the longer the delay, the more time and effort will be needed to restore order.

The Lawyer Child

A guidance counselor friend once related a story about her nephew. He had come from a position of privilege, and had, by the time of this story, just graduated from law school. When he was born, his mother had equated love with protection. This was appropriate, because if babies aren't protected, they will die. However, this mother never quite got off square one. She was "always there" for her son, bailing him out of trouble, doing for him what he was well able to do for himself, and making sure he always had an easy path. She still equates love with protection.

Now the kid is twenty-six years old and out of the protective world of college. He must find a job—or rather, he feels his mother must find him a job. He did make some effort, however. He downloaded the addresses of twenty-three hundred law firms onto computer diskettes. Then he sent the diskettes to his mother with instructions to send his résumé to each of the firms. The mother was frantic. Not because she was finally realizing she had raised a "kept man" who had little concept of what "leaving the nest" meant. No, the mother's concern was how she could get this massive job met within the month timeline the son had set. As I reflect on this story, I realize that this well-educated and intelligent man is in a way more handicapped than many of the disabled kids whose parents and teachers have taught them well.

Covert Messages

Because of how our brains function, we are very influenced by the covert messages that are part of every interaction. Whether called intuition, reading between the lines, or insight, we are all influenced more by what we perceive someone means than by what they actually say. We have all had experiences of knowing that what was said was not what was meant. A story comes to mind.

One day a friend was coming home from an especially hard day at school. As he was driving, he thought to himself, "I hope I only have about three more days like this left in my whole career." He comforted himself, however, with the thought that at least he would have a good meal.

His wife had also had a hard day and was thinking, to herself, "I hope I only have about three more days like this." She comforted herself with the thought that at least she could compensate by *not* having cooking as part of what she would be doing that day.

When the husband got home, what was before him was a nondescript TV dinner—one of those where you don't even know what is in it unless you have seen the package first. He looked at his wife and said, with sweetness dripping from his voice, "You know, Honey, when I was growing up, my mom always had time to get me a good meal."

The overt message was a compliment to his mother. The covert message was a put-down. Which one do you imagine his wife responded to?

Back to the Basics: Cause-and-Effect Relationships

Cause/effect relationships are fundamental to learning. This is an established principle that holds true just about always. That is, kids learn what is really taught via the actual cause/effect and the lessons aren't always what the adults intended. When there is an inconsistency with what we say, mean, and do, the kid is put in the position of deciding which of these three options to respond to. Almost always, the kid will follow the lead of what the adult demonstrates with their behavior.

We have all seen kids in some public place being told to behave only to watch them go ballistic. The admonition to "be good" is often followed immediately with more bad behavior. Although it may seem on the surface that kids are acting contrary to the instruction given at the time, the cause/effect relationship is often consistent with the covert messages transmitted by what the adult does.

Recently, I was meandering down the breakfast-items aisles of our local grocery store. It was a rather slow hour for the store and as I was contemplating what cereal to pick out, I noticed a child, probably about three years old, start working on his mom. "I want that one [some kind of sugared cereal]," were the first words I heard. The mother said she would not get "that one" because it cost four dollars. Although the four-dollar price tag was a sufficient deterrent for the mother, the child evidently did not have the same sense of finance. He upped the ante by whining, and then crying and kicking the cart. Within just a couple of minutes (before I had even made my own decision), I heard the mother say, "Well, I suppose we could get that one this time."

The mother had taught the child well. Perhaps not what she wanted him to learn, but instruction had taken place nevertheless. And in fact, the lesson continued. It was like she was giving him an enriched curriculum in becoming a demanding obnoxious child. Once he got the cereal in his possession, he wanted to open the box and eat some. "Not now, it might spill," was the mother's response. Ah, but the little one caught on quickly and he responded precisely as he had been instructed. I saw them a few aisles later. The kid was pulling cereal out of the box and periodically throwing handfuls hither and yon as though he was sowing some seed. The last statement I heard from the mother was, "Stop that, somebody will have to clean that up!" And the formal instruction continued.

The mother's overt messages were soundly rejected. However, there was a perfect correlation, a flawless cause/effect relationship, between what the mother did and how the kid behaved.

It Happens in School, Too

I recall a situation that is fairly common in special education. A student, new to the district, had been caught selling what he purported to be drugs (they turned out to be over-the-counter analgesics). This was an expellable offense and a hearing before the board had been scheduled. In a last-ditch effort to avoid a predictable decision to oust the kid, he was referred for a special education evaluation. The parent had been told that in the event he were determined disabled, regardless of the outcome of the expulsion hearing, he would have to be provided educational services.

At the meeting to determine eligibility, the parent was bemoaning the fact that the kid was getting F's in all of his classes and had a history of extremely poor academic performance for a number of years. In her words, he had "flunked and was still flunking." Of course, in a sense she was correct, because he had chalked up about as many failing grades as he had classes. However, the question is not what the adults thought or said, but rather what exactly the kid had been taught.

After all, in his previous district he had gone from fourth to fifth to sixth and then to seventh grade. When he moved to our district he was duly placed in eighth grade. His report card said he failed, his parents said he failed, and his teachers said he failed. And yet, here he was, in eighth grade, right on schedule.

What was the more powerful message for him? The overt (the adults telling him he was failing) or the covert (he was progressing through the grades year by year anyway)? The sad thing for the kid was that when reality did finally set in (i.e., he was found not to be disabled and was expelled for two years), he didn't understand and the "system" was accused of being unfair. For the first time, people were consistent in what they said, meant, and did. He was confused and angry. When reality is a surprise, the results are not at all fun.

Few Have Written Plans to Mess Up Their Kids

While it may be true that the covert and overt messages given to kids are sometimes contradictory, there is usually a sincere intent on the part of the adult to act in the best interest of the kid. In all my years in special education I have only known of one parent who appeared to have a predetermined plan to mess up her kid. That kid was literally conceived on a satanic altar and, in my humble opinion, got a bad start right from the beginning.

Most people get into education to help, not hinder, students in their pursuit of knowledge. In my thirty-plus years in education, I can recall only a very few teachers who seemed preoccupied with causing havoc in kids' lives as part of their instructional goals.

Mostly, parents and teachers want their kids to turn out better than they did. And we have all seen adults go to great lengths in their attempts to make absolutely sure this happens. Several types of "direct instruction," including threats, sarcasm, bribes, and begging, are used in pursuit of this goal. However, kids often learn some unintended lessons from a kind of instruction that is even more powerful.

Emotions Precede Logic

These unintended lessons are learned largely because sensory information is processed through the emotional centers of the brain first. The first function of the brain is to ensure survival—first physical needs and then psychological. Perception serves as a filter to interpret facts within a given context. As we think about anything, associations are made from our experiences, temperament, and all of the other variables that make us who we are. The sensory information we receive stimulates an emotional response on a continuum that ranges from nil to extreme.

For instance, I can be sitting at my desk and glance at the clock. I see the time of 2:12. The various levels of emotional reaction to this simple fact might include:

LEVEL I I see the time, acknowledge it is midafternoon, and let it go at that. There is no other meaning than the time of day and very little emotional reaction.

LEVEL II I think about the meeting I have at 3:30 and note that I need to get some information from a file to take with me. There may be just a tad of anxiety that I might forget something, but not enough to cause much stress at all.

LEVEL III The time is the same as the date of Diane's birthday (February 12). I think about how much I love her and that I have time to call her before my next appointment. There is high emotion and I start thinking about what present would really be pleasing to her.

LEVEL IV My kids should have returned from their trip last night, they still haven't called, and I am hoping there is not some sort of trouble. I know I shouldn't get too worried yet, because they may have take a side trip, or they may have returned late and just haven't informed us. However, I heard about some bad traffic accidents on the expressway and hope they weren't involved. I do have a nagging fear and if I haven't heard from them soon, I will start calling myself.

LEVEL V I just remembered I was supposed to be at a messy due process hearing at 2:00 and it will take at least thirty minutes to get to the lawyer's office. I, alone, have the file that contains information that may well determine the outcome and can already visualize the parents, my supervisor, the lawyers, and hearing officer sitting there waiting. Big anxiety! I am mad at myself for not preventing this. I look and feel incompetent and know there is no excuse. This is not a good situation.

To a large degree, stress influences our emotional responses. And when we are under stress, it surely is difficult to see the perspectives of others. Whenever we work with kids in situations that excite those emotional pathways, we need to be careful that wrong decisions are not made.

The Bus and the Wind

Reduced to its essential element, thinking is engagement in a mental activity that is focused on a particular purpose. In the case of volitional behavior, thinking is influenced by what need is waiting to be met. Our thinking, and therefore our actions, will be consistent with whatever we perceive is necessary to meet fundamental needs. This is an important understanding for adults to have, because too often the goal of a student's behavior is misinterpreted, resulting in ineffective interventions being applied.

Some years ago I was asked to participate in an IEP meeting for a student, Joe, who was attending a program out-of-district. Transportation was a service the district was required to provide and a route had been established. However, this student was refusing to go on the bus provided. In addition to the kid not attending school, a major concern for the district was that, on a per diem basis, the transportation was costing more than the tuition. Because of the gravity of this issue, an IEP meeting was scheduled.

Prior to the meeting, staff gathered to discuss the situation and determine why this student was behaving thusly. Of interest was the perspective of each of the members. The vice principal made the statement that Joe was acting this way because he was a jerk. The psychologist had a different take on the situation and concluded that the behavior was a result of a distortion in Joe's cognitive process. Finally, the social worker believed sincerely that Joe's not getting on the bus was a reaction to being adopted. These reasons were mutually exclusive—that is, they could all be wrong, but they could not all be right.

At the appointed time, the meeting began and the preliminaries were taken care of. After indicating the concern over cost, we cut to the chase and directly asked Joe why he wasn't getting on the bus. Joe's response was direct, accurate, and different than any of the adults had surmised.

Joe was good at math and his response reflected this strength. When asked why he didn't use the appointed transportation, he answered with a question: "Do you know what velocity a wind gust would have to be to tip over a school bus?"

No one knew the answer, so Joe told them in miles per hour. He said he didn't ride the bus because of the imminent danger it presented. While his reasoning may not have been consistent with normal logic, the team now had accurate information to consider. In response to this information, the school contracted for a smaller vehicle for him to ride in and there was never a problem after that. Without Joe's input, who knows what the team's conclusion would have been.

Everybody's Theory Is Right—For Themselves

The point to make is that without some guiding structure, we all tend to look at situations in a way that is consistent with how we already see the world. We make conclusions and devise answers that will clarify the situation to ourselves and further confirm our own foundational ideas. It's a form of self-medication to keep us feeling good.

This works really well until we must deal with people on an individual basis. In Joe's case, the hypotheses of the principal, psychologist, and social worker were all equally valid—until their theories were tested. Then it became apparent that their views were valid only for themselves. Since their conclusions were mutually exclusive, they could all be wrong, but could not all be right.

When we work with people, whether little or big, a condition for success is to have a sufficient understanding of their perspective. Unless we have adopted a mind-set that allows for this, our interactions will be overly influenced by stereotypical conclusions. There may be some comfort in believing that all kids with weird behavior problems are jerks, victims of distorted thinking, or misunderstood, but that comfort is short-lived.

When we find out we are wrong, we must either admit our error or work hard to convince ourselves we are still right. How much better to have a way of assessing whether our conclusions are accurate in the first place. As I think about this concept, of course there is another story.

A principal of a large elementary school invited me to teach a course for her staff. One contingent of teachers (they all sat together) seemed rather sullen. I found out later that the principal had mandated their attendance as part of "improvement plan." In actuality, it seemed they were simply improving the very skills the principal was hoping to eliminate.

During nearly the entire course, one teacher was especially visible in her protest. She spent her time grading papers, paging through a clothing catalog and ordering items, reading newspapers, and doing a variety of other activities that demonstrated she wanted to be somewhere else. There was also the distinct impression she was trying to embarrass the principal by this behavior—kind of like a sullen child might do.

The last session of the course was devoted to discussing specific kids. As one kid was being described, the class analyzed the information given and concluded the child was behaving from a basis of low self-concept. At this point, the teacher who had heretofore only demonstrated her resentment nonverbally, made a very revealing statement: "I am so tired of this stuff. I know that kid and she just doesn't want to follow the rules! Somebody should just make her shape up!"

The reaction of the class was interesting. Their eyes went down and no one spoke. They were embarrassed for that teacher, who was so dwelling on her own resentment that she had transferred her anger to the kid. The honest fact is that the "shaping up" technique had already been tried on both the kid and this teacher, and it hadn't worked on either one of them. How sad it was for everyone else to recognize this except the one who would have most benefited.

The Four Key Principles Test

So far, a significant amount of space in this book has been allotted to the Four Key Principles of Love and Logic. Although situations are unique, knowing some of the major characteristics of these principles can make us more skillful in their use. Following are some questions relative to our reactions to problems kids create. "Yes" answers indicate an adherence to the principle.

Self-Concept:
Did I approach the student with dignity and respect?
Did I use implied messages of capability?
Did I use the bonding mechanisms of eye contact, smiles, and (appropriate) touch?

Control:
Did I set limits without waging war?
Did I use enforceable statements?
Did I give the student a "piece of the action"?

Empathy with Consequence:
Did I validate the kid without supporting inappropriate behavior?
Did I avoid giving the student an opportunity to displace anger or hurt?
Did the kid make a connection between the behavior and the resulting outcome?

Thinking:
Did I model a well-adjusted adult?
Did I ensure that the student was more invested in the solution than I was?
Did I orient the student to future planning?

Counterindications

As in all things, there are factors that force us to proceed with caution. I wish there were no circumstances that would exclude the use of these principles, but in the world we live in, we need to recognize the honest fact there are exceptions. For instance, caution is to be used in situations where students' health and safety may be at risk. Potential legal penalties can also override even the best educational methodology. In addition, when students engage in pathological behavior, teachers need to exercise caution and formally review what procedures will be applied. Finally, some students engage in behavior that is nonvolitional.

. . . . .

However, for the vast majority of kids and situations, there will be some applicability of the Four Key Principles of Love and Logic. The following stories demonstrate how these principles interweave with interaction.

Using the Four Key Principles to Get the Job Done

When I first started to use the Four Key Principles as a formal vehicle for teaching, I was discussing these concepts with our twelve-year-old son, Jaben. I told him that I had not been satisfied with my past parenting style and was using a set of ideas to change. In that brief conversation in the driveway, sitting in the car waiting for the garage door to open, we discussed these Four Key Principles. I told him I wanted to interact with him in such a way that he felt good about himself, that each of us would have control over the parts of the situation that were ours. I wanted consequences rather than punishment to govern the outcomes of any action. Finally, although I would be willing to advise, I wanted him to be the one thinking through the problems that confronted him.

As we pulled into the garage, I asked Jaben what he thought of this new way. His response was, "Well, Dad, it's worked for me so far." To be sure, our children, Jaben and Aleshia, had some rough edges. And they learned from the consequences of life. Jaben is a wonderful self-taught musician and makes handcrafted guitars. Aleshia works for a law firm and for ten years raised a child as a single mother.

Both of our kids are independent, responsible, and our good friends. To be sure, they did some things that made us cringe as their parents. They did other things that made for some crying. And they turned out just fine. Both my children and the students I have worked with have given me the benefit of seeing what happens in the long run—a luxury not often afforded to those of us who work with kids.

Aaron's Story

A number of years ago a behavior management plan was being developed for a student who was greatly frustrating his parents and teachers. The most recent plan had lasted less than three days and, apparently, it was time for another. However, at this next meeting the student was requested to be there, a surprise to staff since they had never included students in such meetings (perhaps the first clue as to why the previous plans had not been too effective).

When the meeting convened, the first question to the student was, "Are you the kind of kid that adults can be honest with?" After a little thought (maybe because he had to process a never-before-asked question), he said he was. The second question to the student was, "Do you feel strong enough to work on the problems we are here to deal with?" Again, he answered in the affirmative.

What was the goal of such questions? Not to manipulate, because that, at best, would have short-term success and is usually counterproductive. Rather, the goal was to allow the student to have some ownership and demonstrate that he "belonged" on this team.

As the meeting progressed, past behavior plans were analyzed to find out why they were not successful. One critical factor seemed to be the "rewards." In all cases, the consequence was a tangible reinforcer, the last one being a can of carbonated drink for three days of good behavior. In monetary value, his efforts were worth about a dime a day—not much for a kid who purportedly could earn hundreds for running "errands" for his druggy friends.

He was then asked if he could remember the good feeling he got from accomplishing something he had set out to do. He could, and actually described that feeling in detail. Then he was asked how much that feeling would be worth in dollars and cents. He decided it was too valuable to have a price.

That feeling became his goal. The process was completed and for the first time in anyone's memory, a plan was developed that worked for him. And why? A significant factor was that, for the first time, this student believed he "belonged" as a member of the group developing his educational program. In addition, what he was working for was not some tangible reward the school could work into the budget. There was no cost, because there was no price.

The process used was rather simple. After identifying all of the concerns from those in the room, only those items that had universal agreement would be part of the plan. There were lots of concerns listed—three pages' worth. But there were only three items from that entire list that had universal agreement. The focus of the plan became that Aaron would do all of his work, do his own work, and bring a pencil to class. Aaron was involved in the logistics of the plan, like keeping data and any necessary reporting.

The items selected certainly were not the big issues. They did not address the vulgar language, truancy, and other problem behaviors. However, this plan worked because improvement, not perfection, was the goal. In fact, about three weeks later, Aaron's mother called and said she wasn't sure what magic was being done at school, but his behavior was even better at home. The plan was still working at the end of the year. A virtual personal best for Aaron.

Flunking Versus Being Done

Love and Logic has long emphasized the value of kids experiencing the logical consequences of their behavior. The problem is that teachers and parents are a lot better at giving out punishments and rewards instead. Even those of us who adhere to the tenants of Love and Logic realize the appeal of doling out punishments for inappropriate behavior and rewards for behavior we accept. They are quick to administer and usually have some immediate result. Unfortunately, they also have some aftereffects that can be fairly insidious. We sometimes must be reminded that consequences will be the most effective in the long run and are in the best interest of everyone involved.

Although punishment and reward are sometimes needed tools, they are most effective when we realize their characteristics. They are short term. They generally work only in the presence of the one doling out the prize or punishment, and they often focus the kid away from a feeling of responsibility for their own actions.

Likewise, consequences have characteristics. Consequences are simply events that are logically related, in the kid's mind, between what he or she did and what happened as a result. Consequences are interpreted by kids as a direct result of their own behavior. It is basic cause/effect relationship.

Just as punishment and reward cause pain and pleasure, so do consequences. However, consequences cause this pain and pleasure to come from within the kid rather than from outside. Finally, consequences orient kids toward self-determination, a necessary skill for independence in their adult lives.

In times of stress, the difficulty for adults is to figure out what a logical consequence would be. I am sure we have all been so upset at our kids that we would just like to get our pound of flesh. Adam, a seventh-grade student in a special needs programs because of diagnosed behavior problems, was very effective in creating that feeling in the adults that were a part of his life.

Adam was a likable manipulator. He was skilled at making promises to "be good," but as reported by his teachers and parents, these promises would sometimes not last the hour. Adam had been in special education since fourth grade, and the suspicion was that he had been essentially passed from class to class because teachers didn't want to deal with him any longer than they had to. He was described as being like a bad pregnancy that people wanted to be over in nine months. His parents had also just about had it with him. Their frustration level was rising on a daily basis.

Several meetings had been held about Adam during his seventh-grade year, some of which he even attended. Behavior contracts had been developed. One had a unique provision: He would be able to get out of special education (something he often stated wanting) if his school performance stayed within a normal range for three months. If he could demonstrate he no longer needed special education, he would not be considered disabled and thus would not qualify for services. What a deal!

Although this plan had been well thought out by the teachers, it still had limited effect and within a few weeks Adam was back to his previous behavior. He certainly was capable of doing any of the work assigned, but it was just more entertaining to skip class, make excuses, and watch the adults "dance."

Staff and parents were so frustrated, they called another meeting, this time with a consultant. The adults really didn't have any new ideas, but the situation was of sufficient import that "something" had to be done. As Adam's situation was discussed, the group reviewed his low grades, revisited his inappropriate conduct, such as cutting and disrupting classes, and commented on the general miserableness he was causing the adults. Great mention was made of how he needed to be responsible for his own behavior, and of how frustrating his behavior had become both at school and at home.

Throughout this conversation, Adam was relaxed, listened attentively, and had a little smile the whole time. He had been through these kinds of meetings before. He realized he did not have to worry because, in the past, nothing significant had happened to him, and after all, why should things change now that he was well on his way through middle school?

Adam was not a bad kid—just frustrating to work with. Essentially, he knew how to milk the system. Adam had learned well. He had been enabled by the adults in his world and he had taken full advantage. He was like a kept man. All of his needs were supplied without him having to put forth much effort. Previous interventions had essentially relied on reward and punishment, and Adam was both bright enough know the limits the adults could impose, and patient enough to wait them out.

As the discussion progressed, a thought occurred to the consultant: Adam had never really experienced meaningful consequences for his behavior. Then a question came from out of the blue. Whether a stroke of special insight, the voice of God, or the fact that the concept of consequence prevailed, we may never know. However, the experience etched in the concept of consequence and the power it holds for internalizing the lessons of life.

The ensuing conversation went something like this:

CONSULTANT: Adam, does it seem reasonable that a kid should go to eighth grade when they are done with seventh?

ADAM: Yeah.

CONSULTANT: I was thinking the same thing. When is the last day of school this year?

ADAM: June 2, I think.

CONSULTANT: That's right. This year, most seventh-graders are finishing on June 2. When do you think you will be done?

Keep in mind, Adam was one bright kid and it didn't take him at all long to see where this conversation was going. He engaged in a time-honored technique used by kids throughout history known as the "bird walk." A bird walk is essentially a diversion strategy to get the adults thinking about something else rather than the topic at hand. Also, Adam's mom was starting to experience a mild panic. The whole idea was unrehearsed, so there was no opportunity to prepare her beforehand. (The teacher was also in a mild panic, because she thought she might be facing another year with this kid.)

The conversation continued:

ADAM: You can't flunk me. This school doesn't flunk anyone.

When kids take adults on a bird walk like this, it is vitally important to stay on topic. The encouraging thing is knowing that when a kid does go on a bird walk, you know you are touching a sensitive nerve. In addition, the adults must be honest with kids and refrain from retaliation, unenforceable statements, and sarcasm.

In fact, Adam was right, the district was very oriented against retention. In addition, no one on the team, including his mom, thought flunking seventh grade would be in anybody's best interest. However, flunking was not the issue—being done with seventh grade was:

CONSULTANT: You're right about flunking, and what was the question? Flunking or going on to eighth grade when you are done with seventh?

This was the beginning of a very interesting odyssey. Adam first had to identify what finishing seventh grade meant for him. Since all of the adults had already finished seventh grade, Adam was able to conclude that he should be responsible for finding this out. He declared with an air of bravado that he would be done by June 2 and that, in addition, he would have several A's on his report card.

Not surprisingly, as the end of the school year approached, Adam was not done with seventh grade. He may have thought that this year would be like all the rest. He was relying on teachers not wanting him for two years in a row. However, perhaps for the first time in his young life, Adam had come face to face with an enforceable statement. The adults could follow through with their part.

Adam had a history of adults making threats, promises, and deals. He was always in the driver's seat—even though he was not old enough to have a license. And as he barreled down the road, he pretty much expected everyone to get out of his way. What an unhappy scenario for those who had to live with him.

By the end of the year, Adam had passed all but three classes. Just prior to June 2, he trotted around to his teachers to find out what he had to do to be done with seventh grade. In summer school, Adam paced himself so he would finish just before regular classes started the next fall. He made every tutoring appointment—even after he broke his writing arm skateboarding. That was another opportunity for him to learn a bit about the real world he needed to prepare for.

When he broke his arm, Adam called his tutor to say that he wouldn't be able to do his work. The phone conversation was quite interesting:

ADAM: Hi, I just wanted to call and tell you that I broke my arm skateboarding. The doctor said I would be all right, but it was my right arm. I can't hold a pencil, so I can't do my work. I won't be getting the cast off until a day or two before school starts.

TUTOR: Well, I'm really glad you will be okay, and I have one concern. Could I ask you about that?

ADAM: Sure. (He said this in a happy tone, as though he were thinking, "Since I won't have to do any work, what the heck!")

TUTOR: School starts for kids on August 28 this year. My only question is if you don't do your work this summer, do you think you could be ready to start eighth grade by at least October?

ADAM: But I can't write!

TUTOR: I understand that. Would you like some ideas?

ADAM: I suppose (no longer talking in a happy tone).

TUTOR: Would one of your sisters do your writing if you paid her?

ADAM: Pay my sister! I'm saving my money for a new video game. I think that idea is stupid.

TUTOR: Probably so, but that's the only one I can think of right now.

You can imagine the rest of the conversation. Adam didn't like the idea of paying either of his sisters to do his writing for him and decided that doing some favors for his dad would work out better for him. Since this turned out not to be a problem for anyone, it was a viable solution. In actuality, Adam ended up doing a lot of his writing with his left hand.

During that summer, Adam and the tutor had ample opportunity to talk. They discussed his feelings toward school and he expressed some wonderful insight about himself. This was another situation where the teacher learned from the student—a phenomenon often experienced when Love and Logic is used.

Adam finished August 26—two days before school started. This was not a lad who was going to burn himself out on this project. But the fact was, he was done with seventh grade and could go on to eighth with his classmates. That last day he gave his tutor a soft, plastic Poppin' Fresh Doughboy figure and a mug with the little guy etched on it.

These gifts were symbolic. His tutor had a Poppin' Fresh Doughboy theme in his office (symbolic of an affinity for baked goods) and he added these gifts to his collection. There was never much talk with Adam about "Doughboy," but Adam noticed nevertheless, and knew this must have represented something special to his tutor. As his tutor opened the package, Adam's eyes twinkled and he said, "I thought you would like them." He had basically spent his summer doing schoolwork. He wasn't able to have his own way all of the time. He became more responsible. Anger and revenge just didn't have a place. In fact, his last word at the end of that final session was "thanks."

I saw Adam several times the following year. He smiled and we shook hands and talked about eighth grade. We also talked about an activity discussed previously that he'd said he wanted to do—to work with young kids who were having problems in school. You probably guessed, Adam thought he could help those younger students learn how to behave and get their work done!

Enforceable Bus Rules

One evening over supper, I was swapping stories with Jim and Shirley Fay. Jim told one about an especially recalcitrant student who had been making problems on the bus for some time. The staff decided that a good

. . . . .

dose of consequence would do the child good. All of the adults were part of devising a plan (a critical variable, so there is no misunderstanding or sabotaging). After thorough preparation and rehearsal, the venture was ready for implementation.

As expected, the boy again flagrantly violated the rules. Normally, there would be the usual reprimands to "sit and be good" while the bus continued toward its destination. Today was different. Instead of a lot of talk, the bus driver stopped, ushered the kid off the bus, pulled back onto the road, and proceeded to complete his route.

Since this was a scripted situation, all of the players were on stage and ready for their entrance. The administrator was close behind the bus and in just moments pulled beside the kid, motioned him into the car, and took him home. Remember, this was part of a plan that was thoroughly discussed and known by the parents and staff. The plan was based on using enforceable limits, and although the kid may have had some momentary confusion, he could easily have gotten the upper hand if there were any chinks in the adults' armor.

An added element was the other kids. To ensure they were not scared that the boy had been left in a dangerous situation, the bus driver, once out of view of the "drop-off point," pulled over and explained enough of the plan to assuage any unfounded fear or misinterpretation.

The plan worked as anticipated and the student's bus behavior improved dramatically. He had been hit head-on with a strategy he fully understood. However, as one would guess, he found out about the plan from another student and concluded that he had been set up. He decided that afternoon that he would call the bluff and reassert his status as boss.

That afternoon, as he ascended the bus stairs, he boldly announced to the driver that the gig was over. He knew he had been set up and now he was ready call the bluff. The driver listened to the kid's bravado, looked at him with steady eye contact, and said in a voice that came from an inner strength, "We're ready for that, too." What a learning experience for the kid and a wonderful opportunity to see a demonstration of well-adjusted adults.

Thumbs Up

There are some kids we just have to admire for being honest enough to express how they really feel. However, we often feel uncomfortable around these people because, frankly, they point out our own tendency toward hypocrisy. Rather than change ourselves, it seems easier to get rid of the kid.

One particular kid had this unabashed boldness. He called the shots the way he saw them and he was not intimidated by authority. One year he was scheduled into a chemistry class with a most uninspiring teacher. The kid was dissatisfied with the instruction and had no timidity about stating his opinion publicly. When he had reached his limit (and this occurred several times a week), he would call out with sufficient volume that all could hear—"BORING"—and simultaneously, as though in a choreographed ballet of civil protest, raise both hands with middle fingers extended.

This, of course, raised the ire of the teacher, who reacted by confronting the student and then sending him to the office, presumably for the principal to perform some magic disciplinary slight-of-hand. This happened so often that the kid's credit was in jeopardy and the principal, not knowing what else to do (and probably not wanting to keep the kid another year), called the school psychologist for advice.

The psychologist knew that simply trying to get the student to stop the offending behavior would not work. Even if by some psychological prestidigitation he could do so, the kid would fill in the empty space with some behavior that might even be worse. Instead, the goal would be to develop an alternative behavior that would provide the student with at least some expression of his feelings yet not result in his getting kicked out of class.

To get some background, the psychologist visited the class to see for himself what variables might be instrumental. His conclusion was that the class was, indeed, extremely boring, so trying to convince the student otherwise would be counterproductive. He also concluded that talking to the teacher about making some unilateral changes at this point would be futile. So, throwing caution to the wind, the psychologist made the decision to work just with the kid. Relying on the positive relationship he and the kid had developed, a plan was made.

The key to any behavior intervention plan is to identify a replacement behavior that will address the same need for the student as the inappropriate behavior did. If the student simply ceases the maladaptive behavior, a void will be left that will be filled with who knows what. At this point, two behaviors are the focus: the gesture and the vocalization.

First, the psychologist asked whether there was enough mutual respect between them that the student would be willing to try something, even if it didn't make sense at first. When the student agreed, the psychologist asked about the possibility of thinking the word "boring" instead of actually saying it. This was a stretch for the kid (given the fact that the teacher was not willing to initiate any change), but he said he would give it a try.

The second change was in reference to the gesture. Knowing, again, that replacement behavior was the key, the psychologist asked the kid if instead of raising his middle fingers in protest, he could raise his thumbs. Again, the psychologist confirmed that this would be a stretch for the kid, but asked whether he would do it anyway—just to see what happened.

Upon returning to class, the kid encountered the same teacher situation. This time, however, he only thought the word "boring" and raised both hands with thumbs extended upward. Of course, this immediately caught the teacher's attention. The student's change in behavior resulted in a difference in understanding on the part of the teacher. His reaction to the "thumbs up" sign was far different than when he had been given "the finger."

In actuality, he thought the kid was expressing a level of approval (kind of like at the Roman Coliseum of old). When the teacher approached the kid this time, it was without the confrontation he had demonstrated previously. As a result, the kid had a slightly different perspective as well. There were no big changes, just enough small reciprocal ones for the kid to stay in the class.

What Is Kept Is What Has Been Taught

There is a work of art by Anita Caldwell Jackson titled *What Is Kept Is What Has Been Taught*. The scene depicts a young Native American boy surrounded by a book, notepad, and pencil. Also surrounding him are the adults from his culture. Superimposed are several other children. It is a haunting picture and one that causes the viewer to ask, just what will this child keep from his education? The answer is in the title. Although the books are open, the boy is learning what he hears and sees from the values conveyed through the interactions of the adults and other children.

Kids respond more to the covert messages from their formal instruction than to what teachers are actually trying to teach. Even though there may be a level of lip service for kids to be involved in the educational process, in actuality the adults usually make the decisions, determine the rewards, and even have the negative feeling when learning doesn't occur as expected. Whenever there is inconsistency in what adults say, mean, and do, it is what is done that actually conveys the covert messages kids internalize.

As important as books and technology are, what kids believe their magic people (significant others) believe is what will remain. Kids will never be fooled by words when those words contradict actions. Actions convey the most powerful message, a fact that has been recognized for millennia. God help us if we work with kids and don't realize this.

PART 3

The Human Factor

CHAPTER 8

The Love and Logic Teacher

Some Kids Really Do Need a Teacher

Many years ago I heard about the "Goldilocks and the bears" theory of education. The idea purported that there are three kinds of students. One kind would actually do better without the teacher. The educational system can tangibly interfere with their progress. For other kids, the system is just right the way it is and they prosper. The third kind of kid will suffer damage from school without the compensation teaching can provide.

Our system of education has evolved as have many institutions. One of the advantages afforded to those of us who have been in the profession for a while is realizing that cycles are more prevalent in education than trends. Many theories that were once in vogue, then out of vogue, often come back. Usually there is little change at all—just a new name for the same concept.

Unwittingly, Grandma Used Strategies Not Yet Invented

My grandmother was a teacher in a one-room schoolhouse in rural Iowa many, many decades ago. Certainly, she faced some very different circumstances in her career. For instance, teachers then were qualified to instruct whatever grade they had completed. Grandma finished eighth grade, so she could teach all of the elementary kids. Since many students had no need for further schooling, Grandma was the only teacher some kids had.

Another difference was that part of her pay was room and board. Each month she rotated living with the families of her students. This was perhaps the ultimate in parent/teacher conferences! Imagine the effect of everyone sitting down to supper and the parents starting a conversation with, "How did school go today?" Grandma was responsible for starting the fire, pumping the drinking water, cleaning, and oh yes, teaching a roomful of kids ranging in age from six to sixteen.

When I first started my teaching career, I often talked to her about all of the new concepts in education, especially the strategies that were being devised to instruct special needs kids. I recall one methodology I had learned about in one of my professional journals. It had a good research base and had been piloted for two years before being published. I was especially excited about implementing such a program with my own students.

The technique was called "cross-peer tutoring," a term I thought sounded especially sophisticated. I obtained all of the information I could and teamed with a colleague who taught learning-disabled students in one of our district's elementary schools. In brief, my middle school kids with reading problems taught her kids, who had similar deficits. In the process, the older kids were building their own reading skills as they taught their "students."

The program was good for everyone. The middle school kids worked unbelievably hard. The elementary kids thought being taught by the "big" kids was the coolest thing. We stopped only because the district was a bit freaked about my driving kids hither and yon—liability and all. But regardless, the program was more than successful and well worth doing.

On one visit to Grandma, I told her about this wonderful, innovative, researched, and piloted program. She listened as Grandmas do and then said she also found that way successful when she used it in the one-room schoolhouse. She just called it "the big kids helping the little kids."

You can imagine her response when I talked to her about differentiated curriculum, full integration, and direct instruction. Now keep in mind, she had kids who were bright and dull, young and old, skilled and unskilled. She had them all in one room, all by herself, all day long. She taught reading, writing, arithmetic, and everything else required at the time.

To Grandma, differentiating instruction was not some theoretical construct that required a deep research base and extensive training to implement. And to the question of full integration—where else would the kids go? There was only one room, one teacher, and one school! And the discussion we had about direct instruction must have been especially amusing to her. After all, she reflected, how else could you teach what you wanted the kid to learn? Upon reflection, education may have become more technical since then, but I don't know whether it's any better.

Good teaching has always been good teaching, and special needs kids require precisely that to learn. What desperately needs to be recognized, however, is that instruction doesn't always have to be from the teacher to the kids. If the truth be known, some of the best instructional resources are often so obvious that they are overlooked. The amount and quality of "educational consultants" resident in each classroom or school is phenomenal. Two stories come to mind.

The Classroom as a Teaching Community

The Teacher from New Jersey

A third-grade teacher in New Jersey had just been told by her administrator that a severely handicapped student would be transferring into her classroom in about two weeks. Although this teacher had a master's degree and had taught for a number of years, she went into a mild panic. The news put her into a condition of stress and the frontal cortex of her brain shut down. She couldn't imagine how she could effectively teach this new student.

You see, the new student was multiply handicapped. She was medically fragile, cognitively disabled, restricted to a wheelchair, and had a bunch of other conditions whose terms were hard to spell. While the teacher felt confident that she could meet the challenges posed by her other students, she didn't have a clue what to do for this new girl.

What the teacher did may seem ingenious, but was really just the only thing she could think of at the time. After telling the class about the anticipated student, she instructed them to get into their cooperative learning groups to discuss what they thought could be done.

After about twenty minutes, the teacher reconvened the class, wondering whether she would later consider this exercise a waste of time or, worse, some lame effort to hide her own insecurities. What happened instead was an opportunity for this teacher to gain a valuable professional insight. In the few minutes allotted, the kids came up with seventy-three ideas for incorporating the new student into the classroom. Of these, the teacher determined that sixty-two of them were pedagogically sound.

What a revelation to this teacher. Her students, who had not yet completed elementary school, had no problem figuring out what to do. What this endeavor did confirm was that, absolutely, this new student needed a teacher. But instead of her having only a few adults to fill that role, she would have a classroom full of "assistants." When the girl did arrive, there was no need for the other kids to adjust. They were looking forward to this new classmate, and to implementing their ideas.

Tom and the Math Lesson

The second story is from Tom, a fifth-grade teacher. His district had adopted a new math series and the lesson of the day involved multiplying fractions. Tom waxed eloquent for the twenty-minute lesson. He had prepared well and was quite pleased with his performance. As we are all wont to do, Tom thought it would be appropriate to have some feedback from the class to validate his success. In fact, he was thinking that a "Teacher of the Year" nomination might be in order.

He asked for all who knew how to multiply fractions to raise their hands. Two of the twenty-eight kids responded. Just two. This, of course, gave Tom pause and he decided to review his presentation for any flaws. He needed some time to do this and asked one of the two students if he would come to the board and demonstrate his understanding to the class.

Tom took a seat at the back of the room. Because he was deep in contemplation about how to present this topic more effectively, he was only half listening to the kid's presentation. By the time the student was done, Tom had another idea about how to make the necessary clarifications. Before he started again, however, he asked, "How many of you now know how to multiply fractions?" Twenty-six hands rose to the sky.

The real lesson of these two incidents was identified by Tom's comment at the end of his story. He had enough self-esteem and personal security to say, "I never want to teach so long that I can't be taught by kids." That statement may not be the whole of teaching, but it certainly represents a foundational quality that effective teachers have.

. . . . .

Getting Kids Ready for When We Are Gone

What is the ultimate goal of teaching? Sometimes it's getting to the end of the book by the end of the year. Sometimes it's getting kids primed to take some high-stakes test. Sometimes the goal may even be just holding on until the end of the day. All of us face these circumstances, but unless we have a very firm understanding of the eventual goal of teaching, we will pretty much live in a perpetual state of being off balance. In the most basic of terms, the primary goal of both teaching and parenting is to get kids ready for when the adults are gone. This goal is important for nondisabled kids—it is essential for those with handicaps.

I have often thought that the real test to determine whether a class is disciplined is if the kids behave even when the teacher is out of the room. Likewise, the test to determine kids' moral values is what they do when there is no chance of getting caught. And, not to be morose, someday we will all assume room temperature—we will die. Then will come the test of all tests: to see if the kids are ready for life. And along the way to getting kids ready for this unavoidable event are many hurdles.

Parents and teachers soon realize that kids don't come with an owner's manual. Even highly qualified professionals face issues never anticipated from their training. Very often, what most significantly influences the classroom has little direct relevance to the education of students. Economics, politics, and legal issues all have their impact. Groups with hidden agendas and ulterior motives plague the educational structure. Perhaps there should be a mandated course in teacher certification programs dealing with irrelevant issues that vex education and can drive the weak from the profession.

Special education is most certainly a hotbed of controversies that can divert time, money, and effort from the instructional process. Endless IEP meetings, parents with untenable demands, school staff who know precious little about procedure, and students who hold Guinness World Records for educational enigmas are often part of the daily routine.

However, there is a factor that supersedes the destructive power of any external influence. That factor is when individual teachers fail to manifest the essential qualities of effective teaching. Whether these qualities are referred to as attitude, demeanor, or outlook on life, there are some characteristics effective teachers have and ineffective teachers don't.

Like many other concepts, there may be an initial difficulty with creating a precise definition, but you know it when you see it. I am also willing to accept that these characteristics are innate. I am fully convinced that good teachers can become better; I very much doubt that it's worth the time, money, and effort expended to keep bad teachers in the field. And, unless we monitor our own ranks, there will be no need for an enemy from the outside—we will destroy ourselves from within.

A Teacher on Purpose

We have all probably known teachers who are in the profession by default. Some may have been forced into the field by family pressures, others because they didn't think they were smart enough to be anything else. I remember one superintendent who commented somewhat sarcastically that the three main reasons some choose to be teachers are June, July, and August.

Sadly, there are those who fit these descriptions; however, the vast majority are teachers on purpose. They care about kids and care about learning. These are the people who make a positive difference for kids and they have some universal characteristics, one of which is not to bring attention to themselves. Some of the most effective teachers are not known outside their personal sphere of influence. And that is all right with them because self-aggrandizement is of little interest. They are the proverbial unsung heroes and display a true humility.

There is a persistent question of what identifies an effective teacher. I have known hundreds of educators in my career and can attest that some of the more common stereotypes don't hold true. Size, gender, and age are basically irrelevant. I have seen diminutive female teachers in absolute control of a class of overgrown behaviorally disturbed boys. Conversely, I have seen males who are as big as line-backers intimidated into submission by their students. Some seasoned teachers still don't have a clue about being effective, while some, from their first day in class, perform like the experts they are.

What characterizes good teachers is not so much training, degrees, or their GPA in college. It doesn't matter if they teach in content areas, special education, elementary classrooms, or fine arts. Rather, it is more what they feel about themselves, their view about the kids, and their

. . . . .

belief that life has purpose. I have not conducted an extensive research study on the subject, but of all the teachers I can recall, the good ones had the following characteristics, the bad ones didn't.

Demonstrate a Sense of Presence

One characteristic, for lack of a better term, is presence. Effective teachers believe in themselves and they believe in their kids. They have an unconditional love for both themselves and their kids and they demonstrate what they believe. They have an inner strength and confidence that comes from an understanding of their inherent worth, and because they have few negative issues with their own self-concept, they convey a presupposition of kids' innate value as well. When they make mistakes, they either fix them or live with the consequences—and then go on with life.

Mary, a teacher friend who has since passed from this world, was one very neat lady. She had a strength of spirit and a brightness of personality that were exceeded only by the intensity of her red hair. She was presenting at a conference sectional and told a story about an incident that had happened to her some years earlier.

She was hired as a temporary teacher for a tough group of kids in a tough inner-city school. She was the sixth substitute that year, and it was not yet November. The class prized themselves as being a "sub killer" and so far they were winning, five to zip. When Mary walked into the room that first day, she was greeted by a dozen kids, one of whom was standing on his desk, screaming at the top of his voice. Mary approached the boy and asked that he get down. The boy answered her request by spitting on Mary. As she turned to wipe the "gob" from her eye, the kid jumped on her back.

When she finally got him off, she looked at him with a steadfastness the kid had perhaps never before encountered in an adult. Then Mary said some prophetical words. In a tone of calm alert she said, "I'm scheduled to be here for about six weeks. By the end of that time, you and I will be okay with each other."

She demonstrated on a day-to-day basis that she had the inner strength to control herself, and over time this transferred to the kids. With Mary there was a consistency in what she said, meant, and did. Of course, it was hard work, but she knew that the first order of business was for her students to feel accepted and to see what a well-adjusted adult looked like. These were two experiences the kids had seldom encountered—at school, home, or anywhere else.

Mary also had one other technique that was a tangible expression of her character. It is a strategy that never wears out, and when administered correctly allows one to pretty much rule the world. Her strategy of choice was to find something unique about each kid, in a subtle and personal way, and share that information with them. She would mention to one kid that she saw him hit a home run. She would ask another kid about becoming an uncle for the first time. For another kid she would ask if the parts for his car had arrived yet. Obviously this had to be done from a basis of sincerity and required a level of research, and the results enabled Mary to make connections with her kids when no one else could.

In essence, the kids fell in love with her. She met their basic affective needs and they bonded with her. She had "control" over the kids because they trusted her. In fact, she had so much real control that the kids would do things for her they wouldn't even do for themselves.

Mary actually stayed in that class through the entire school year. A few weeks before summer vacation, the kid who had spit on her the first day threw a book at another student. The intended victim had the audacity to duck and the book flew through the open window. Adjacent to the school an old lady who lived next door had planted a small garden. The book's trajectory landed it right in the garden and broke one of the tomato plants.

Looking out the window, Mary and the student surveyed the damage. She put her arm around the kid and said, "I want you to go over to that old lady and apologize for breaking her tomato plant." That was probably the hardest thing this kid had ever been asked to do. You see, he had no trouble slashing tires, bullying other kids, intimidating the adults, shoplifting, and worse. But apologizing to an old lady for breaking her tomato plant! That was hard. In fact, it was so hard he would only do it for Mary.

Mary's sense of presence set the tone for her relationships with the kids in that room. She demonstrated the confidence, poise, and self-control she wanted her kids to have. By using modeling, one of the world's most powerful teaching techniques, she conveyed a lesson to her students they could not sabotage.

. . . . .

Balance Role and Status

I once heard a statistic that 80 percent of misbehavior follows a compliance request—another commonsense fact that research has "confirmed." One hopes there wasn't a lot of money spent on that particular research project. But the question is whether opposition is engendered by the actual request, or by how the "request" is presented. But many compliance requests aren't met with resistance from kids. A coach telling the team to "Go out there and win!" Asking a kid to go with you to get ice cream. These are compliance requests, but there isn't an 80 percent refusal rate in such cases.

In previous chapters much has been said about the concept of shared control. Giving choices, providing options, and sharing alternatives are all excellent strategies. However, there is a "teaching dynamic" that can make or break these, or any other, ostensibly effective techniques. That vital factor involves the concepts of role and status.

The balance of any relationship is "different role, equal status." Relationships become unbalanced when one or more of the parties have a belief that translates into "different role means different status." Think of this in the context of husband/wife, parent/child, teacher/principal, or any other association that involves differentiation. When those in each position interact with equal respect, the resulting balance allows happy productivity. However, when this balance is disrupted by one position treating the other as inferior, relationship and productiveness deteriorate.

Sometimes this differential is obvious, but mostly it is subtle. How often have we heard phrases like, "She's just a custodian" or "He's from a bad family" as a way of discounting a person's position? The presuppositions of language betray what people really believe, regardless of how nice or sophisticated their public words may sound. What is exceedingly sad is when professionals in education try to validate themselves by lowering the value of others.

The Psychologist and the Kindergarten Teacher

A psychologist had just recently received a Ph.D. and was conducting an IEP meeting for a kindergartner. Armed with his new credential, the psychologist, who had tested the kid for about two hours, was reading from his fifteen-page report. He dominated the meeting and made several declarations about the kid's condition. As he concluded, the kindergarten teacher, who had seen this kid every day for seven months, said, "What you [the psychologist] say from those tests doesn't describe the kid I have in my class."

Evidently, the psychologist took this as a challenge to his authority. He raised his butt off the chair about four inches, pointed his finger at the kindergarten teacher, and said, in a tone of voice that dripped with an empty superiority, "I have a Ph.D." A strange comment, indeed, because there had been no previous reference to his degree.

The teacher, who had been in the profession some thirty years, was unabashed. After all, she could manage a couple dozen five-year-olds at a time—one egotistic Ph.D. was hardly going to intimidate her. She looked past the psychologist's finger, and said with a calmness of voice heard only from well-adjusted kindergarten teachers, "You tested the kid for two hours. I've known this kid for seven months. I win." She did.

First-Grade Terrorists
Just as with adults, the balance between role and status determines our effectiveness with kids. My most favored Love and Logic tape is the interaction between Jim Fay and two little "first-grade terrorists." This is an interaction Jim recorded a number of years ago of two youngsters who had been sent to his office for playground fighting.

Although the use of given strategies and principles is certainly apparent in that interaction, there is a dynamic that constitutes the foundation for Jim's success. I often use that tape in presentations and after a general discussion is completed, ask the group, "If the voice track were separated and you only heard Jim's voice, could you tell if he were talking to kids or adults?"

The answer is always that the group couldn't tell the difference. Jim demonstrates this essential quality of "different role, equal status" as he lays some pretty heavy consequences on these two kids. He is the principal, they are the two little kids in trouble—a different role, to be sure. However, all three actors in this play have the same status. As such, they all are afforded dignity and respect as well as being held accountable for their decisions.

Believe in Learning from the Kids

Another characteristic of effective teachers is an attitude of reciprocity. That is, they anticipate learning as much from kids as they hope kids learn from them. I have become convinced that adults can't think like kids and as a result are not effective in solving kid problems. Without this sense of reciprocity, adults too often reject a solution that would allow kids to effectively solve their own problems. Such rejection is interpreted by kids as a put-down. They very soon form the opinion that being involved in problem solving is not worth their effort.

I recall one incident that happened on a quite blustery day in November. A student had come to school in only a flannel shirt—no coat, no hat. This kid had truancy problems and was on the automatic suspicion list. The teacher called the parent, because she, too, would be upset with the kid. Two adults to one kid should tip the odds in the adults' favor.

The adults were prepared to give this kid his umpteenth lecture on the stupidity of his actions. The lecture would include the zinger that what they were only telling him was for his own good. After all, even thinking of going out in this type of weather without being properly bundled was stupid and he was probably doing it just to make the adults mad.

The scene was set. Two adults and one kid in a stark room. The first question, I am sure, was meant to be rhetorical: "Why didn't you wear your coat?" But the kid's answer basically ended the conversation. You see, the adults were anticipating some irreverent comment and they were "psyching" themselves up for a lengthy argument. What the kid said was totally unanticipated. "I promised my mom I would stay in school today. I didn't wear a coat because I knew if I did, I would have skipped. I knew it was cold and if I didn't wear my coat I would stay the whole day." Talk about a lesson learned.

Validate the Kid's Personhood

There is a strategy in the arsenal of Love and Logic referred to as the "Two-Minute Intervention." The technique has a simple format:

1. Invite a kid to talk with you for two minutes a day, for as close to ten days in a row as possible. Obviously, there are weekends

and other interferences, but ten days seems to be the optimal time frame.

2. Listen with full attention to whatever the kid wants to talk about for the two minutes and then end the session with a descriptive statement that is positive, personal, and true. For instance, the kid may have been talking about horses and the teacher concludes the session with, "I can sure tell you like horses."

That's it. It's so very simple, but also so powerful. To be listened to with full attention validates our personhood like nothing else. One teacher related the following experience:

I will give a little background on my student, James. He lives in Milwaukee and is part of the Chapter 220 Program [a court-ordered desegregation plan]. . . . James has the reputation of being a child you don't want in your classroom. This year he was placed in a sixth-grade classroom of a new teacher. As the year progressed, so did James's bad behavior. James's teacher was quoted as saying, "He just won't do what I tell him to do. I tell him to sit in the blue chair, he'll sit in the green one. It's a constant power struggle and I won't let him win. It will be done my way only!"

Needless to say, his approach didn't work and James's parents insisted he be taken out of that classroom immediately. With ten other sixth-grade classrooms to choose from, guess where James ended up? You're right—my classroom. Lucky for me, James was given to me the Monday after my first weekend of classes on "Discipline with Love and Logic." Taking in all the information, readily, I planned my approach. I decided to try this two-minute teaching technique, and asked James if he would do me a favor. I told him that I chose him because I didn't know him very well and it would be a nice opportunity to get to know him. Just the thought of James helping me (the teacher) with my homework excited him! And this is what I discovered.

The teacher then summarized the conversations they'd had. Topics included what James did on weekends, arguments he had with his siblings, and how he liked his current class better than the previous one. He talked about his girlfriend and being "grounded" from the telephone. On the ninth day, James forgot to come. On the tenth and final day, the teacher reported:

> He was concerned about missing yesterday because he knew this was my homework. I told him that was okay, but I missed our talk. James also asked if I needed help with any other homework. I said, "Not at the moment, but if I do, you'll be the first one I ask." James smiled and walked away. He paused at the door and mumbled something. I think he said, "Thank you."

The teacher concluded with the following comments:

> I was amazed at the results. James has never given me a discipline problem since he's been in my class. I hope that since our time of talking is done, things stay the same. If not, I will continue our two-minute "chats." The best thing about this is the other teachers' reactions. They wanted to know what my secret was to keep James in control.

Shooting from the Hip

Sometimes this validation must come spontaneously. I have a terrible time remembering names. The part of my brain that performs this function was either damaged at birth or never installed in the first place. Walking down the high school hall one day, I saw Jim, one of our special needs students with behavioral problems, and caught his eye. He smiled until I said, "Hi, John." Jim's older brother was named John and many of us know what it is like to be referred to by a sibling's name. Even our parents do that. It was some years before I knew my name was just David and not "Linn Errol Duane Rolan David."

However typical it may be to call a kid by the wrong name, Jim's disappointment was apparent. "This guy couldn't even remember my name," was the clear message from his expression. A recovery was in order.

Since I had made the mistake, the cost should accrue to me, not to Jim. I thought a monetary fine was in order. Later that day I motioned Jim out of his classroom and said, "I've decided that every time I call a kid the wrong name, I owe them a dollar." As I handed him his money, his demeanor changed. His smile resumed and he said, "From now on, you can call me anything you want." This became a connection between us and every time I saw him in the hall, he had a smile on his face, a twinkle in his eye, and he always asked, "What's my name?"

Give Unconditional Regard

There is a power in unconditional regard. This concept reflects the "love" in Love and Logic and is an underused resource for teachers. When kids have a sense of acceptance, even those who seem hardened to the system respond.

I would never refer to any kid by some cutesy name. Especially a six-foot-three, 230-pounder who had just been released from a juvenile institution for hardened boys. But June, a teacher of the behaviorally disturbed at the local high school, did. She had a pet name for each of her kids, and Barry would be no different.

When Barry was released, the school had to take him back. However, there was a dilemma: Who would take him? A meeting of all potential staff members was convened, with Barry off to the side and the teachers sitting around a massive conference table. The principal started the rounds and one-by-one asked each of the teachers if they would take Barry into their class.

Each had a unique and individual reason not to. The social studies teacher declined because she had Barry's brother and was not going to have another kid from "that" family. The math and English teachers took one look at Barry's test scores and determined he could not meet the academic rigor required to be successful in their classes. The science teacher had an argument based on the safety of other students: after all, if Barry were to be allowed in a lab, the inevitable result would be that the school would succumb to a massive explosion, or worse. In brief, no one would take Barry.

Barry, of course, heard the entirety of each of these conversations. In all probability, he was resigned to dropping out or at least being transferred to some alternative program outside the district.

There was one more teacher, however, who had yet to voice her opinion. When it came June's turn to speak, she said, "Hey, what the heck, he can come to my room. I think we'll get along all right." And they gave him

. . . . .

to her—all day long. He was her "Barry Bear" from that moment on.

Picture this massive student sitting at a standard one-piece student desk, wedged in like he was wearing jeans that were three sizes too small. But he was learning and he was with someone who believed in him.

One day he demonstrated the effect of the relationship that had been developed between him and his teacher. The door to the room had a small window with chicken wire embedded in the glass—kind of like what one might see in a solitary confinement cell in a prison. Presumably this was to give a view to the world outside the room. One day a school jock peered through the glass and made some crude facial gesture, not at the kids, but at the teacher, whose back was turned.

Barry saw this, worked his way out of his seat, walked to the door, and with no apparent regard for the window or what might happen to him, punched through the glass at the kid. The action was dramatic enough, but what he said was of more importance: "Nobody looks at my teacher that way." He was determined to defend this person who had defended him.

Certainly, this caught the attention of the staff and administration, and once the incident was resolved, June talked to Barry about paying for the window. She only had to ask and he did it to honor her. He allowed her that control because of the bond between them. At a cost of over seventy-five dollars, Barry had to work a lot of hours to pay for that piece of reinforced glass, but he did. This story is not to justify what he did. What it demonstrates, however, is the effect on what people are willing to do when they feel accepted.

Put Thinking Before Problem Solving

As mentioned earlier in this book, when I first heard of Love and Logic, I had a queasy feeling it was a bit wimpish, what with "Love" in the title and all. What I observed, however, was that those who adhered to this process were some of the most intact and strongest people I had known. One especially visible characteristic was their penchant for waiting until everyone is thinking before discussing solutions.

Several years ago a panic call came from the bus company that was transporting three high school boys to an alternative school. The dispatcher reported that of the sixteen drivers available at the beginning of the year, fourteen had quit or refused to continue transporting those kids.

This dispatcher had the gift of conveying implied messages. Without hearing another word from her, the school person receiving the message concluded that if the other two drivers quit, he might be adding "bus driver" to his résumé. Therefore, he was very invested in the solution. (It has always interested me that the experts in "applied psychology" seem to be people who've never had formal training.)

In actuality, for two of the kids, the problem was fixed pretty quickly. There was a meeting with all concerned, the kids said they would shape up, and they did. Usually, two of three isn't bad, but the third kid, Jerome, still had to be provided FAPE (Free Appropriate Education). Jerome was a challenge, and, in fact, so was his mother.

To give a perspective about Jerome, note the following comments from the bus drivers' reports:

> *Jerome is the worst—extremely foul mouthed! When being picked up for school [he] makes bus wait as long as five minutes before coming out. Called the driver a "fat, f--king, white bitch."*
> *Jerome is the leader [of the three boys riding the bus].*
> *[Jerome also said:] "If we get white man back we're going to kick his ass."*
> *[Jerome was] feigning masturbation and other obscene gestures to following traffic.*
> *[Jerome is] refusing to board bus—until finished smoking.*
> *[Jerome flashes] gang signs and other obscene gestures at following traffic.*
> *[Jerome] called [the bus driver] a "lesbian bitch."*
> *Jerome told [the bus driver] to watch her back—she doesn't know how crazy he really is.*
> *Driver asked Jerome if he talked to his mother like that: He said, "She's a bitch, too."*
> *[Jerome] threatened to urinate on the floor.*
> *Jerome [is the] main problem.*

When Jerome and his mother did not show up for the group meeting, they were called to "reschedule." No one answered and the following message was left on the family's answering machine: "The bus will start picking Jerome up again depending on what happens when we meet."

Admittedly, this was a pressure ploy. Jerome had been court-ordered to attend school and further truancy would be a real hassle for the parent. Jerome's mother left her own message in response: "Jerome didn't do anything wrong and if the bus company says he did, they're full of shit!" Interestingly, in the background Jerome could be heard giving his mother verbal encouragement.

Jerome's mom was mad and she was big. She was well able to beat just about anyone into submission and she was not one to argue with.

Jerome was no dummy either. He had a fantastically high IQ and wanted to go into some esoteric archaeological field of which he was already pretty much an expert. To engage in a debate with him would also have been a losing battle. First, it would be two against one. Second, he could easily outthink most adults.

The key in these situations is to be sure everyone is thinking with calm alert. One effective method is for the professional to assume the role of scorekeeper rather than umpire. Jerome and his mom were afforded the same opportunity to respond as the bus drivers. On the surface, this apparently sounded good to them; however, when asked to put their position in writing (like the drivers were asked to do), and have a decision rendered by a mediator (who had no vested interest and would only look at the provable facts), the issue of who did what was dropped. With the current vote of fourteen to two in favor of his guilt, the odds were against Jerome winning.

Once past this hurdle, the district representative offered two ideas, with the added comment that he didn't think the mother would like either one of them. However, she was somewhat curious and the conversation continued.

The first option was that the district could develop a transportation contract with the mother and pay her mileage for taking Jerome to and from school. The other was that Jerome could be taught at home. Of course, neither of these alternatives was acceptable. The mother didn't at all want to drive her kid, and certainly didn't want him home alone most of the day. Jerome was seeing his mother's support deteriorate right in front of him and he basically knew the gig was up.

In spite of Jerome's behavior, he had a high regard for keeping his word. The problem was reconciled with a verbal agreement and a handshake. The whole meeting took less than thirty minutes and as the two left, the mother whispered, "I know Jerome is not an angel." In reality, he was very far from being an angel, but the comment represented a level of trust on the mother's part. Not a lot, mind you, but more than she had been able to demonstrate in the past.

Jerome finished out the year without further reportable incidents. I trust he is now digging up artifacts and doing well.

Deal Honestly

A "one-liner" I ask kids at the start of a serious meeting is, "Are you the kind of kid adults can be honest with?" The answer, so far, has always been affirmative. This establishes a point of mutual agreement and lessens the chance that defense mechanisms will be erected as an initial response. However, this statement only provides a one-way commitment, and reciprocity is essential if change is to be accomplished.

To establish this reciprocal commitment, a follow-up question is often necessary. Although circumstances will determine precise wording, the question basically asks, "Are you the kind of kid who will be honest in return?" People amazingly and consistently open up when the opportunity is presented this way. Lying, deceit, and manipulation tend to lose their appeal under such conditions. If this process is undertaken, however, the adults need to be honest, and this can be uncomfortable at times.

Bryan's Song and Dance

Bryan was a kid whose thinking was distorted, and he often went into intimidating rages. In addition, he was an expert at bird walks. Even as a fourth-grader, he was an absolute genius at getting adults off track and talking about everything except his part of the problem. And frankly, the soft-heartedness of his teachers contributed to his maladaptive behavior. Somewhere in their training it seemed they picked up the idea that kids should only hear nice, positive things so their feelings don't get hurt. The teachers' idea of "Children First" somehow resulted in the adults being last.

Let's have a reality check. When adults contribute to kids' distorted thinking, they perpetuate the problem. Some kids have so much baggage that they will never get better until they start over. Being syrupy is all right for some kids, but there are others who need a tidal wave of honesty before they perceive a need to change. In Bryan's case, watching him use the sincere intentions of the adults to bludgeon them into senselessness was, frankly, becoming annoying.

Bryan had a fantastic memory for the minute details of what everyone else had done to him. According to Bryan, nothing was his fault—absolutely nothing. At one meeting, his mother said, "If Bryan stumbles on a stair, he yells and hits the step and blames it for tripping him." This kid had some serious emotional problems and the "feel-good" techniques his teachers and therapists were using were ineffective at best and may even have been delaying a remedy.

Something different had to be done. First, a list of what wasn't working:

1. Reasoning and explaining his own lack of logic.
2. Telling him to ignore the other kids.
3. Trying to talk louder than him.
4. Appealing to human virtues like kindness, longsuffering, and forgiveness.
5. Rewarding him for being good.
6. Punishing him for being bad.
7. Laying a guilt trip on him.
8. Asking him how the other kids feel.

Since all else was failing, honesty sans euphemism seemed worth a try. The following narrative occurred after blocking Bryan's repeated attempts to shift blame. The only question of the day would be his behavior, and his behavior only. He was persistent, but every time he strayed from the predetermined topic, the facilitator's response was a simple phrase, repeated as often as necessary: "I'm only interested about what you do." Sometimes it took a dozen repetitions of that phrase, but eventually Bryan got the message. Then the real instruction could take place:

FACILITATOR: Bryan, what would happen if you acted this way on a job?

BRYAN: I'd get fired.

FACILITATOR: That's right. And how many times could you get fired before nobody would want you to work for them?

BRYAN: Probably two or three times.

FACILITATOR: That's what I would guess as well. So, does it seem we're thinking alike about that? If some changes don't happen, it will be hard for you to have enough money to buy food, get a car, and do other stuff you might like to do.

BRYAN: Yeah.

Actually, these questions constituted a kind of diagnostic test to determine Bryan's level of contact with reality. Remember, he is just going into fifth grade, but since his answers evidenced appropriate understanding, the process could continue:

FACILITATOR: Bryan, how old are you?

BRYAN: Eleven and a half. (Bryan was on the extended plan to get through elementary school.)

FACILITATOR: How old do you have to be before your parents don't have to let you live at their house?

BRYAN: I'm not ever leaving!

Behold the bird walk technique. What was interesting at this point is that Bryan looked at his mother and realized, perhaps for the first time, that she was just biding her time. The conversation continued:

FACILITATOR: Bryan, you answered the wrong question. How old do you have to be before your parents don't have to let you live at their house?

BRYAN: I don't know.

FACILITATOR: Eighteen. So, it looks like you have a little over six years left. Do you think you are getting ready for this as fast as other kids your age are?

BRYAN: (Shrugs his shoulders.)

FACILITATOR: And, Bryan, another question you might think about. Someday, your parents will die. Even if you live in their house after you're eighteen, someday they won't be here. Will you be ready for that? Or do you think your little sister might let you live with her? (His little half-sister was three years old and already disliked him.)

. . . . .

Bryan had no more argumentative answers. In fact, he quit talking altogether. Another interesting observation was the conduct of the other adults in the room. The teacher, who had been lightheartedly cajoling Bryan, when in actuality she wanted to get rid of him, dropped her false smile, singsongy talk, and artificial laughter. The therapist, who had appeared to be walking on those proverbial eggshells (because she wanted to appear sensitive to Bryan's inner self), dropped her clipboard, and left it on the floor. The mother, who had taken every opportunity to tell Bryan how bad he was, said, "Yes, Bryan, that's what scares me to death" (and it didn't seem she was making a play on words).

The only "technique" was to talk directly about the real ultimate issue. The great hope was that the adults in Bryan's life would realize how their interactions with him were contributing to his sickness.

The following year, the people working with Bryan were willing to take a more direct and honest approach with him. He had some very serious emotional problems that would not get better without his facing the eventualities of his behavior.

The Accrued Benefits

When these characteristics of effective teaching are internalized, there is little emphasis on defense mechanisms to fortress a position of superiority. This, in turn, provides the wherewithal to effectively intervene with even fairly extreme and unexpected situations. When the teacher is not preoccupied with self-justification, the kid doesn't get the expected reaction. This initial confusion is a "start-over" point and forms the basis for new learning.

Take, for instance, the normal expectation of some kids walking into a room and stating, "I hate this damned school and all you f--kin' teachers!" The usual reaction involves some sort of reprimand and removing the kid. That is what Mike, a kid from a small Wisconsin district, anticipated. What he got during one of his performances, however, was something a bit different.

For Mike, getting kicked out of class was a normal occurrence. He didn't like school and had developed this rather unsophisticated way of getting some school-approved time off. It had worked every time—until he walked into Marian's class that fateful day.

Marian had decided to become a teacher now that her son and two daughters were all in school. She was completing her student teaching, and the day of reckoning had arrived. Her college supervisor was in the class to observe, and today Marian would be totally responsible for the class. She was pretty much preoccupied with getting things ready, and in fact was already a bit behind schedule when Mike made his grand entrance. With full confidence in his ability to get himself removed from class, he shouted his signature statement. Because of Marian's view on life, she did not interpret Mike's comment as a personal affront. Her reaction, although consistent with her view on life, was not at all what Mike expected. Marian barely looked up from her preparations when she said, "Mike, I'm really busy now and I'm about three minutes behind. Could you come back in about an hour and a half and say that again? I think I could handle it better then."

No yelling back at Mike. No telling him he couldn't talk like that in her classroom. Not really even kicking him out. Rather, it was more like rescheduling an appointment. In fact, Mike did come back, and with a much different demeanor. No one knows where Mike went, but he didn't get into any trouble and he didn't leave school. Actually, a relationship developed between the two that influenced Marian to eventually become a special education teacher. One relatively isolated incident resulted in a very great benefit.

A Humble Test Maybe We Should All Take

Some years ago a group of our staff attended a two-day conference addressing the issue of including disabled students in regular education. One of the speakers had significant limitations as a result of cerebral palsy and was a convincing advocate for those with disabilities. As a result of the meeting, those in our group, including two other men, offered glowing reports about the insights they had gained.

Then came the test. During the following school year, one of our teaching aides faced a minor emergency and was going to be away from school for several days. Part of her assignment involved assisting one of our students who could not independently take care of many of his personal needs (including eating and toileting). To prepare for this absence, the building administrator made a request to the male staff to help toilet this student. When no one offered to assist, the administrator called me for some advice. Although she would be willing to step in, she thought it would be much better if a male could assist the student.

When she called, my first comment was that she should ask the two men assigned to the student's school who had gone to the conference the previous year. After all, they had supported the idea of dignity for the handicapped. They knew this high school student was incapable of helping himself, and this opportunity would be perfect for demonstrating their commitment.

When I mentioned this to the vice principal, she said she had already spoken to these men. In fact, she had spoken to them first, thinking that since they had participated in the conference, they would certainly be willing to follow through. Evidently we had both been naive. The two men declined on the basis that it wasn't their job and that they were not trained in special education. I was so ticked! What training did they think there was to help a kid use the toilet? There is no course called "Butt-Wiping 101."

The indignity was not that this kid needed help. The indignity was when someone thought helping him was below their status. Twice a day for the next week I drove across town to help the kid use the bathroom.

Several days later, the kid's mom and I were both attending a meeting. Since we had known each other for some time, we sat at the same table. At the break, she handed me a package. At first I thought it might be some book she wanted me to read, but instead it was a framed certificate. She and her son had designed a humorous, but very professional-looking document, declaring that I was now a "Certified Urinal Technician."

That "credential" hangs on my office wall in a black document frame along with degrees and other recognitions accumulated over the last three decades. It has an added significance as a tangible reminder that the indignity of being handicapped is not the disability, it's not even the reaction of those who don't know any better. The true indignity is when professional educators treat the needs of kids as "not their job."

I hung the plaque on my wall and somewhat basked in the "honor" I had received. But that was pretty egocentric. Each time I saw it, I was increasingly quick to think, "What a good little boy am I." Then I learned a lesson I should have known all along. One of our teaching assistants saw the plaque and made a comment that she had been toileting kids for almost two decades and had never thought about getting an award.

The best teachers aren't the ones who write books, they don't present at conferences, and they haven't received doctoral degrees. The best teachers are those who get their kids ready for when they are gone. And when these teachers are gone, the kids cry for a time, remember the important lessons, and then go on with life the way they were taught.

CHAPTER 9

The Other People
of Special Education

The Parents' Role

Parents are the other people in special education. They are important not only because they have given birth to and reared their disabled kids, but also because they have been given a unique position by law. Regardless of training, background, intellectual capacity, or motive, parents of special education students possess substantial rights in making educational decisions that affect their children. In large measure, these rights were granted because of inequities that included a sometimes flagrant disregard of parental input.

Although parents now have a plethora of designated rights, there are no commensurate imposed obligations. As a result, the school can find itself in a position of not being able to compel parent participation or follow-through, even if such action could result in noticeable improvement in the student's performance. Given these factors, it becomes vitally important for school personnel to know how to work collaboratively. When the parents and school have the same focus, the process works as intended.

When there are irreconcilable conflicts, the district could initiate mediation or due process (in fact, the district is required to pursue these courses under specific circumstances). However, these legal entanglements are expensive not only in terms of monetary cost but also in terms of the time and effort that could be utilized toward a more satisfying end. In addition, even if there is legal action, most often the kid will continue to be educated in the same system and the adults involved will still need to work together. For the most part, the time spent developing a positive relationship pays better dividends.

Two Kinds of Parents

The experiences afforded to me over my career have pointed in the direction of simplification. In this quest, dichotomizing has become a useful tool. Frankly, I don't think there are as many gray areas as are often purported. Good/evil, yes/no, male/female, young/old are often quite effective in giving an order to the world. It was especially comforting to me to find out that even the most complicated computers run on devices that are essentially minuscule on/off switches.

It's not so very different with parents. Although parents come with as many nuances as kids, there may well be only two basic categories. The first category includes parents who focus on their kids, the second is limited to those who focus on themselves. This may seem a bit simplistic, and even mean-spirited at first, so bear with me.

Parents Who Focus on Their Kids

Parents who focus on their kids demonstrate a wide range of attributes. This group includes those who are capable, understanding, grateful, competent, and overjoyed that their kids are getting help with their learning. These are the parents who are often referred to as "easy to work with" and who provide teachers with pleasant feelings.

But being the diverse group they are, this category also includes parents who are angry, worried, depressed, alcoholics, too young to have children, irresponsible, crazier than their kids, neurotic, fuzzy in their logic, and mad at the system, to name just a few. These are the parents who are often referred to as "hard to work with" and who are largely responsible for providing teachers with opportunities to refine their professional skills.

Certainly, this group of parents express a wide range of negative affect, because they are scared about what the future holds for their kid. They want fulfillment for their child, and although extraordinary amounts of time and effort may be required, they (eventually) respond to genuine good-faith efforts of people who demonstrate they care.

. . . . .

Parents Who Focus on Themselves

This is a fairly short list, because there are so few. Parents in this group, under the guise of advocating for their child, use their kid's disability for their own self-promotion. Since they are empty of honor, they put on a show of support for their kid, but are hypocrites of a special kind because they sacrifice their own children to satisfy the god of their own ego.

In my thirty-plus years in special education, I have known hundreds of parents in the first category. I can recall fewer than three in the second.

A Lesson Learned

It is important to differentiate the two groups, because good-faith efforts will work only with the first. Some cases will take lots of time, effort, and even tears. There will surely be frustrations and setbacks; however, once these hurdles have been passed, progress will be made and a positive relationship can be developed.

Spending resources on the second group is likened to shoveling water. These parents take more time than they are worth. I know this because I have spent more time with them than they were worth. My experience is not unique, and from the discussions with peers about this subject, these parents seem to have three consistent characteristics:

1. Such parents hold teams hostage by dominating the meeting with superficiality and minutia. They may put on a show of genius or knowledge of the law, but betray their lack of understanding with faulty logic, inaccurate application of instructional strategies, out-of-context legal references, and mispronounced acronyms. Sadly, these parents often intimidate IEP teams and take over meetings because school staff are inadequate in their knowledge of legal parameters, limits imposed by procedure, and the role of educational methodology.

   In one instance an IEP meeting was lasting longer than anticipated and the room was needed for another activity. The group was asked to move and they continued the meeting in a classroom a few doors down the hall. The parent protested and later filed a complaint to the state education department that the IEP was invalid. His reason was that the written invitation had not properly notified him that the meeting would be moved to a different room.

2. Another common characteristic is for these parents to scrape the bottom of the professional credibility barrel in finding "experts" to support their claims. Shopping for psychologists, therapists, and lawyers is evidently a favored pastime. And there are always those with sufficient credentials who can present what seems to be impressive research, test data, and opinions to support whatever these parents want. Research, to be sure, is important, but caution must be exercised when group studies are applied to individuals. Statistics and findings may sound quite impressive; however, unless there is sure evidence of a valid and undeniable connection between the kid and the analysis, there may be very little relevance to diagnosis or programming for the student.

   In one instance, a parent demanded that a particular psychologist be involved with an independent educational evaluation. The district complied with this request, but when the findings from the parents' chosen psychologist did not conform to their liking, they demanded still another. Eventually, they obtained the services of a "qualified consultant" located a fair distance from the district. (Interestingly, this person's professional organization was in the process of revoking her license for unethical practices.) During the actual meetings (there were several) she recited research as though it were gospel. However, when asked to verify that the findings she was reporting specifically applied to the student in question, she could not. In a classic bird walk, she then explained how this information related to the solution for her own daughter's school difficulties. It was confusing why one invalid argument could be remedied by another equally void of credibility.

3. A third characteristic is that these parents get especially defensive when evidence is presented indicating that their kid is getting better. They are not at all enamored with having effective remediation, since their goal is to increase their own status through power and control. Even when test scores substantiate progress, that evidence gets twisted. Without a "defective" child, these parents no longer have a base of operation. Teachers are often

accused of lying, deceit, and worse in a "righteous" attempt to discredit reports of improvement.

It must be emphasized that there are not many parents in this second group. The school should actively avoid placing parents in this category simply because they may be difficult to work with. However, the honest fact is that there are such parents and that they will drain the efforts of school staff to no avail. When dealing with this type of parent, it is especially important that schools follow correct procedure and keep accurate documentation. Unfortunately, involvement of legal counsel may often be the only option.

One Person's Job Is Another Person's Kid

For some teachers, disabled kids represent an employment opportunity. For many, these kids provide an educational challenge. For others, kids with disabilities represent little more than a curiosity—an opportunity to experiment. Regardless, teachers have an eventual respite. There is an end of the school day, an end of the school year, and even an end of the student's school career. At any rate, the teacher's job is eventually done.

For parents of a disabled kid, the end of school represents a loss. A loss of security, a loss of a place where their kids can go. What teachers look forward to is often a fearful and regrettable event for parents. This part of having a disabled child is scary.

"This Was Not Our Plan"

For someone who started out as a classroom teacher, I have had some unique opportunities to work with parents. In addition to attending literally thousands of meetings involving evaluation and programming for disabled kids, I often speak with parents after workshop presentations. What continues to amaze me is how freely parents bare their souls. Although a very few are seeking attention or justification for their own behavior, the vast majority are desperately seeking some help with their kids. They love their kids and they don't know what to do.

Not expecting to have a disabled child is the universal experience for parents of special needs kids. They remember when the pregnancy was confirmed. They remember anticipating the birth. When their child was born, they remember the exhilaration of contemplating what could be. But at some point, parents became aware that their expectations would not be fulfilled.

I recall speaking with one couple. They desperately wanted a child. They went through all sorts of unnatural procedures to conceive. Finally, relatively late in life, their son was born. However, there were some serious genetic defects that were a permanent part of who this child was. There were both physical and cognitive deficits that would significantly limit this student's ability to perform in school as well as in life. In a private conversation with the father, he confided, in quite an understatement, that this was not what they had bargained for.

For a long time, they didn't seem to accept the fact that their son was handicapped. They looked for a way out. They didn't know what else to do. During one informal conversation, the father showed a picture of an uncle who "didn't do very good in school either, and they thought he was retarded, but he did okay." The uncle had the same first name as their son and they were hoping, beyond hope, that the story would be repeated.

It is no trite saying that it takes a village to raise a child, and some parents don't even have an intact family. The educational community may be the only resource for some parents, and unless they can find support, the school may lose an ally. Often, developing these relationships will not be an easy task, but without parental support, programming for the kids will be incomplete.

The Need for Both Hope and Help

Anyone who has been in special education for any length of time has had some dealings with parents who pose significant, and often irritating, challenges. Sometimes these parents are angry, sometimes demanding or even threatening. Others might be passive-aggressive and during meetings give the impression that all is well only to call administrators and board members with their gripes later. However, fear is a basic motive for these actions. For the most part, parents expressing these emotions are scared spitless about what will happen to their kids when the support they have from the school and other agencies is gone.

As educators, we would do well to recognize and accept that we are involved not only with the kids, but with the parents as well. It is a special irritant to me when parents are told only what they have done wrong, the grim details of their kid's abnormality, and the fundamental dynamics in their family that must be changed immediately to prevent further damage. It is even more irritating after the meeting when the "professionals" have no other intention than to lament about the inadequacy of the parents' skills in raising their kids.

I am not opposed to pointing out problems. But leaving parents to wallow in guilt and frustration has little purpose. Regrettably, parents are too seldom guided into what to do other than some cursory command. In what other profession would it be acceptable to believe responsibility ends at identification? If parents knew what to do and had the where-withal to do so, they probably would. And frankly, educators might be more prone to providing the necessary help, but they often don't know what to do either. Otherwise, they might be more willing to work with parents to effect change. It is a relative no-brainer to identify what is wrong. What takes professional skill is to identify what is needed to remedy a situation.

This, of course, would take time and require change. At the very least, however, we can recognize that parents, like everyone else, need some validation. I recall a situation when a parent and her son had recently moved to the district. She was a single parent and the placement had some unique complications. During the initial conversations it was easy to see that the parent was emotionally overtaxed. She thought getting her son to school was going to be her responsibility and didn't know how she would juggle that with getting to her job. When she was told transportation would be provided, she was quite relieved. A simple comment was added that it seemed she didn't need that stress in her life. When the conversation was done, she said, "That's the first time anybody from a school seemed to be thinking about me. Thank you."

That simple phrase of empathy set the tone. Verily, her kid was a handful (and the mother was too), but from the start, the school had at least one positive connection. Of interest was the comment by the kid's former teacher that the mother had a bipolar disorder. So what! Are the criteria for treating people with respect connected with them having no conditions identified in the current edition of the *Diagnostic Statistical Manual (DSM)*?

How encouraging it is to parents when a school member of the IEP team says, "Would you like to have some ideas to use at home?" And it's only fair, isn't it? I have never quite understood why the school believes that its issues are all-important without any responsibility for reciprocity. It's quite commonplace for the school to tell parents about the importance of setting aside time to do homework with their kids, to read to them each day, and generally to instill the importance of formal education. However, if a parent would ask the school to help with sibling rivalry or teaching the kids to be more responsible for doing their chores, that request would be rejected out of hand. One wonders why.

The Turnabout

Life is full of imponderables that have some rationale in their history. I remember learning some time ago that men wear ties because some long-ago king had a goiter on his neck he wanted to hide. We shake hands because there was a need in the past to show there were no hidden weapons. The presumption that the home should support the school is so strong that many educators are actually offended when there is the suggestion that the school should likewise support the home.

Maybe it's simply tradition. Maybe it's because there is such diversity represented by individual families. Maybe it's because it seems too much work. Maybe it's because teachers don't know what to do for home problems anymore than parents know what to do for school problems. Or maybe it's because nobody has asked.

I have sat in on countless IEP meetings during which the parents are virtually ordered to provide a structured homework time, parent more consistently, and generally get their act together. Sometimes this is spoken from professional educators who themselves give unstructured assignments, provide an inconsistent model, and generally need to get their act together. I have heard insensitive psychologists tell parents, in the same manner that they report the kid's age and birthday, that their child is emotionally disabled because their family is dysfunctional .

If the parents were to place similar requirements (or accusations) on the school, they would be considered difficult. This one-way street may be one of the last vestiges of education's authoritarian past. I wonder what

. . . . .

would happen if more parents would send letters like this one composed by a mother of four kids (the last of whom had Down's syndrome):

Dear Teacher,

I come from a long line of moms who believed it was their duty to follow through on all of the requests the school made. We set aside structured study time, read thirty minutes a day to each child, and made sure homework was done. We also made sure lunches were packed with items from the "approved" snack list. In short, we did everything we were told to do because . . . well, just because we thought we had to.

I have been teaching my children a lesson that I don't think is going to help them when they get out of the house. I think I have taught them that since the school can "order" me to do things, home must be less important. I got quite good at teaching them to think that if they have school assignments, they don't have to do their chores at home. That frazzled me and then my kids started to think moms are frazzled people. I think I can reverse this with my first three kids, but with Jimmy's problems, I don't think I have the luxury of holding off. I have a plan that I think will help both of us.

I want my kids to do good in school. I also want them to be able to get along with others—and that includes their brothers and sister. So, if you call me about their not getting along on the playground, let's use the same amount of time talking about how they cannot fight in the van when we are going to the grocery store. If they don't get their homework done for you, let's have a good talk about getting them to do their chores at home. I am sure that with any other school problems, there will be something similar at home.

I've got some really good ideas for how you can work with my kids at school. I think you have some really good ideas for me at home. If we can have this agreement, I will look forward to calls from school. I think this will be healthier for both of us and the kids, too. Thanks.

Sincerely,
Mrs. G—

Procedure and Trust

It is extremely unfortunate if there is an understanding that the school and parents are predestined to be oppositional. However, because the perception that schools have the expertise and power to conquer the naive and unsuspecting parent is so prevalent, a whole industry of parent advocacy has cropped up. Therapists, psychologists, and lawyers advertise their services, promising to get parents what they are due. It doesn't need to be this way.

The need for these adversarial actions is lessened when procedure is properly exercised. Procedure is a legal element that balances the parental desires for the best for the kid and the school's need to work within constraints. It is more than just filling in all of the blanks, and deals with the appropriateness of provisions within the IEP.

The importance of someone on the school team who is knowledgeable about procedure cannot be overemphasized. How often have teams been schnookered into providing some service because the parent or advocate said the law required it? And just as frequently, how many times have teams overlooked some fundamental requirement and had to pay dearly for the omission?

Ignorance Is Far from Bliss

A number of years ago, a parent, wise to the parameters of law, wanted a particular wording included in her child's IEP. Her son was orthopedically impaired and she wanted him to go to a school that was not wheelchair accessible. The wording she wanted in her son's IEP was "educated with familiar peers." This doesn't seem so bad, except that, unbeknownst to the team, this would have required the student to attend his own non-wheelchair-accessible elementary school. The "familiar peers" were the kids in his school, and they were all going to the school preferred by the parent. The principal, serving as the local education agency (LEA) representative, was ready to accept that wording, thinking it meant little more than "kids the student's own age." Little did he know, if that wording had been incorporated into the IEP, the school would have had to install an elevator and other modifications to the building or engage in some equally expensive legal action.

· · · · ·

Fooling the Parent—Not a Good Idea

I recall another situation where a parent indicated she would not be able to attend what everyone thought would be a simple placement decision. Because there had been no previous indication there would be any surprises, the parent indicated that the meeting should proceed. However, information was presented that took this meeting far from its intended purpose as a simple placement determination. A number of issues, including residency, increased aggressiveness, and the necessity of hiring additional staff, became known to some members of the team only at the meeting. This new information significantly altered the course of events.

Because the student would not even be placed in the same district, let alone the same program or school, the burden of who would be telling the parent arose. In response to this quandary, the special education administrator said that since the parent was not in attendance, she had given up her right to appeal. What a total inaccuracy. And what a deception to the parent. Had this error been acted out, the repercussions would have been a legal no-brainer. This is but one instance of the importance of procedure serving to protect everyone. The parent was protected from what amounted to a social insult and the district from an automatic legal defeat.

What the IEP Says, the District Must Do

Keep in mind that the IEP identifies the services to provide the disabled student with an appropriate education. It essence, it is a rather sophisticated "truth in advertising" document. What it says is what must be done. For instance, one undeniable provision is informing parents of the student's progress toward IEP goals periodically throughout the year. Too often, the IEP is written, filed, and reviewed in a year. Although this violates a fundamental provision of the current law, the practice persists.

At one especially sensitive IEP, the parent indicated she had never been informed of her child's progress, even though the wording on the actual form said reports would be made quarterly. Only at the annual review did she become aware that her son had made virtually no progress. The teacher, perhaps in a futile attempt to defend herself, made the statement that she didn't know she "really" had to follow through with that reporting. Then she essentially dug her grave deeper when she said she had not so informed any other parent and no one else had complained.

. . . . .

In the world of special education, procedure has a vital place. It protects all parties and in essence defines what special education is. It is not to be taken lightly and if violated can result in a nasty bite.

Keeping a Balance

A table with three legs represents an analogy to explain relationships within the special education process. As the analogy goes, the kid is a like ball placed on a table, with the legs of the table representing the parent, school, and procedure. The goal is to keep the table even so the kid does not fall off the edge. The parents want what is best for the kid and schools want what fulfills their educational obligations. Procedure is focused on the legal and substantive factors that identify the boundaries defining special education.

Given these three influences, there are two ways to maintain a balance. The first is competitive and requires each party to hope their strength can resist the influences of the other two. The second is cooperative and has the goal of each party holding their end at a level with the others. The second takes a lot less strain but relies on concerted efforts to develop trust.

Thirty-four Hours and Counting

But trust is not without its burden. I recall my longest IEP meeting. It lasted thirty-four hours over several weeks. As I look back, about four hours were spent developing the content of the IEP. The rest of the time was spent in developing trust. However, once that trust was established, subsequent meetings took on a different tone. Eventually the parents developed a level of confidence in some of the school staff that they had previously extended only to their advocate. The process of creating this relationship took time (over two years), but given the fact that the student would be a district responsibility until he was twenty-one, the investment was well worth the time and effort expended.

Interestingly enough, a tradition of "pizza party IEPs" originated with this family. The father, a construction worker, always wanted the meeting held at the end of his workday. In his job, if he didn't work, he didn't get paid. This was one issue, but another was that if he didn't work, eight other men didn't either. The staff, who didn't know this latter fact, had the impression that the father wasn't willing to cooperate. Meeting after

. . . . .

school hours posed some special difficulties. Finding childcare and working "after hours" were but two inhibitors to this practice. Situations like this may be solved only by thinking "outside the box."

Since this marathon IEP meeting had gone on for almost thirty hours already, everyone was favorably inclined to closure. The suggestion was that if all parties would agree that the IEP would be completed at the next session, the school would have pizza delivered so we could work until we were done. (We also agreed to chip in for baby-sitting for the teachers with young kids.)

The school footed the bill for the pizza, the parents brought the drink, and some teachers brought dessert. A great time was had by all and the IEP was done by 9:00 P.M. that night. The following year, the same suggestion was made. That time, the parents volunteered to bring the pizza! The IEP was completed in two sessions of a couple hours each. Maybe this arrangement would not work for every situation, but the point is that being considerate of the needs of the parents and finding solutions that will address the needs of all involved can have very big dividends. (Variations I have used on this carbohydrate theme include ice cream, bakery goods, and even just simple cookies and milk, but any combination of calories and caffeine usually works.)

The Dynamics of Trust

If trust is that important, the question is how it is established, especially between those who may have had a bad start in building the relationship. The first step is to identify the four component parts: mutual experience, no ulterior motives, predictability, and humility.

1. **Mutual experience.** It is easy to relate to those who have a shared experience. In such cases the development of trust is facilitated. Teachers who have disabled children themselves can form emotional connections with parents and the trust relationship is easier to build. However, in many cases, there will not be such a direct link. In those instances, the consideration of empathy is vital because it serves as the vehicle for one person validating the other. There is a caution, however, because insincere attempts at empathy can be a powerful separator.

We often use phrases in a somewhat habitual manner without stopping to consider what they imply. When people say "I'm sorry" or "I understand" out of habit, there is a tendency to dilute the other person's feelings or point of view. True empathy is to make emotional connections and support the one who is hurting.

I remember a number of years ago hearing of a conversation between a teacher and a parent whose kid had fried his brains on drugs. The kid had become so incompetent that he could not care for himself. He didn't even recognize much that should have been familiar from his past. Like a bad audition from a poorly written script, one teacher said to the parent, "What a tragedy. I know I would be devastated if that were my boy. I completely understand. You must feel terrible." The response from the parent was not pleasant. The mother was especially vitriolic and stated in no uncertain terms that it was degrading for the teacher to be so pretentious. Mutual experience is a powerful connection between people, but the results of "empathy gone wrong" can take immense efforts to heal.

2. **No ulterior motives.** Perhaps one of the worst feelings is when faith is betrayed. How many of us have believed someone was acting in our best interest and later discovered we were simply being manipulated? Trust is fairly easy to obtain, but once lost, it is very hard to regain.

   Years ago, when I was highly involved with behavior modification, a friend challenged my ability to shape behavior. The bet involved whether or not I could get my wife, Diane, to wear a particular skirt on a designated day. I used my best "positive reinforcement" techniques and won the bet. Then Diane found out and I lost her trust. I remember her saying it took four years to recover from that feeling of being manipulated. I learned a heavy and painful lesson.

   Feigned honesty is not a way to develop any relationship. Like a sophisticated bait-and-switch maneuver, parents of special needs kids have too often been told one thing, only to have something else happen. Teachers may temporarily keep parents at bay by indicating that all is well, when in reality the kid is failing miserably. Other parents are told that the kid is doing wonderfully well in school, only to realize the falseness of this claim when the kid graduates or ages out and can't do squat. Why we don't think we can be honest with people, I am not sure. Maybe because we aren't honest with ourselves.

3. **Predictability.** Consistency is important in any relationship and especially in the development of trust. But consistency is often understood only to mean doing something the same way each time. Certainly, that is one valid concept, but predictability is another aspect that is more meaningful in context with people. That is, if I can anticipate what a person will do, a foundation is set for knowing what to expect.

   This aspect of trust is perhaps the most difficult to implement. Often, promises are made in all sincerity only to be hampered by some unexpected variable. To be true to our word may take some additional effort. When trust with parents is in the process of being developed, extra effort on the part of the educator may need to be expended. Remember, no one promised that teaching would be convenient.

4. **Humility.** Arrogance has no place in the development of trust. There are many professionals who I wish had internalized the concept that "But for the grace of God go I" when it comes to dealing with the parents of disabled kids and especially those with behavior/emotional problems. It is so easy to pontificate from a point of advantage and not realize that each of us is a hairsbreadth away from being in the same situation as the parent being judged. If educators approach parents with an air of superiority, the trust connection will be difficult if not impossible to make.

   Another part of professional humility is acknowledging that parents know some facts about their kids that we as teachers don't. Sometimes the results of sophisticated tests are considered gospel and the observations of parents are put aside as opinions ranging from naive to biased.

   Additionally, even if we try to hide weaknesses, we can sabotage the goal of trust. I learned long ago that a person can only be blackmailed by things they are trying to hide. This is not to say that we are to discuss the intimate details of our own inter- or intrapersonal issues, but having an openness demonstrates that a person is human. Recognizing that we all make mistakes gives an opportunity to demonstrate to others that we can understand when they make mistakes.

A friend once told me of a school psychologist who seemed to take delight in telling parents that they were the primary reason for their child's dysfunction. He repeatedly stated, both in his reports and at the meetings, that if they had parented correctly, their child would have turned out a whole lot better. To the point of smugness, he was more than ready to associate the student's behavior with cult activity, sexual dysfunction, or ignorance on the part of the parents.

In these diatribes he gave the impression that he had full control over his own daughter's behavior—and that appeared true until she was fifteen. Then a level of rebellion started, the likes few have ever seen. She got heavily into drugs and sex. However, the psychologist had so much invested in his "theories" that he accepted no responsibility at all. He declared that it was his wife's fault for not following through with his strategies and techniques. An unhappy time was had by all.

The Benefits of Trust

"If you say 'FAPE' one more time, I'm going to hit you right in the face!" is not a phrase often heard in an IEP meeting, but this parent was mad. It didn't even seem to matter that his lawyer was there. Four years later, we were still having to think hard about programming for this man's son. An idea was presented that would be somewhat controversial, but with enough cooperation and monitoring, could be done. The father, who had made the threat a few years prior, said, "Dave, we will go along with whatever you think is best."

Whereas before he was ready to fight the system and the individuals within it, he now trusted that the school would be working in the kid's best interest. There were problems, to be sure, but now the parent and school were focused on the same goal and no energies were dissipated

. . . . .

fighting each other. With this element of trust well established, the problem was the problem rather than the people.

Getting to that point took a calculated effort to apply the principles of trust. The outcome, however, was worth every erg of energy expended. As a result, a number of precedent-setting practices were established in the district. We were able to try new ideas—and the kid was the beneficiary.

When Knowing Love and Logic Can Come In Handy

Much of this book has reflected an application of Love and Logic to kids and their school performance. I will readily admit, however, that having these tools available in my work with parents has probably been just as vital. There were times when my exposure to Love and Logic let me know what to say to parents when things were bad. There were other times when my relationship with a parent essentially bought me time to fix mistakes. And sometimes, things were terribly wrong and I needed to mend fences. I have learned that trying to solve a problem without having a positive relationship is very like walking through our grandson's room without turning on the light.

The Path of Perception Is Always Well Traveled

Since everyone's behavior is consistent with their perceptions, parents (even those who are difficult to work with) will always act in ways they believe will get their needs met. Having this understanding with even an angry or unreasonable parent will allow the professional to interact with fewer defense mechanisms. Otherwise, there is a tendency for those involved to get into a cycle of defending themselves and attacking others. The key to moving a person from one perceptual set to another is to start with a point of mutual agreement. Once this has been accomplished, parents are quite likely to feel understood and their anger will dissipate.

Ariel's Mom

A parent had moved into the district and enrolled her son. When the previous district was called for records, mention was made about how difficult the mother had been. Although Ariel was one big boy, he was mercilessly picked on by other students. Eventually, the fights that occurred as a result of this teasing left Ariel in jeopardy of expulsion. When an IEP meeting was being arranged, the mother asked for it to be held at 4:00. She explained that she had just taken a new job and didn't want to jeopardize her position by asking to leave early.

Rather than making any overture to accommodate the parent, the case manager said he didn't have to schedule that late because he didn't have to work after his contracted day. What a wonderfully efficient way to start things out badly. The mother was mad in the first place and this just made her madder. Provoked by the time issue, she loaded her guns for a bear hunt. Her response was to bring legal proceedings against the district with specific mention of the case manager, principal, and selected other staff.

My first direct encounter with this mother was via a phone call. After playing phone tag for a while, we agreed I would call her on a Sunday afternoon. I had completed a class and had ninety minutes of uninterrupted time as I drove home. For over forty minutes I was exposed to some of the most foul language I have heard from anyone. She was extremely angry and did not let polite talk get in the way of what she wanted to say.

Often, when I have related this story to others, they have told me they would be disgusted or offended with such verbiage and would not tolerate someone talking to them like that. Perhaps one benefit of having a name like "Funk" is that I early on became immune to foul language. The other factor is that I had learned long ago from Jim Fay that anger is a surface emotion for fear. Look for what is scaring people and you'll probably find the starting point for solving the problem.

As this mother was venting, she made mention that in addition to the stress from school, she also had the burden of taking care of her rapidly failing mother. She said that at least four times a week she and her son had to stay the night with her mother. Bingo. This is where a connection could be made. I mentioned that my mother-in-law was in a similar circumstance. She, too, was failing mentally and I knew how difficult it was to watch someone who had been strong and vivacious deteriorate so rapidly.

It was at this point that the mother's tone changed. She was still mad, but her defensive stance was moderated just a bit. Eventually, a level of trust was developed to the point that she gave me her unlisted phone number (in exchange, I gave her my pager number). I was the only one who could call her at work. The exchange of these phone numbers was another step in the trust building. One night she paged me as I was walking into the local Blockbuster video store. When I returned the call, her first words were, "I am so sorry to bother you this late at night." This is the same lady who would have had the head of everyone in the district on a platter just a few weeks prior.

She did pursue her legal action against the district. In the documents drafted by her attorney, there was one comment that I will long remember: "Dave Funk was the only one who tried to understand." This story is not intended to aggrandize any one person. The point is that even difficult situations can be redeemed if a few principles of human dignity are observed.

Principles: What Works for Kids Works for Parents, Too

Much has been said about applying the Four Key Principles of Love and Logic to students. They can be just as powerful when working with parents. One of the emphases intended by this book is for educators to constantly focus on the development of their own professional skills. As in any other work-related endeavor, tools are critical. In the pursuit of working with people, the principles advocated by Love and Logic are basic tools that can be adapted to meet specific requirements.

1. **Self-concept.** As discussed previously, self-concept is highly determined by what we think other people think about us. Parents, especially those who are involved with special education for the first time, can feel extremely intimidated. Imagine a bunch of professionals talking about their kid. Words like "below average," "disturbed," and "deficit" punctuate the meeting. As these words are being used about the kid, many parents are associating those same words with themselves.

   Parents are well aware that in our society, ability, achievement, and worth are often woven so closely together that there is little differentiation. Parents who have special needs children are faced squarely with the fact their kids are looked upon as damaged. And there is the too often instance that parents feel they did something wrong. To the extreme, parents may have the feeling that they are facing some cosmic punishment.

A vital factor in special education is to validate parents. It is an observation that most of us would rather be understood than agreed with. This is no less true of parents in an IEP meeting where their child is seemingly being autopsied and their worst fears are being rehashed. Listening to parents with full attention without contributing to any neurosis they may have is a professional skill. This "therapeutic" listening demonstrates that the other person has worth and is an effective tool for working through even difficult problems.

2. **Shared control.** Sadly, some parents feel that using anger and intimidation is the only way they can get needed services for their kid. Interestingly enough, federal laws (and, subsequently, state statutes) require a high degree of shared control in the special education process. The balance of "different role, equal status" is especially relevant in this aspect. Actively seeking information about the kid from the parent in the evaluation process is but one application of this principle.

However, this practice can be threatening to some educators who use knowledge as a way to control others. Knowledge is power, and secret knowledge is even more powerful. Special education is replete with nomenclature and acronyms that make no sense. When educational staff throw around phrases, concepts, and terms that have little meaning to the lay person, we set the stage for conflict. Who knows what "FAPE" means anyway. Special education is also quite guilty of imbuing common words with esoteric meanings.

Maybe some educators obtain a sense of power from discussing test results as though only they have some holy grail of knowledge. This concept of shared control requires educators to adopt the attitude that parents will have knowledge and insight about the student that will assist the team (of which they are a part) to make appropriate determinations.

I recall a situation some years ago where the school and parents were at loggerheads. The parents insisted that the student demonstrated certain skills at home but the staff said he didn't at school. The result of this long argument was that the parents were convinced the school was not effective with their kid, while the teachers thought the parents were lying.

The honest fact was that the kid did demonstrate skills at home that he never did at school. The key was to examine the variables. He was an only child and had lots of adult attention at home. At school, he was one of twenty-plus students in a classroom. Basically, he preferred to perform when he got lots of adult attention. Once this was known, both the teachers and the parents could be more effective with him.

3. **Empathy with consequence.** One of the tasks of special education teachers is to know enough about the real world outside school to accurately identify what the kid will face. What are the opportunities, barriers, and prerequisites? For the most part, educators have been in school since they were five and it may be the only world they know. However, it is highly unlikely that special needs kids will follow the same path.

Another task of special education staff is to identify the long-term consequences of decisions. For instance, often parents demand one-to-one aides for their students or a particular intervention. They believe this additional adult will be the answer to their child's academic progress and social involvement, as well as the basic solution to all other school-related problems the kid may have. In the short term, there may be some advantage; however, the hard fact is that short-term advantage can result in some permanent loss. When the parent sees only one solution, the professionals must be especially skilled in their interaction at saying no by saying yes to something else.

Giving Kids Too Much

Reynald had come to our district from another state. He was disabled both cognitively and physically and he had a personal aide in his previous district from the time he entered school. The philosophy of that district was, come hell or high water, every kid was going to be fully included all day in a regular education classroom. To accomplish this for Reynald took a high level of resource. It also required the aide to do virtually all of his work, make the social contacts, and run interference whenever pressures arose.

When Rey came to our district he was at an age when his school career was nearly at an end. At our first meeting, his parents were cooperative, but quite vocal in their disappointment that Rey would not have a personal aide as he had in his previous district. There were some accusations that we didn't care for kids enough and were obviously too concerned about money.

Very soon, however, the parents realized the folly of past practice. Rey had never learned how to function without a personal attendant. He had not developed enough independence even for sheltered employment. It took an additional two years for him to gain enough discipline and social skills to be accepted by a training center for the developmentally disabled. The resources expended to keep Rey in a regular classroom essentially prolonged, and to a degree prevented, him ever from being as ready as he could be for adulthood. His parents and the educational "pioneers" felt good for the first eighteen years of Rey's life, but he paid after that.

4. **Shared thinking.** Being in the thinking rather than the emotional state is important when working with kids; it is vital when working with adults. It is wise to be ever mindful of the role of nonverbal language. The 7/38/55 rule indicates that only about 7 percent of a communication is conveyed through the actual words; 38 percent is conveyed through the nonverbal aspects of language such as pronunciation and intonation. However, a majority of the meaning in a communication is conveyed by the covert or implied messages conveyed through the presuppositions of language.

   Early in my experience with Love and Logic, I heard Jim Fay tell a story about an irate parent who wanted her kid removed from a particular class. Jim's phrase was, "If we can't come up with something better, I will support you in that decision." How often I have personally used that concept when working with parents who are angry or confused, or who have simply given up. Part of this skill is to understand what the parents mean, regardless of what they say. When a parent says, "I want my kid in the regular classroom," often the meaning is, "I want a normal experience." Once there is no reason for the emotional response, thinking has a much greater chance of taking over.

What Is Remembered

There is an experiment that might be of interest. Look at your own school records and try to recall what you learned in each of the courses listed. My guess is that there will be some classes you don't even remember taking.

I mentioned this to a colleague and she referred to a graduate course in school finance. The class was a semester long and cost her a bunch of money. All she could remember was that "there is something called a TIFF district" (she didn't know what the letters meant), that a "mille" was a thousandth of a dollar, that the teacher's name was Bobbi, and that the teacher had moved to Albuquerque.

At the end of every year, Laurie, a fifth-grade teacher, has her kids list five things they remember from the nine months they have been in her class. She says that what is amazing to her is the narrow range of responses. Most kids come up with the same dozen or so ideas. One year, every kid wrote about the time Laurie fell off her platform shoes, and how everyone was sad for her when her father died. Certainly, the kids learned content and skills, but what they remembered were the connections they made with their teacher.

That conversation gave me cause to think. My mind went to a history class Diane and I attended together the first year we were married. I remember that the professor was a short bald man who ran everywhere and said, publicly, that women didn't belong in history class. His tests contained material not covered in his lectures nor in the assigned readings. His theory was that if students were interested in history, they would be vociferous in their own personal research. Since it was impossible to know what would be on the tests, there was very little incentive to prepare.

I remember another thing. On one of the tests, Diane and I both received D's (which, by the way, was the standard grade in his class). The professor's comment at the top of each of our papers was, "Having marital problems?"

That's what I remember from a whole year of college history. I don't remember the brilliant insights the professor made. I vaguely remember that he had credentials up the kazoo and could speak several languages, but what I took with me was the impression that this was an egocentric, insolent little man hiding behind the excuse of academic excellence. Oh, yes, I recall one more thing. I pretty much turned off to history for a while.

I once heard a generalized statistic that if someone is satisfied with the service a business provides, they will tell three people. If they don't like the way they were treated, they will tell twenty. I don't think it is much different in schools. In the context of this chapter, the question would be, what do we want parents to remember from their experiences with their kid's school? Just like kids will probably not remember the details of some history or math lesson, parents will probably not remember the statistical validity of some test. What they will remember will more than likely be whether or not someone seemed to care and whether there was someone to trust.

The Experience

For me, the hardest part of writing each chapter is ending it. There are so many other stories to tell, but another book the size of *War and Peace* may not be very usable. So, to end this chapter as well as this section, I have chosen to relate a painful personal experience when, as a parent, I wished some educators would have known and applied Love and Logic.

When our daughter, Aleshia, was in the latter years of high school, she decided she had had enough of being a good girl. The result was a discipline incident at school serious enough to require a meeting with the superintendent and psychologist. I had been to innumerable meetings to discuss similar situations regarding wayward kids; however, this was the first time I had been to any such meeting as the parent of the recalcitrant child.

Upon entering the room, the very first thing I realized was that Diane and I were the only ones without a folder and written report. Since these two items are the shields and weapons of special education, we had no armaments of defense, of arms of offense. I also knew that whatever I said could be misconstrued. You see, the foundational premise of special education is that dysfunctional kids come from dysfunctional families. No matter what any parent says, their words can be translated into whatever the professionals want.

From that experience, I adopted a professional practice of never having anything the parents don't have. I want them to have as many pieces of paper as I do. If I have a form, so do they. If I have a report to refer to, so do they. There have been numerous times that I have participated in an IEP meeting when the case manager is the only one with paper. I know how that feels, and it is demeaning.

I also determined that I would never read from a report. You see, that's what the psychologist did to us. Thirty-one pages, typed, single spaced. Essentially, my kid was reduced to a test subject. I only remember the ending, when the "diagnosis" was made. Diane and I waited in great anticipation, holding each other's hand for security.

Aleshia was declared to have "isolated oppositional behavior," as though this was some great psychological insight. I knew what that meant. She was stubborn in a few things. Everybody who knew Aleshia knew that about her. That little piece of information cost twelve thousand dollars. Quite a hefty price for what we already knew.

That was a very hard time for our family. We made it through and got a grandson, Edrik, out of the deal. Aleshia turned out better than good. Not from the therapy sessions, but from having to live with some very heavy consequences of her behavior. The relationship we have now, I wouldn't trade for anything. I wouldn't ever trade Edrik for anything, either.

Guilty or Not Guilty

For good or ill, Love and Logic is what kept me in education. Whether with the students, parents, educators, administrators, advocates, support staff, or even lawyers, the principles advocated by Love and Logic are applied every day. In workshops and classes, I often ask, "If you were accused of being a good teacher, would there be enough evidence to convict you?" My continuing hope is that I stand in the ranks of the guilty.

CHAPTER 10

Lessons from
the Kids

And How Are the Children?

A few years ago I spoke at a consortium of Catholic schools in Chicago. It was the rally meeting to prepare teachers for the beginning of the school year and the principal introduced the day with a story about an African greeting:

> In our culture we commonly greet people by asking, "How's it going?" It's a polite phrase and we don't think much about how nebulous the comment is. Such phrases fill in the empty spaces when we don't know what else to say. Among the most accomplished and fabled tribes of Africa, no tribe was considered to have warriors more fearsome or more intelligent than the mighty Masai. It is perhaps surprising then to learn of the traditional greeting that passed between Masai warriors. "Kasserianingera," one would always say to another. It means: "And how are the children?"

An oft-heard comment during workdays when only the teachers are at school is how much easier the job would be without kids. Mostly, this remark is made in a lighthearted manner, but regardless, kids are sometimes looked upon as an intrusion—especially those who are hard to teach. However, lest we forget, kids are what keep teachers employed. If we take time to consider how the children are, we can gain an insight that would not otherwise be realized.

John—It Takes a Village

I grew up in rural Iowa pretty much in the middle of the twentieth century. Special education was not very sophisticated then. Kids who had trouble with academics went through school hovering at the bottom of the class. Eventually, most dropped out and went to work. Many who had cognitive problems were eventually taken to institutions. In many other cases, the families more or less took care of their own.

John was the first cognitively disabled kid I remember knowing. Our small rural community grew up with him and, as a result, "backward" kids (the term we used) were not scary to us. John stayed in elementary school until he could no longer fit in the seats. After that, his family took care of him.

John was a common sight at our house. He would stop in to "visit" quite a bit and when his parents died, his brother "saw to him." John helped a bit on the farm, visited some, and on occasion went to church.

There is a common phrase that it takes a village to raise a child. The lesson from John is that it is most fortunate to have a village to "look after" the disabled even when they grow older. How we take care of the handicapped has become quite institutionalized. This is a reflection of our society and may be to everyone's detriment. When schools substitute for families and agencies substitute for the village, we will have an irreconcilable loss.

Another John—Kids Are Our Best Teachers

For the first several years of my teaching career, I had little concept about the real reason kids misbehaved in school. Although I was always sure my own actions had justifiable motives, I was quick to attribute wrongdoing in others, especially kids, to some innate character flaw. It was one way to shift blame from myself whenever something went wrong.

But John, who was in my very first class and the only kid I sent to the office, was always on my shoulder, kind of like a voice of conscience. He was a nagging reminder that if I always did what I thought was best in any given circumstance, maybe everybody else did too. Could it be that John felt he was better off being sent down to the office because it was less painful than staying in my class?

. . . . .

Whenever these thoughts would surface, I was fairly successful in suppressing them. That is, until I became terminally involved with Love and Logic. Then it became infinitely harder to excuse my own behavior by blaming others. If I wanted to orient kids to owning and solving their own problems, I should do so as well.

The way school was set up was not a good fit for John. Academics didn't seem to be his strong suit and I am now convinced his behavior was more a reaction to the relative irrelevance of how I was teaching than to anything else. Because I didn't know how to analyze or provide for his needs, he had few other options than to misbehave. It was his only way to demonstrate that I was ineffective. Unfortunately for John, I didn't realize the lesson he had to teach until a decade and a half later.

An additional two decades later, while writing this chapter, I mustered the gumption to try finding John, to learn how I had affected his life. I had thought of doing this for some time, but it's a fearsome task to undertake. As long as I didn't know, I could always speculate.

I did an Internet search and, in the whole database, there was only one person with his name. I had hoped there would be hundreds, because one of my primary reasons for not doing this sooner was the presumed enormity of the task. I had convinced myself that it would be impossible to locate one person more than thirty years later. When only one name showed up, I realized that excuses for inaction are just that—excuses for inaction. It would have been relatively easy to find John a long time ago.

I called to find out whether this John was the same kid I had in eighth grade. When the phone rang, I told the woman who answered that I was looking for a student from my first year of teaching. John was not home at the time, so I told her the city, school, and year. We had a match.

When I called back, John and I had a wonderful talk. He gave a summary of his life since eighth grade. After finishing his GED, he tried college for a while, and traveled around the country. He told me of his three kids still at home and about the daughter he hadn't seen for twenty-two years. He told me of his house-painting business and how he ended up in Indiana.

John also remembered Todd, the kid he got into a fight with in eighth grade, but didn't remember getting kicked out of class. Funny, isn't it, how one incident is so permanent for some and so transient for others?

John made it in this world in spite of his eighth-grade experience. He may well have been more of a teacher for me than I was for him.

Donna—Overpowering Doesn't Work

Donna was the only student I didn't want to want to like. She was a chronic liar—I couldn't believe anything she said. She would tell me several times a month that her period had started and ask to go to the restroom. She knew she had me because, of course, I couldn't say no. Often she didn't come back and she knew I couldn't go get her. When I was around Donna, the power I thought I needed to control kids oozed away from me like honey off hot fry bread.

In my effort to win, I often did some fairly stupid things. One day I set up a video camera to catch her. I thought her behavior was so atrocious that few would believe me unless they saw it for themselves. In addition, I planned to use that video so Donna could see firsthand how she really acted. Surely, I hoped, this would shock her into behaving better. However, my room was so small (twelve by fifteen feet) that keeping her in the view-finder became an effort in frustration. There were a lot of power struggles with Donna, and she always seemed to win.

Donna was the only girl student I hit. The year she got braces, I hit her in the mouth and she bled all over the floor. I had just laid some carpeting that was left over from redecorating the Board of Education room and now there were bloody stains all over it. My room looked more like a crime scene than a place for learning.

About fifteen minutes after Donna got home that afternoon, while I was still at school, there was an all-call on the intercom: "Mr. Funk, please report to the office." I had been called to the office as a kid, and just like riding a bicycle, one never forgets the feeling.

The principal was fair and he let me tell my side of the story. Then he said that hitting kids was not a district-approved procedure (with state laws banning it and all) and I concluded that I would need to find a different way to control kids. Ironic as it seems now, Donna was instrumental in my eventual involvement with Love and Logic. She taught me that trying to control kids by taking away all of their power was not an effective long-term instructional strategy. It was a good lesson, but one that would take a while to lock in. I did, however, have the sense to know I had better start looking for other techniques to deal with kids' behavior.

Ken—Manipulating Doesn't Work Either

Whereas Donna was the only girl I hit, Ken was the last kid I hit. I had learned from Donna that overpowering kids could get me into trouble. In response, I looked for another way to assert the control I thought good teachers held over kids. About that time I had started my master's degree and one of the first courses was on behavior modification.

What a godsend, I thought, and just in time. Although I didn't always agree with the logical extensions of operant conditioning (e.g., the mechanistic view of people as little more than stimulus-response organisms), at least it would prevent me from wallowing in a morass of inaction. In addition, I could bypass the touchy-feely, warm-fuzzy strategies that were so prevalent. I could go straight to working on a kid's behavior without worrying much about how they felt emotionally.

By the time Ken was in my class, I had become pretty good at manipulating kids. In fact, I started my consulting career by showing teachers how to set up operant conditioning programs in their classrooms. Of course, these strategies needed to remain covert to be effective. If kids found out they were being fooled into behaving, they had a tendency to sabotage even the best of plans.

One day, Ken stubbornly refused to respond positively to my very good efforts to conform his behavior to my expectations. I was fully engaged in the two major strategies of behavior modification: ignoring the inappropriate behavior, and reinforcing the desired behavior. Neither was working, and when new things don't work, there is a tendency to go back to the old.

I didn't really mean to hit him that hard. It seemed more of a reflex than anything else. I kind of backhanded him in the solar plexus and he left my room broadcasting, as best he could given his limited ability to breathe, what he thought of me as a teacher, of school in general, and of special education in particular.

Then, like "déjà vu, all over again," fifteen minutes after Ken got home that day, there was an all-call on the intercom: "Mr. Funk, please report to the office." This was about three years after the "Donna Incident" and it was the same principal. He listened attentively to my side of the story and then used a baseball analogy. I don't know much about sports, but I did recall something like "three strikes and you're out."

I had a wife, two kids, and a mortgage, and I was actually pretty good at my job. Ironically, this was the same year I received a "good-teaching" award from the state special education director's association. But I knew that all of the professional accolades in the world would not be enough if I hit another kid.

Whereas Donna was instrumental in my understanding that overpowering was not effective, Ken taught me that manipulating kids doesn't work all that well either. However, in all probability, were it not for those two kids, I would have remained content with whatever strategies wouldn't get me into trouble. Had that been the case, there would have been little initiative to become involved with Love and Logic. Strange, isn't it, how very painful experiences may be the impetus needed to motivate a desire to change?

Ricky—Mean What You Say

Ricky had a natural talent. He could sound just like a police siren—thus his nickname, "Ricky the Siren." He'd coerced school busses into pulling over more than a few times with his version of a police car in hot pursuit.

Ricky was also very nimble and quick. One time he bolted from a class and pulled a fire alarm. The principal felt, of course, that Ricky had to be found and brought to justice. A commando team was formed and a search-and-capture mission was under way.

They never did find him that day. The staff radioed each other several times about sightings, but Ricky was never lured into their trap. Eventually the mission was aborted and Ricky was simply waylaid when he came back to school the next day.

His behavior became increasingly counter to the goals of the school and eventually he was put on the "homebound" program. Interestingly, his behavior problems were attributed primarily to the fact that his dad was old and had already retired when Ricky was born. Diagnosing the cause of behavior problems was so simple back then.

I took the job as his homebound teacher. I was only a few years into my career and welcomed the extra $7.50 per hour the job paid! Ricky and

I had a deal. The first half of the instructional session was for work, the other half was for playing pool.

Playing pool was not to some people's liking, but then nobody wanted Ricky to come back to school, either. Although I was nowhere near an expert on behavior, the fact was, Ricky had been working zero amount of the time before and was working half the time with me, so I figured we had made some gains.

One day I went to the home at the appointed time and Ricky was cleaning his air pistol. I sat across the table from him and as he put the final piece together, he picked up the gun, dramatically lowered it until it was pointed straight at my head, and said, "Pool or work—what do we do first?"

I had little time to think, so I just quoted what first came to mind: the classic "Grandma Principle": "First we work, then we play." I took out the math assignment, he put the gun away, and there were no more such incidents. That was one of those "teachable moments" we hear so much about in education. When I first heard Jim Fay state, "Say what you mean, mean what you say, and do what you say you will do," the scene with Ricky was pulled from my memory. As with most kids, Ricky needed consistency and boundaries. I believe that this is what happened that day, so many years ago. But it was an accident—a fluke, really. I hope I am now better able to do that on purpose.

Ricky and his family moved to a southern state before that school year was over. A few years later I found out he had become a state trooper. I presume he drives a squad car and maybe even provides some sound effects.

Jimmy—Courage

Some kids never have a chance to experience a normal childhood. Sometimes this happens because their country is devastated by war, natural disaster, or even economic collapse. Sometimes kids have the misfortune of being born into a family so dysfunctional that there is little chance of growing up in a typical sequence. Other times the child is born with a disability and normal development is not possible.

Jimmy and his twin sister both had cystic fibrosis. There were not a lot of effective medical interventions in those days and eventually Jimmy couldn't come to school anymore. I started working with Jimmy as his homebound teacher about a year after his sister had died.

I remember his coughing and the contrast between his frail body and strong spirit. Every day, Jimmy had his homework done. During his last days, I sat next to his bed, teaching him algebra. That's what he wanted to do, and that's what we did.

I didn't shed tears for very many kids, but I did for Jimmy. Toward his last days of "class," we had wonderful discussions. Although we had to hold back from laughing (because it would cause him to cough), we smiled a lot. Jimmy died during his junior year of high school. This kid, who was in the process of dying the whole time I knew him, demonstrated a level of courage I doubt even a soldier in battle could supersede.

Brittany—The Basis of a Child's Worth

Brittany was one of the last foster babies to come into our family. In the seventeen years we were involved with infant care, Brittany was the most medically involved child we had. I still remember the medication regimen that had to be followed. One had to be administered within a fifteen-minute window (6:45 to 7:00 at night). Too early or too late, too little or too much, could put her into a seriously compromised situation.

Brittany had had a stroke in utero and when she was born had only a partial brain. We were not quite sure what she could see or hear, but she loved to feel textures. I remember Diane carrying her around the house and letting her touch the curtains, furniture, and carpets. Brittany would reach her little hand out in anticipation. This may have been her best window to the world.

When we first got Brittany, we were told that her time on earth was limited. When she came to us in April, it was anticipated that she would die before summer. One day I came home and Diane was visibly upset. I knew she had taken Brittany to the doctor that day and I presumed the announcement had come that Brittany would not be with us much longer.

This, however, was not the issue. The doctor had given an informal suggestion that when Brittany died we should calculate when best to call 911, because she would "be a good little organ donor." His further instruction was for us to have a couple of drinks. We don't drink alcohol, and what an insult to Brittany if we were to try dulling our senses.

The comment by this doctor, who often spoke of his own "gifted" children, excelling in a prestigious private school, demonstrated his view of what gives children worth. Those who have intact bodies and minds have value. Those who do not have such endowments are good only for what can be harvested.

Brittany, with all of her limitations, left a legacy that only she could leave. Because of her neurological condition, she often lapsed into what seemed, for lack of a better term, absolute terror. She would wake up screaming like no baby we had ever had before. When we would pick her up and hold her, Brittany would mold into our arms. She would still startle, but calm would eventually take over. That little girl taught me the value of being comforted. I now realize that others, including my beloved wife, had tried teaching me that before, but I just didn't catch on.

A wonderful young couple adopted Brittany that summer and she died about a year afterward. At her funeral, as opportunity was given to speak, six people made the statement that Brittany had taught them about the value of being comforted. There was no prompting, and I had spoken to none of them previously. Their comments came simply because that is what Brittany had taught them.

I wish no children were damaged in mind, body, or spirit. I am not of the opinion that God makes children handicapped or that they are little angels in disguise. What I do believe, however, is that children with disabilities force us to ask questions we might not otherwise contemplate. One of the biggest: On what basis do we value children?

Annie—Altruism

Annie was becoming stiffer and stiffer. Her joints were fusing and her back was curling up like a shepherd's hook. She was to undergo spinal surgery—a procedure purported to be 97 percent effective. She was among the 3 percent who came out worse than when they went in. After the surgery she was a paraplegic and basically had no control of her body from the waist down.

When Annie was in middle school, her mother died suddenly. Her father had remarried less than a year later. His new wife would put Cinderella's stepmother to shame and openly declared at an IEP meeting that Annie was too much trouble and was to be out of the house the minute she turned eighteen. Her father acquiesced. He was the only parent I purposely did not shake hands with.

Annie often confided in the staff at her school. A few days after the "big announcement," she asked a question that demonstrated her true spirit. She was worried about who would help her younger sister with homework—that was her first concern. Her second question was whether it would be okay if she didn't want her dad and stepmother to be happy.

This frail girl, who did not know where she would be living in a few months, was concerned about her younger sister. I often think of Annie in the midst of listening to people's complaining. It's a way to balance out the "bitch and moan" syndrome so prevalent in our society.

Jeff—The Satisfaction of Honesty

It was Jeff's last year in school and he was bussing tables at a local restaurant. Since this was part of his vocational training, he needed to be observed periodically by school staff. During one of these reviews, the teacher and I decided we might as well have lunch, since we were at the restaurant anyway. When we got there, Jeff was busy working and looked proud in his white shirt and bow tie.

As we sat at the booth waiting for the server, Jeff exercised his employee prerogative and brought us iced tea in the biggest glasses I had ever seen at a restaurant. How pleased he was to say, "No charge" as he put the drinks on the table.

I remember my dad often commenting that with six kids at the family table, he hardly ever had dry feet by the end of a meal. Tipping over full glasses of liquid was somewhat of a family tradition. Whether from that background or from the simple fact I am a motor klutz, as if on cue, my arm caught the rim of that huge glass and iced tea cascaded over the table edge, completely soaking the bench seat I was sitting on. The teacher I was with would have been soaked, too, if she had not been so quick to exit her side of the booth.

I never realized how spongelike wool suit pants were until that day. My estimate is they can absorb well over a quart under ideal circumstances. I also found out that wool retains cold like you would not believe. I think the "wicking effect" I have heard so much about is greatly overstated.

. . . . .

Part of Jeff's job was to clean up after inept customers. He came over to our table, towels in hand, and as he started wiping up the mess he stated, "Oh, oh, looks like somebody was clumsy." He was so matter-of-fact about the obvious cause.

He began the cleanup operation by drying the tabletop, although there wasn't much left to soak up. Then he started on the bench where I was still sitting (I had decided that to stand up would serve no useful purpose). After asking if I could "lift up a little bit," Jeff commented that I had a really wet hiney. For a second time during that scenario he had simply commented on what was obvious. His honesty without condemnation was somehow quite comforting.

So often we presume some social faux pas is going to result in some great embarrassment. In actuality, it's probably more the perceived reaction of others that makes us feel awkward. This cognitively disabled kid with an unpretentious honesty taught a lesson: Mistakes happen. Sometimes they could have been prevented, but they still happen. He also taught that if you sit in what you spilled, your hiney gets wet, and when you think about how cold it is, you are more careful the next time.

Zeke—The Power of Relationship

The power of relationship is not always demonstrated in a dramatic way. Sometimes, it's the unspectacular events that offer the most valuable evidence.

Zeke had been a hellion in elementary school. He had challenged his teachers since early childhood. It was only once he came to middle school that the good teaching he had received started to "kick in." I had an opportunity to work with Zeke over a number of years and was able to see his growth over time.

Zeke, now an eighth-grader, had joined the wrestling team and asked if I wanted to see the video his dad had made of his first meet. As we were watching it in my office, the superintendent walked in, sat down, and watched it with us. Zeke didn't win, but it was interesting to watch him analyze his own performance. It was like he was his own coach.

During the performance I was munching on tortilla chips and salsa (the superintendent didn't want any and Zeke had declined because he was in "training"). As Zeke was leaving, he commented on the brand of salsa I had been eating. His dad worked for a company that made "the best" and Zeke suggested that I really should not be spending my money on those inferior brands. As he left, he said, "I'll talk to my dad—we'll take care of this for you." I felt like I was in a *Godfather* movie where someone was going to be made an offer they couldn't refuse.

A few days later, Zeke's dad delivered several jars of the "good" stuff and since then I have had a steady supply. The relationship I developed with this kid was so strong that he was looking out for me even in the little things. I started my career believing that taking away kids' power was the only way to have control over them. Zeke is a recent confirmation that I was wrong to ever have believed that.

Andrea—A Message for Us All

Andrea was a high school student who engaged in all sorts of behavior that was of concern to those who knew her. She was fortunate, however, to have found an adult within the school who cared enough to see past the behavior to the kid inside. Andrea wrote a poem to this special person that revealed something about this young woman whom many had already discounted:

Kay,

No one seems to see anything of me but the surface side
The side when I'm at school
Or just going about my days.
But there is another side of me, an inside
That people seem to never see.
I have a thousand thoughts,
A part that wants to show love and have friendships,
A part that tries, desires, and learns.
The inside of me has so many moods
And once in a while it may show outside of me.
For once in my life, though,
I've been trusting someone implicitly.
I look up to someone in an understanding way.
I know it's ok to let that trust in
That I can let my emotions be free.

It's not an everyday thing going around
And feeling safe and secure,
But when you listen to my troubles
I can sort things through.
You have seen me be sad and mad.
You are the person I go to
When I'm doing real bad.
I trust you with my words
And I know you try to help me.
I've never said it,
But I'm real thankful to know someone like you.
It's like you're a second mother
And a close friend too.
I may be a teenager,
But you seem to understand me real well
And when I walk into school
I know I'll have someone to talk to.
I want to say thank you
For just being there
Caring and sharing
Your time
And talking with me
Like I was your own child.

Merry Christmas, Kay. I know this may not be much, but I wanted to give something that could mean something more than just a card. Remember, I never write things I don't mean. You have really helped me through school, not only that, but my outside life. Believe it or not, I do listen when you say things and I take it into consideration.

Love from Andrea

What Are Disabled Kids Trying to Get?

What are kids trying to get with all of their complicated behavior? Nothing more than the rest of us. Sometimes we need to be a bit more creative in our analysis and sometimes we need to know how the kid is thinking. But we are all pretty much the same.

The stories in this chapter involve only a very few of the kids I have known. The first come from early in my career, a couple happened as I was writing this chapter. Basically, they represent over three decades of reminders that we are never so expert that we cannot learn from kids. Our students provide us with professional training that can't be obtained in any workshop, graduate course, or even a book.

We all have our own stories. The lessons we have learned from our experiences with kids are an integral part of what we have become. My best calculation is that I have been directly involved with somewhat over twenty-one hundred individual disabled students. I don't remember them all and wish I would have kept a journal. Once in a while, usually at weird times like sitting in traffic, I remember a particular student. These are the times it really locks in that when we forget a kid, we lose part of ourselves.

PART 4

Implementing Behavioral Interventions

CHAPTER 11

Short-Term Interventions

Differentiating Strategies for Different Purposes

One way to differentiate behavioral interventions is to divide them into short-term, transitional, and long-term strategies. Each has a different function, and provided they are administered consistent with the Four Key Principles and consider the student's perceptual set, they are effective for their intended purpose.

The role of short-term strategies is to stop or redirect a behavior. That is what they are good for; when applied for a different reason, they quickly become ineffective. Just like cramming for a test does not establish learning, using short-term strategies for long-term problems will have very limited success.

Transitional strategies serve an intermediary function. Because the shift from the short term to the long term is a significant jump, transitional strategies are designed to form a foundation for the development of long-term strategies by creating situations where students can process, change perception, and establish the elements of a trusting relationship.

The purpose long-term strategies is to develop reciprocal trust and relationship. In terms of influence over volitional behavior, this is the most powerful type of strategy. They take time, do not have immediate effect, and are often discarded before their purpose can be carried out. Unfortunately, when students change teachers every nine months, these particular strategies often do not have time to take root.

Categorizing strategies is somewhat arbitrary. They could just as well be divided into strategies that are effective before, during, and after a behavior. But regardless of how the interventions described in this section are compartmentalized, they are all focused to a common end: validating the student's personhood. This does not at all mean that we justify or excuse inappropriate or maladaptive behavior. What it does mean is that none of us has the right to degrade any human being simply because we don't agree with them, or worse still, as a defense mechanism because we don't know what to do.

The purpose of these final chapters is to give the reader some broad concepts about interventions, rather than a specific recipe. Because kids do not usually misbehave in a prescribed and predicable manner, teachers will need to make adjustments to fit the situation—that is the skill of teaching. In addition, strategies that can be implemented within a normal school setting and without the necessity of specialized training are also included here. Admittedly, some students require techniques and interventions that call for high levels of sophisticated preparation and even certification. Those strategies cannot be learned from reading about them in a book and are therefore left to others.

Our Penchant for the Instant

Perhaps it started with instant oatmeal, but whenever a presentation is given about behavior management, the obvious expectation of a majority of the participants is that they will leave the program with an idea that will efficiently quell the behavior problems that prompted them to come to the program in the first place.

In response, presenters give a number of strategies, some of which are unique. Stories of their effectiveness heighten the anticipation on the part of many participants that they, too, will be able to go back into the classroom the next day, invoke the strategy, and sit back and watch the magic work.

And it does work! But this initial success is a bit insidious for two reasons. First, it feels so good to have a successful strategy that the tendency is to hang on tenaciously and use it again—and again, and again, and again. Very soon even a very good strategy quits working. It doesn't take long for a short-term strategy to lose its effectiveness with a given kid or situation.

Second, the fact that a strategy was initially successful leads many to believe that when its effectiveness wanes, all that needs to be done is to intensify or refine it, when in actuality the short-term strategy has run its course. It has served its purpose and now must be replaced with a strategy that will sustain the appropriate replacement behavior.

Without this understanding, a number of false conclusions will be made. Discouragement will set in and many will lose faith in the efficacy of the strategy. Some will become cynical and wonder if the presenter was some kind of charlatan—giving a false hope by giving ideas that won't work in the real world.

In fact, something far different is more likely taking effect. Most of what teachers are taught about behavior management falls into the category of short-term solutions. These strategies work with many of the kids much of the time. However, when a long-term problem arises, teachers are often ill prepared. Short-term strategies are sometimes intensified, but will ultimately become ineffective.

Short-term strategies are not very effective on long-term problems. As in emergency medicine, immediately effective strategies may stop the bleeding, but eventually a long-term solution needs to be put in place. Behavior management has conformed to a societal norm of immediate gratification. We want satisfaction now, and seeking to change a kid's behavior is no exception.

Short-term strategies are appropriate in situations that do not need to be or cannot be sustained. Short-term strategies can also be used to stop or redirect a behavior. In brief, short-terms strategies are not designed to sustain a student's performance.

One-Liners

"One-liners" fall into the category of short-term interventions. Upon first meeting a student and especially when the student first participates in their IEP meeting or in the development of their own behavior plan, a common introduction I use is: "Are you the kind of kid adults can be honest with?" There are all sorts of variations on this question, but the point is usually to cut to the chase.

A one-liner is a question or statement that meets the kid at the point where intervention can be sabotaged. That is, if the kid is a chronic liar, that factor is addressed with a question like, "Do you give any clues so I can know if you are lying or not?" If the kid is known to use tears a lot, the question would address that factor (e.g., "Do you think you will be crying during this conversation?").

Frankly, this strategy is one of my favorites, not only because one-liners are effective, but also because they fulfill a sense of creativity. One-liners are quick, to the point, and effective at setting the direction of subsequent interaction. Following are a few examples and the circumstances in which they have been used. I want to emphasize, again, that individual circumstances dictate what, how, and when any particular technique or modification is used.

> "Are you the kind of kid adults can be honest with?" (When I don't
> know a kid very well and there will be some serious topics discussed.)
> "Do you see yourself as a kid who will take six years to get through
> high school?" (When a kid is failing because of bad choices.)
> "What would happen if you did that on a job?" (When a kid does
> not acknowledge the inappropriateness of the behavior in school.)

As you can imagine, such one-liners can only be used selectively. Can you imagine asking the same question day after day, situation after situation? I would guess that after a couple of times, its effectiveness would be finished, especially if it is not used as a conduit for less transient interventions.

Walk Up and Whisper
edited from the work of Jim Fay

This strategy is an extension of the one-liner with some refinements. There are many situations where we could wander up to a kid, smiling on the way, and say, "Would you mind saving that for Mr. Clark's classroom?" Do you think the kid would be able to keep from smiling? What's going to happen to the immediate behavior and, more importantly, to the attitude? My guess is that both are probably going to be a little bit different.

Now some will say that this isn't fair to Mr. Clark, but keep in mind that Mr. Clark can do the same thing. He can say, "Save it for Mr. Funk's classroom." Or, if you don't like that, you could always say, "Could you save that for the playground or for after school?" Sometimes just a question like, "Is this the best place for that?" can be effective. Those kinds of questions leave the kid thinking, and feeling some sense of control. What's happening to our relationship? Is it getting better or worse? My hope and intention is that it should be getting better.

Some people have questions about attention-getting behavior on the part of kids. There is always a possibility that other kids may want that same kind of attention and might act out in their attempt to get it. In light of this, teachers often feel that ignoring a behavior might be the best option.

My thought on that topic is that often the kids in my class who will never give me a hard time, who are rather compliant, nice kids, can get really scared if they see another kid embarrassed in front of the class, and they live in fear that it might happen to them someday. As a result, they may spend too much time worrying over it and often become more inhibited as far as making suggestions and generally taking the thoughtful risks necessary to learn and grow. If they have any doubt about themselves or what they might say, they may think, "Oh gee, what if he talks to me like that in front of the class?"

Of course, there will be times when we must talk to kids in front of others, but I'm not so worried about this if I can keep the kids' dignity in tact. What I'm trying to do is to provide the optimum condition for changing volitional behavior. In my experience, the "whispering technique" (i.e., keeping the conversation private) has usually proved effective.

I think this technique is effective because there are several things going on. First of all, this student can see that I'm not afraid of them or the situation because I am more than willing to come directly to them and talk. I also want to demonstrate to the kid that this situation is not really a stress-producing problem for me. I demonstrate this by having a smile on my face so all can see my perspective on the situation.

Some may be thinking that using the whisper technique on a child might encourage other kids to misbehave so they'll get that extra attention too. That could happen, but an awful lot of misbehavior in the classroom has to do with kids not feeling good about the teacher and looking for a chance to get a little revenge. Being private helps short-circuit this cycle because now the nice kids in class don't have to be afraid when they do misbehave, and the acting-out kids have little reason for retaliation.

When the teacher is whispering to avoid embarrassing a student, the other students can say, "Hey, I'm safe in this classroom. The teacher is not going to embarrass me. It's a lot safer to risk and to be here and enjoy myself." Their anxiety is greatly reduced.

Changing the Student's Location
edited from the work of Jim Fay

Changing the location of the student is interesting because it's often far easier to change a kid's location than it is to change behavior. Although I have not been able to figure out all the psychological reasons for this, from my observations it seems that there is some kind of magic involved when we change where the kid is placed. I don't know exactly what it is, but I've seen it work over and over. The only thing I have been able to figure out is that somehow when the location is changed, the emotional tone is changed.

The first time I really took note of this phenomenon was at Stapleton Airport. I was waiting for an airplane and saw a man standing, if you can believe this, next to a little ice cream shop, holding a three-year-old. Now nobody holds a kid in front of an ice cream machine, but he did and this kid was going crazy. "I want some ice cream! Why can't I have some ice cream! You've got some money, I know you've got some money!"

As I watched, I was thinking, "That guy is probably going through a lot of stress right now, but anybody dumb enough to put a little kid in that situation deserves everything he gets." But suddenly my respect for that gentleman changed. I saw him, without one single word, take this child, put the kid down on the floor, take her hand in a very determined way, and just start walking away from the ice cream machine.

The kid was trailing along behind him, and with every step the volume of that whining little voice got softer and softer until six or seven steps away, the kid was completely quiet. And to my surprise, Dad had not uttered one single word. He then picked up the kid and deliberately walked right back to the ice cream machine. I thought the kid would start all over again, but that never happened.

Other times I've seen this same phenomenon in classrooms where I have done demonstration teaching. Sometimes when schools hire me to do some consulting, I will show how to use some of the Love and Logic techniques by teaching an actual class. As part of the deal and to balance the situation, I tell the teachers that they can choose the class, and I get

. . . . .

to choose the subject matter.

Usually I divide the class into two teams and set up a game that's competitive between them. In addition, I might go in and change all the chairs and desks around so that now we have the makings for chaos. Then I set up a bunch of rules that are a bit hard to follow, and if not followed allow the other team bonus points.

Often the teachers will try to "challenge" me by planting some ringers. They will pick some really rough kids in that school and stick them into that class. Then the teachers wait to see what "the expert" will do with these kids who have been driving them up the wall all year.

What humors me is that it is fairly easy to find out who these transplanted kids are, because the others are looking at them and saying, "What are you doing here today?" But the really funny part of it is, those kids hardly ever act up, because the teachers have already done for me what I might do if I were confronted by a disruptive kid: change their location. For a short period of time they're a little bit off balance and they don't act up. Instead, they watch and listen and really don't cause a problem at all.

What also humors me is the teachers' reactions. They will watch with great anticipation and afterward ask with a bit of reverence, "What did you do with those kids? We want to know what you did with them." I almost feel like saying, "Well, it's classified information," but after basking just a while in their awe of my skill, I let them know that they were really the ones responsible for changing the kids' behavior because they changed their location.

But from time to time, there will be a kid in this class, and it's usually one who doesn't have an attendance problem—he's there every day for the teachers—who starts to act up. Not to brag, but I've kept a tally on this, and the technique has worked thirty-five times in a row. This is not to say that it will work the thirty-sixth time. I'm only saying that thirty-five times in a row so far, I have walked over to one of these kids who has been acting up, approaching in a calm fashion with a smile on my face, and asked, "Would you mind sitting over there." Thirty-five times in a row the kid has moved before figuring out what was going on and finally asking himself, "What am I doing over here?" By the time he has figured it out, the behavior has changed.

At this point, let's remember our goal with behavior management. That goal is to change the offending behavior. It's not to do therapy. The technique we have just described is not going to work for the long term. Eventually, he may act up over there, but for right now we've completely changed the tone of what's going on and that gives us additional time and opportunity to work on the relationship.

Now I must be ready for one eventuality. Someday, some kid is going to say to me, "No, I'm not moving." Now, would it better to talk first and smile later or smile first and talk later? I would go for a smile, and say something to the order of, "Would you humor me?" And the best way to say that is in a whisper, so that he knows that our conversation is as private as I can make it. Again, once in a while the kid will say no and it is then that we especially need to buy some time and get the kid to do the thinking.

As in the example above, I'll continue to rely on questions. One of my favorite in a situation like this is, "Did I ask in a nice way?" If I have been treating the kid with dignity and have truly asked in a nice way, the kid is pretty obligated to say, "Yeah, you asked in a nice way." I follow that up with, "And you're still not going to do it? Wow. Really? That's hard for me to believe."

What's happening? Is this kid eventually going to grin? Probably. And when he does, the behavior has changed. I then have an additional opportunity to build a relationship. In fact, right now, this kid may not be acting up anymore because he's so busy listening.

But of course there is the chance that I will encounter a really tough kid and decide I may not be able to avoid a big power struggle if I keep up this line of interaction. At that point I may just say, "Hey, that's okay, I've changed my mind." I'm still okay. Because I didn't go in there right away and say, "Hey, move!" That would sound like an indictment of the kid. I realize that I may be the one who pays the biggest price if I go over and say "Hey, move!" to a kid who's not going to move in any way.

Now what is the secret—why is it that these kids so often accept requests when we say, "Would you mind, would you consider?" It is a simple matter of choices. They feel like they have some control. It's not a command. Now I won't guarantee that choices will always work, but I firmly believe that they significantly raise the odds that I will engage in a win/win situation.

The comment may be made that this sounds like a lot of time-consuming interchange, so let's go back and review the scenario. We must be conscious of the amount of time we are taking in the classroom. As I am describing the interaction in this book, it may seem inordinately long, but if I time the actual interaction, I find that only a very few seconds are actually used.

Let's suppose a kid is acting up in the back of the room. I ask, "Would you mind sitting over here?" But she says, "No, I won't do it." My next response might be to say, "Humor me." Now I've looked back at the class and I am back to teaching. I've used less than ten seconds so far. Then I'm back to looking at the group and seeing how things are going, asking them some questions, and proceeding with my teaching. Then I notice that she (the disruptive student) hasn't moved and is showing no indication that she intends to comply with my request.

One important thing about asking the question in this instance needs to be mentioned. Notice that when I asked her the question, I didn't ask for an answer. When I do go back to her and she says, "No way, I'm not going to do it," my response will probably be, "Did I ask in a nice way?" I'm still in tune with the rest of the group and my teaching has not stopped. The interchange between me and the misbehaving student is still private. The rest of the class still doesn't know what's going on, although they may wish they knew.

I'm basically asking, "Does that mean you're not going to do what I asked?" When she says, "No way," I change the rules—another fifteen seconds total. And during that time I have not abandoned the rest of the group. I would not like for that kid to think that I'm going to make such a big deal over her misbehavior that I would take time out from teaching the class. In fact, the message that I'd like to send in this situation is, "Hey, this a piece of cake—I won't have to take a lot of time out from my teaching for this. No sweat."

And if the other kids want to know what I said to her later on, I would probably say, "Hey, you know, I would never share with the rest of class the things I say to a kid in private. That's kind of private stuff, but thanks for asking anyway."

There is one more question to consider. Let's suppose you're doing just fine with this kid over here. She's handling it okay. You're handling it okay. And now we've got her counsel over here, a lawyer from the fourth row back, telling her what to do and lending a little moral support. I would probably just look back and smile and say, "Good try" or "We'll talk about it later" and move on.

Dr. Foster Cline teaches about an idea called "the assumption of compliance," which is incorporated into the techniques we have been discussing. What we have observed is that when we talk to a kid in a way that portrays our assumption of compliance, the odds are raised immensely that the kid will do what we ask. When I smile and say, "Thank you" at the end of a request and then move right on to what I was doing, I have given the implied message of expectation that the kid will cooperate.

The assumption of compliance is just as powerful in the negative sense. If I say, "We'll talk about that later" and then stare at the kid, I am basically saying, "I don't believe you're going to do what I'm asking. Let's have our power struggle right now." The messages are nonverbal, but they are definitely saying, "Hey, keep it up." And keep in mind that our nonverbal messages are much more powerful than words could ever be.

Let me give you one more thought on this, because in order to change a kid's location, it's essential that we give a message that says, "There are actions I want you to take, but this is not a threat." To do this, we need to use words that will convey respect and dignity.

Systematic Suspension
edited from the work of Jim Fay

Increasingly restrictive interventions involve appointments with the administrator regarding consultation, parent conferences, and student suspensions. The only thing you don't see on that list is systematic suspension. This is a very specific technique that obviously must be used with considerable forethought.

The parties of systematic suspension are the principal, the teacher, the parents, and the kid. All need to get together to draw up the arrangement. If the student is enrolled in a special education program or has a "504" accommodation plan, we already have a potential vehicle for this strategy. In other cases, a contract can be formulated. Whatever is used, the plan basically says that this student is allowed to attend school for as many minutes or hours per day as he or she can be there without interrupting what's going on in the classroom. The teacher identifies specific misbehaviors, and when they see these, it is time for the child to go home for the rest of the day.

That is not something the teacher can do unilaterally. It's going to be tough because the parents may attack us and say, "But if my kid is out of school that's just what he wants. He's not learning a thing."

If this happens, we need to state, "You are absolutely right, that's what we're worried about, too. When he's out of school he's not learning anything. And we've also discovered something else. When he's at school acting like he has been, he's not learning anything either. We're beginning to wonder if it matters where he does not learn. What does matter is that we can still run school and that other people can learn."

When we get to the point where we fear the parents who send us responsible kids as much as we fear the parents who send us irresponsible kids, we will turn this nation around. We have too many kids in class today creating situations where they do not learn and nobody else learns because we're afraid to enact a systematic suspension.

Another thought I want to convey is that for every technique you can imagine, you can find a kid it won't work on. These techniques work wonderfully to maintain a classroom, but often when teachers say that a technique didn't work, what they mean is that it didn't do therapy for the kid. He is not now cured of his problem.

Some kids bring problems to school that will only be cured with some pretty intensive therapy. Some kids come to school from such a bad life that there isn't a technique in the world that would work other than putting them somewhere and letting them calm down for a while. The interventions we have just covered will not do therapy. However, they will help maintain the classroom. They will build better relationships, but we need to always be aware that some kids may still need special professional help.

The purpose of short-term strategies is not only to redirect a student but also to serve as the conduit for setting the foundation for transition and long-term strategies. Often, the three are mutually interdependent. Especially with difficult situations, the long-term strategies can't be instituted because the student's current behavior is so disruptive that these strategies doesn't have much of a chance to take root.

CHAPTER 12

Transition Interventions

Using Point B to Get Point A to Point C

As with many things in life, there is a transition that must occur between dissimilar events. At my age, when I drive for long periods of time, the transition from sitting in my car to standing is the hard part. Once I am upright for a while, my muscles and joints are just fine.

Transitioning from short-term to long-term strategies will also often require the use of mediating strategies. Essentially, these are unilateral relationship-building strategies. That is, the teacher takes the initiative and reciprocity is not a criterion. The "Two-Minute Intervention," discussed in Chapter 8, is an example of a transition strategy. This chapter gives examples of other interventions, based on the Four Key Principles, that serve to mediate between short- and long-term techniques.

Stay Until You Are Done

One of the alternative schools I have worked with has a wonderful transition type of strategy. It is effective and probably has the highest guarantee of success of any technique I have seen. However, there are certain variables that need to be in place before even trying it. The strategy is that kids stay at school until they are done with the day's work. Now, in a public school, with teachers hardly able to wait until the day is over, there will definitely need to be some soul-searching and planning for this to work.

In this particular alternative school, staff do not look at this extended day as a negative—they look at it as overtime pay. They would stay with the kids for hours—in fact, the longer, the better. And it doesn't much matter why a kid refuses to do work. For some, it is oppositional. For the kid whom our district placed in this school, it was because of a pathological shutdown. That's what got him there in the first place. He would shut down at school and his teachers just could not get him out of his funk (no pun intended). Then, the last bell would ring and the kid would go home.

The first week he was at this new school, he tried his stuff. He did a wonderful job of shutting down—he had practiced for years and was an expert. However, rather than ending with the ringing of a bell, his day continued. Actually, it continued until almost 8:00 that night—more than five hours after the other students had finished their day.

His teacher earned a few extra bucks that day, and the kid learned a lesson that was priceless. He had subsequent mini-shutdowns, but they lasted for minutes, not hours. He stayed after school one more time (for about half an hour) and the situation never repeated itself.

This strategy does take some effort and preplanning. It can be very inconvenient. But it works. And the real value lies in its transitional effect: it prepares kids to be receptive to the real goal of behavior management—long-term behavioral change.

Time-Out

edited from the work of Jim Fay

Time-out has been terribly abused in America. I would never tell parents I used time-out in my classroom, because they have probably heard all the wild horror stories. Because the term has a negative connotation, I would call it things like "the office of productive thinking," the "think-it-over place," or better yet, I'd have the kids name it.

The kids in my classroom named it "Australia." It was behind the filing cabinet and they had a big sign they had made themselves that said "Australia" in huge letters. It had a picture of a beach and palm trees and kids could go to Australia when they wanted to get away from the other kids. They could go there when I needed them to get away from me.

Originally, time-out was a strategy advocated by a school of psychology that determined that kids needed to have an opportunity to get away from their teacher for a while, and that the teacher needed an opportunity to get away from the kids. It was intended to be a way to maintain the integrity of the teaching environment.

Time-out became abused when people started using it without its intended options and choices. The original design allowed children to come back to class when they knew they could handle the limits that were placed upon the group. So basically, a kid could stay there for thirty seconds, he could stay there for thirty days. It didn't make any difference. The kid was in control of that.

Well it wasn't too long before people started abusing time-out and actually giving the kids an opportunity to use the concept of time-out as a way to escalate the power struggle with the teachers. Teachers did this by saying to the kid, "You go over there and stay until I tell you to come back" or "You go there for twenty minutes" or "You go there for an hour."

Then teachers started giving kids additional opportunity to resist by saying, "And you do your work while you're in there." Then the kids really had something they could use as a club. The sad part for those people who use time-out in this way is that often kids can get themselves together in three or four minutes. If they've been put in time-out for an hour, they have plenty of time to figure out how to get even.

I had a little girl back in the days when I did not know this. I had sent her to time-out with the instruction to stay there until I was ready for her to return to the class. About an hour later I went back for her. What I found was that while she was there, she'd done $370 worth of damage to a solid oak door with a nail she had picked up somewhere. That's what she did with all that extra time. Nobody heard it, nobody saw it. She didn't have the money to replace it, neither did her parents.

As I look back on the situation, I realize that she probably got herself together in three minutes and had fifty-seven minutes left to figure out how to get revenge. Does anybody want to give a kid that much power? I don't ever again want to give a kid fifty-seven minutes to figure out how to get even with me.

There are some other commonly asked questions I would like to address. Many ask if work should be sent with the kid. I prefer not. Time-out is a think-it-over place. Another question is whether we should prescribe a certain amount of time. Again, I prefer to have the kid in charge of when to come back. This involves shared control, which might avert a needless power struggle.

A tricky question is whether the kid should have some counseling when he or she comes back from a time-out session. My answer to this is that counseling is not always necessary. For some kids, it's appropriate and they will respond positively, but for most, I would say probably no. However, I would emphasize that this is a judgment call based on the circumstances and the kid.

Another commonly asked question concerns what to do if you don't have a time-out area in your room. If that is the case, I would suggest making one. I know of one teacher who brought a beach umbrella to school and just put it down on the floor in the back of her room. It was big enough to provide a visual barrier and the kids just went behind it. Some teachers move bookcases around to create a little place where a kid can sit and be alone. It's basically a place where there's no visual contact with buddies.

If you have kids who prefer to be in time-out for massive amounts of time, they're telling you something. They're telling you that they have some kind of problem and that it may not be solvable within the classroom setting. They may be telling you that they need some professional help, because basically kids want to be around other flesh and blood.

This brings us to another issue that can arise where kids are repeatedly sent to time-out, come back on their own accord, and start acting up again. Now if that happens, we need to consider something different. It may mean that we need to go for a more intense level of time-out. If this is the case, I would want to involve the parents.

When I mention parental involvement, I may strike a nerve with a number of teachers, but if we handle the situation in a certain way, there need not be much anxiety. In situations where the parent is involved, I would probably have a discussion similar to the following script:

JIM: (Addressing the parent:) I'd like to have a little talk with Joyce (the student). I realize you know her better than I do, so when I get done with this conference with her, I'd like to get your reactions to our discussion.

Notice how that comment gives the parent their role. It's well defined. Then I get close to Joyce with good eye contact, a smile, and a positive attitude. The dialogue would be something like the following:

JIM: Joyce, do you think I have been sending you to time-out because you're a bad kid or because I just can't teach when there are distractions? What do you guess?

JOYCE: Misbehaving?

JIM: No. I'm sending you because I get distracted and when I get distracted, do I teach well or not teach well?

JOYCE: Not well?

JIM: Exactly. Yes. So I don't teach well. Now we've established that I'm not sending you there because you're bad, just so that I can teach. So, then who's in charge of deciding how long you stay there. Have I been deciding or have you?

JOYCE: Me.

JIM: You've been. Right. So you come back when you decide, and lately I've noticed that you've been going out and coming back in quite a bit, so would you say you're spending a lot of time or not much time going to time-out?

JOYCE: Lots of time.

At this point, Joyce's mother needs to hear about the amount of time being spent in time-out from Joyce's mouth, not mine. She'll believe Joyce. Then I would continue, this time involving the parent:

JIM: So I guess what we're here to decide is what would be a reasonable number of times to go to time-out in one day. It's kind of like I'm asking this, Joyce, if you went "x" number of times, you'd say, "Well, that's pretty normal for a kid," but then if you went one more time, it would be like saying, "I guess I just can't handle class today." So what do you think would be reasonable—three or four?

JOYCE: (Nods in the affirmative.)

JIM: I guess I could put up with three easily enough. Would you say that's reasonable?

JOYCE:	Yes.
JIM:	Then, if I'm hearing you right, if you went on to the fourth time it would be like waving a flag and saying, "Guess class is just too hard for me to handle today." Does that sound reasonable?
JOYCE:	I agree with that.
JIM:	Well, put it there. (Jim and Joyce shake hands.)

(Turning to the mother:) It looks like Joyce is saying that three times would be pretty reasonable and then the fourth time it would be like she's saying she can't handle it here today. Let me tell you what works the best and then you tell me how that affects you, because we don't want to make a problem for you just because Joyce is making a problem in the classroom. Fair enough?

MOTHER:	Fair.
JIM:	What seems to work the best is if we could have you say, "Joyce, when this happens, go down to the phone, call home, I'll come over and pick you up. I'll take you home and let you sit in your room the rest of the day and think this over so you can get all prepared to go back the next day."

Now this would be with no lectures, no questions. Nothing but sadness. "Oh that's sad it didn't work out." Now that seems to be the thing that works best. How does that affect you?

MOTHER:	Well, since I don't have a job it might work out all right.
JIM:	It might work out all right while you don't have a job, and what I hear you saying is that if you go to work we might have to change? Since that might happen, let's discuss the next best way just in case we need that.

The second best way is to use a room we've got in the school. It's unsupervised, but it's safe. We could, at your written request, allow her to go there for the rest of the day and then try regular school again the next day. We would also give no lectures, no threats, no telling her how bad she is—none of that. Now that's a possibility. Would that feel any better to you or not better? What do you think?

. . . . .

MOTHER: That would work out really well, especially if I were out and you couldn't get hold of me.

JIM: So, what I'm hearing is that this would work out well if we couldn't get hold of you. Okay. Well, thank you.

(Turning back to Joyce:) Joyce is there anything else we need to talk about? Can you think of anything else you'd like to say here?

JOYCE: No.

JIM: Are you feeling that this is fair or not fair?

JOYCE: I guess it's fair.

JIM: Well, I guess let's shake on that. Thank you.

Notice that throughout this entire scenario, although I have not said that Joyce must stay in time-out for a given amount of time, I have given a strongly implied message of how long that time might be. For instance, I could have determined the amount of time by saying, "You can go there and think it over and then you're welcome to come back the next day." Notice how the delivery can take a lot of the threat out of the penalty.

What should the time-out area be like? I think the ideal would be a little room with a bare light bulb and a chair. However, we don't have a lot of those kinds of rooms available. At any rate, I prefer not to put a beanbag chair where kids can put their feet up and be really comfortable. I also don't want it to be a really negative place. So any place where there is no human contact, a place where the kid can easily get out, would be appropriate.

One of the most effective time-out areas involves a reciprocal agreement with other teachers. In other words, teachers make an agreement to use each other's rooms for a time-out spot. There may be some details to work out, like sending only one kid at a time, or if the kid is disruptive in the time-out area he or she is returned to the original teacher.

This method is effective in large part because we are also engaging another factor discussed previously: changing location. Using another teacher's room is also usually more acceptable to the principal, because the kids are supervised.

Now at the high school level, time-out takes a totally different form. There, the message is, "Hey, I don't want to force you to be in class, I don't want to make life tough for you, please feel free to be somewhere else." We will need to negotiate with the administrators to discover an acceptable place for kids to be when they're not in the classroom.

I once talked to some kids at Roosevelt High School in the Portland area. They were talking about the teachers they liked the best and teachers they didn't like. That day I talked to the eight toughest kids in that high school.

One of my questions was, "What kind of teachers do you like?" Their answer surprised me: "Well, we like teachers who will try to understand us and give us help when we ask for some." That's all they were asking for. Somebody who knew and responded to them as a person. Some might think that these really tough kids would want the world's greatest, perfect teacher, but they just said they wanted somebody who was friendly, somebody who cared about them. They wanted somebody who treated them with respect.

That's the bottom line for all of the interventions discussed here. I encourage teachers to treat kids with dignity and talk to them with the language of respect, in a way that we would talk to a best friend. That's the kind of teacher the Roosevelt kids were asking for. That day I also asked them what teachers they most disliked being around. They had a quick answer: "Oh, the ones who only know how to say three things: 'Sit down, shut up, go to the principal.' It seems that for some teachers, that's all they know to say."

That was a fun and informative day. The kids were a delight. Those kids are always a lot of fun for me and it always appears that they know more about the real world than the kids who behave all the time. They had some opinions about teachers that I thought were insightful. When I asked about what they were really looking for in a teacher, I found out that they didn't have impossibly high standards. It seemed they just wanted somebody who knew them personally, liked having them in the classroom, and was willing to answer their questions when they had some problems.

What they definitely didn't like was people who came in with the purpose of making them be or act in a certain way. And they certainly didn't like the people who said, "Sit down, shut up, and get out," because the kids were really nasty in the way they talked about those teachers.

A lot of times kids come to school already thinking that they're not so great. Their self-concept is pretty damaged and they have a tendency to listen for the messages that teachers send that confirm this view of themselves. Even sadder, they tend not to hear the messages from teachers that say, "You're okay." The teacher with a kid who is always looking for the negative message will need to be especially aware to keep this cycle from repeating.

I am painfully aware that this cycle often starts in the early elementary years, and we can even see it beginning in kindergarten. In fact, students who quit school when they are sixteen probably dropped out in the second grade. Their bodies were simply removed in high school. They have dropped out as soon as they have said, "Hey, school is not for me. The other kids are better students, the teachers like the other kids better, and I have no place here." Finally, when they can't stand the pain anymore, out they go.

To enhance the effectiveness of time-out, I will often focus the kids' thinking with the following five questions:

1. What happened?
2. How did I feel?
3. What did I do?
4. How did it work out?
5. What am I going to do the next time?

I allow the kid to go to time-out and either think through the answers or write them down. Notice that the questions are oriented to having the students think about a cause-and-effect relationship. These questions also focus students on how they have reacted in the past and whether they think it is best for them to continue their current behavior.

Sometimes there will be kids who want to act like time-out is a joke and try to sabotage the technique by peeking around the corner or yelling out to their friends. With those kids, I simply tell them that this is a quiet, think-it-over place, but that there is another place that they can go if they need to. In other words, I'm not saying that the behavior is bad, just that it's misplaced.

I may need to negotiate with the principal on a different time-out place for those kids. One that is secluded, but safe. Ordinarily that requires involvement of the parent. When all are in agreement, we can sit down and say, "Sometimes kids need places where they can swear, stamp their feet, jump up and down, kick, scream, peek around the corners, and all that kind of stuff. We have a perfect place like that right outside. You're welcome to go out there when you need to, and you're welcome either to come back to class or to go to the quiet time-out area when you get all of those behaviors out of your system."

Providing Natural or Logical Consequences with Empathy
edited from the work of Jim Fay

The key word to emphasize for this intervention is "empathy." Imagine that Al has been caught fighting in the parking lot and has been sent to the principal's office. Let's further suppose that the school rule for this behavior is a three-day suspension. If we were going to issue a negative content message (you're out of school), we can balance it with a positive ego message (we'll miss you). The following conversation would be typical:

JIM: Looks like you got caught fighting again. Those guys must have really made you mad to fight like that. I bet I would have felt the same way. And a fight like that will earn you how many days of suspension?

AL: Three.

JIM: Three. That's right. So we'll get to see you when?

AL: Monday.

JIM: Monday. Well, we'll look forward to seeing you. I'd appreciate having you stop by when you get back. Okay?

The consequence has fallen and Al will be out for three days. If he is like most kids, he will be hurting inside and will be asking the question, "Who caused all this pain for me?" In all likelihood he will run down the list of possibilities and when he gets to the principal will probably say, "It's not him; he was concerned for me and is looking forward to my return." Our hope is that his ultimate answer will be, "This pain was caused by my bad decision." This acknowledgment of responsibility is a key to internalizing control, and the conditions to encourage this acceptance can be determined largely by the interaction of the adult.

The key to this orientation is empathy in conjunction with the consequence. So often we dispense the consequence with anger, retaliation, or threats. And then what happens? Imagine the same scenario if the principal, in "attack mode," had said to Al, "You're not going to fight around here, understand? That's three days' suspension! You're out of here, don't come back until Monday! We've had it with you! We're not putting up with that stuff! You're history!"

And as the kid leaves the classroom, he is no longer history—he's making it because he will probably be asking the same question as in the first example, "I'm hurting, and who caused all this pain for me?" There will be no question in his mind that the principal is responsible. When that is established, the kid will have no hesitation to seek revenge through vandalism or other acts of retaliation.

It is vitally important to go through this process with suspensions so that the student does not view the circumstance as a vacation. This is what happens far too often.

Informational Letters and Phone Calls
edited from the work of Jim Fay

Informational telephone calls and informational letters have about the same effect, so it doesn't matter which we use. However, it does take a professional judgment for us to decide whether it would be better for this kid to call his parents to notify them of his behavior and tell them about his plan of action so he can involve them in his thoughts, or whether it would be better for the student to write down this information. Some kids are better off writing it down, because you have more control over what they actually deliver to the parents.

If they are going to make an informational phone call, I would recommend contacting the parents ahead of time. Fill them in about the situation and what the kid will be talking about. Be sure to tell them that you don't want them to take on the problem. Instead, ask if they could just listen to their child talk about the problem and about the solution. Then, when the child is done, ask the parents to end the conversation by saying, "Thanks for sharing. Is there any way I can help?" When that happens, we have a true informational phone call.

If the parents agree to cooperate, I ask them to not let the kid know that I called ahead. It's interesting to see what happens if the kid has a different story, because most people will believe the first person they hear on a given subject. I've seen kids half get killed over the telephone, and I didn't need to be the bad guy.

Sometimes these informational letters need to go to businesses or to neighbors, because a lot of older kids are real adept at stopping by the mailbox to see if anything has a return address from school. We can outsmart the kids if we take our time and plan our actions while we're in the thinking state.

Sally Ogden has some wonderful informational letters. One of them says, "Dear Mom, you're right, it happened again. I'm going to get an 'F' in French. Please don't blame my teacher. She's worked hard. I've just been messing around too much. I'm going to get my act together." Signed, "Daniel, who loves you dearly."

It's amazing the impact these letters and calls can have.

Contingent Restrictions
edited from the work of Jim Fay

Sometimes having kids simply submit a written plan works great, sometimes it doesn't. Sometimes kids come up with wonderful ideas, but they don't work. If so, we move on to restricting the student. With this intervention, students are still restricted from the area of the infraction, but on different terms. Once they come up with a new plan of action and describe to you what they're going to do to replace the infractional behavior, they are given permission to regain privileges one day at a time.

Each successful day earns students one more day, but they do not assume that they have this privilege on a permanent basis. Students follow a schedule that reviews their performance on a daily basis. The following dialogue would be typical:

JIM:	Okay, Ralph, we are going to let you go out to the playground on Thursday. If you have a good day on Thursday, what's your guess about Friday?
RALPH:	I get to play.
JIM:	Right! And if you have a good day on Friday, what about Monday?

. . . . .

RALPH:	I get to play again.
JIM:	Right! And if you blow it on Monday, what's your guess about Tuesday?
RALPH:	Don't go out.
JIM:	Good thinking. Hope it works out for you.

We may need some additional instruction at this point. Ralph, in our example, has come up with a new action plan to manage his own behavior and it's in line with what you, the teacher, want him to do. It may seem that we have indicated that he's now seeing playground time as a right he earns for good behavior or something you restrict as punishment.

I think I see the situation a little differently. I'm not looking at going to the playground as something he has earned. First of all, he has a new behavior, but it's an action plan he developed. He says, "Here's what I'm going to do instead of the old behavior." So the odds are that he's going to be able to behave a little bit better now. But when he does go back onto the playground, what we're really looking for is proof from him that he is demonstrating his establishment of self-control and trustworthiness. We're not saying he's earning a privilege, he's just showing that he can demonstrate self-control on a day-to-day basis.

As people read this, I assume that they are thinking of adapting this intervention to various situations they have experienced. I want to interject an additional thought. The trick is to have the child do the adapting. All you do is say, "Well, that's not working out too well in the classroom, you're welcome to come back when you can figure out a new behavior." Or, "That's not working too well in the halls. Glad to let you use the halls when you can come up with a new behavior." Or, "That's not working too well in the lunchroom. Feel free to come back when you've got a new plan of action."

These are all opportunities for the kids to do some thinking, and they orient kids toward internalizing controls.

I Messages
edited from the work of Jim Fay
When talking about "I Messages," I'm often asked about a specific situation in which we have a chronic liar. This is the kid who says his dog died

and gets a lot sympathy. Later we find out that none of the story was true, and we feel we've been played for a patsy. However, to redeem this circumstance, we could use this as an opportunity to teach the kid a valuable lesson for life about the benefits of being trustworthy.

Before we go further, I need to say a couple of things about lying. First, lying can captivate adults like nothing else. When that happens, we often aren't aware of the really important things that are going on. Simply put, we can get too involved in lying.

Let's also keep in mind that there are two kinds of kids—kids who lie and never get caught, and kids who lie and do get caught. When kids lie, they present us with an ideal situation for an "I Message." When I know a kid has lied, I might say, "When I hear stories from you that I later find out are not true, it takes away most of my fun of listening to what you have to say."

Some teachers would say that this sounds a little wimpy. There are many teachers who think that when a kid makes the trip to the principal's office for lying, or for any other infraction, the experience hasn't been effective if they don't see any trail of blood as the kid leaves. Without an understanding of "I Messages," it's very easy to say that they are not effective.

We need to keep in mind what our goal is when working with kids. Do we want them to be burdened down with some kind of heavy guilt, or do we what them to consider the long-term consequences of their behavior and make a volitional decision to change? Do we want to lock the kids into the emotional state, or do we want to usher them into the thinking state?

If kids want you to listen to their stories and now realize that, because of their lying, you have much less interest in hearing them, my guess is that the kids will do some pondering—deep thinking about what they are doing. They already know the lecture on trust, and to repeat the moral harangue may simply lock them deeper into their behavior.

There is another very important piece of information about "I Messages" that needs to be discussed. Thomas Gordon taught people how to use effective "I Messages," but a problem often arose—the other person ended up having the last word. This left a situation where the "listener" could neutralize the effect of the "I Message" by ending the interaction on a negative note.

So the question of the hour is how the speaker can have the last word without escalating a power struggle or otherwise compromising the value of the "I Message." And there are times when we do need to have the last word. Not so much to save face, but to indicate to kids that they don't have unilateral control of the situation, or perhaps to bring closure to the situation quickly.

For instance, let's suppose I go over to a kid and say, "I get distracted when there are pencils tapping." This is a respectable beginning to the "I Message," to which I could reasonably expect a cordial reply. However, instead of reciprocating my respect, the kid says, "I like distracting you and besides, I can think better when I'm tapping my pencil, so bug off."

To have the final word in these situations, I need to use a self-referencing statement—one that will be difficult to counter as invalid. I might say, "I just wanted you to know how I felt and I was hoping you might take that into consideration." With this statement, I haven't ordered the kid to stop, but I have given him some additional information and there is little for him to react against.

It would be satisfying if we said a statement like this, had the last word, and had a clean final closure on the interaction. But we have all had kids who, if we give them the "I just wanted you to know how I felt" statement, would simply respond, "I don't really care how you feel." People will respond this way for any number of reasons. Sometimes to save face in front of their pals, sometimes to strike out, sometimes to gain control, and sometimes as just a knee-jerk reaction. Whatever the reason, we need to be prepared with a continuation of the self-referencing statement that says, "That's probably true, but I was hoping that telling you how I felt would make a difference." Again, the purpose is to apply the Four Key Principles in a way that can leave us both winners.

Give the Student an Appointment to Talk About the Problem
edited from the work of Jim Fay
The next intervention is to give the student an appointment to talk about the problem. This strategy is especially effective for kids who use hit-and-run techniques. Have you ever seen those in the classroom? A kid shouts out, and when you say, "You can't do that in this room," the kid says, "I already did." In those situations, effective consequences are extremely difficult to think of and administer on the spot.

That's the time when I want to cruise by and in a very quiet way say, "We'll have an appointment to discuss that." Then I give the kid some control by saying, "School is out at 3:00 and I could meet you at 3:15 or at 3:30, which would be better for you?" If the kid says, "But school is out at 3:00, why can't we meet then?" I simply respond, "My early appointment is at 3:15 today. Good thing it wasn't yesterday. You know what time the early appointment was yesterday? After the faculty meeting. So, what's your choice?"

Now, do I make a big deal when the kid comes in for this appointment? No. Here's my dialogue with Al:

JIM: Al, thanks for coming in for the appointment. I just wanted to let you know that this afternoon when you were shouting out in class I got so distracted you probably noticed I did a crummy job of teaching. So I just wanted to share that with you. Thanks for coming in. You have a nice evening.

AL: You kept me here all this time just to say that?

JIM: Well, you know, I wanted to say it when I was calm. You have a nice evening.

Now, will Al need to think about that a little bit? My hope is that he will think a lot. Does that mean the problem is cured? Probably not. He might need another appointment down the line. If the problem happens again, I would probably make another appointment the same way. And this time the dialogue would be something like the following:

JIM: Al, thanks for coming in. You remember the discussion we had last time about shouting in class?

AL: No.

JIM: You don't remember that? Well, there's the problem right there. Thanks for being honest about it. So let me go over it again. When I hear that shouting, I get distracted and then what?

AL: You can't teach.

JIM: At least I can't teach well. So that's what this meeting is all about. Now, did I not do a very good job of explaining that to you last time, or did you decide you wanted to be disruptive anyway? I'm just kind of curious where you are on this. Have I done something that makes you so mad that you want to get even with me? If so, maybe you might want to share that with me and see if I can change. Do you have any thoughts on this?

AL: Not now.

JIM: Not now? Maybe this is a bad time to talk about it then. I have a lot of papers to grade. Why don't I just give you a quiet place to think and maybe later on you might have some thoughts on it. So take your time. There's no big hurry.

At that point I will probably just start working on my papers. If by the time I am ready to go home, he still doesn't have any thoughts, I might continue the dialogue:

JIM: Still don't have any thoughts?

AL: No.

JIM: Tell me this, are you planning on continuing to shout out or not continuing? What do you think?

AL: No.

JIM: What does "no" mean?

AL: No shouting.

JIM: You're not going to shout out anymore. Well, I appreciate that. Thank you for coming in.

You might be thinking, "But what if he doesn't show up?" Well, that's a good possibility for many of the more resistant kids. The nice thing about school is that the kid will probably show up sometime. I haven't lost my opportunity to work with this kid. I could get my blood pressure up and go home tonight and eat holes in the bottom of my stomach with all the black bile that I create over this whole issue, or I could call the parent and say, "Al didn't show up for his appointment today. With your permission, I would like to reschedule this for tomorrow. Please don't tell him that I called, but I want to pick him up from his last-hour class and have the discussion then."

I work out any details I need to with the parent like transportation, being late to other activities, and so on. The next day, I let Al get all the way through to the last class period. Prior to that time, I have made arrangements with the last-hour teacher to hold him for me. Then I meet Al at the class and say, "Hey, Al, remember the appointment yesterday? We didn't get it done. So let's do it now?"

Typically, kids will kick in their most creative powers and will think of a way this plan would get the teacher in trouble by involving another teacher, activity, or even the parent. This is why preplanning is so important. So, when he says, "But I got football practice and the coach would be really mad and the team would be let down, so I can't come now," I simply say, "No problem. I talked to your mom and the coach. They both said being late for practice would be all right, under the circumstances. They said you can go after we have the discussion."

If the kid is worth his salt, he won't give up. We can expect him to say, "Well, this is stupid!" We've already rehearsed what to say to counter this: "Probably so, and you are free to go to practice when we have had our talk." Maybe he's going to say, "But I ride the bus." My reply, "No big deal, your mom said she would come over and pick you up. By the way, she also said you should be prepared to pay for her gas and time."

When we have used this technique a couple of times, we will learn to cover all the bases ahead of time. We can actually outthink kids if we don't do it in the heat of battle. If we try to make decisions when we are in an emotional state, all of our other responsibilities will come to mind and the kids will probably outthink us.

CHAPTER 13

Long-Term
Interventions

The Focus of All Intervention

The element of long-term strategies is reciprocal relationship based on trust. The components of trust, discussed in Chapter 9, bear review. A prime characteristic of long-term strategies is unconditional regard, but with high expectations. That is a skillful balance, because the expectation is not generated from obligation, but from desire that accentuates and preserves the value, worth, and personhood of all involved. Characteristics of trust exemplify the elements of these strategies.

The basis of long-term strategies is fairly simple to state, but a bit more complicated to implement. It is, pure and simple, reciprocal trust. That is, there is an interactive involvement in which I believe the other person has my best interest in mind. Interventions that create this kind of bond are absolutely the most powerful. Think of the effects of trust in real-life situations of two people deeply in love, gang-member affiliation, those who have been in military battle together.

The significant factor in these kinds of strategies is that their development takes either time or an event charged with high emotion. Usually, the more damaged the student, the more time or emotion needed. The fact that our school system requires kids to make major moves every nine months, involving new teachers and new situations, is a fundamental problem, because it often takes at least that much time to form trust and relationship. In the area of special education and behavior management, the consistency of staff is vitally important.

Rather than listing only specific strategies, I will also present one of the most poignant stories I recall hearing from Jim Fay. It involved a teacher in Watts and exemplifies the essential characteristic of trust and relationship—the essence of long-term strategies. My hope is that from the information previously presented in this book, the reader will be able to apply this story to specific kids.

The Teacher from Watts

edited from the work of Jim Fay

Some time ago I went to Las Vegas to give a keynote address. Between sessions I had an opportunity to listen to other presenters and, like so many conferences, this one had a lot of presenters who did very, very good things back at their schools and were now coming to share what they were doing. But the problem for some was that they were not experienced speakers.

I went to listen to a woman who was noted as one of the outstanding teachers in the inner-city schools of Los Angeles. She was a teacher of problem students at the high school level and taught what was, in essence, an alternative program within a conventional high school. She had all the kids whom nobody wanted. She had the kids who could not read, kids who could not write, and the tough kids of the school.

She was trying to give a presentation in the same way she had seen it done at her staff development academy. She had all the slides and the overheads and the audios and all the visuals. She had lots of research to share with everybody—but the audience was bored to tears.

In fact, one guy, who was rather straightforward in his communication and probably not the most gentle person in the world, said, "Can it! Look, if you're supposed to be so good, tell us one thing we can take away from this conference that we can use with our kids right away."

You can imagine that this comment just threw her back. But when she recovered, she started talking from the heart and said:

Well, I guess if there was only one thing I could depend on, it would be relationships. All of these kids that I work with are bigger than I am and they're tougher than I am and you can't threaten them with anything. They're not scared of anybody. So I have to rely on getting them to fall in love with me.

. . . . .

And then she said something that made several of us think:

Now, I know that there are a lot of people who hate to hear that phrase, "fall in love with me," because you know so many people, especially your gestapo-type teachers, who have an attitude that says, "I expect these kids to respect me," which basically says, "I get to do anything and they are supposed to respect me because I am an adult."

She went on:

A certain kind of teacher doesn't like to hear the word "love," but with those tough, tough kids, that's what I've got to use. I've got to get them to fall in love with me so deeply that they will do things for me that they would not do for anybody else and especially things they would not do for themselves.

In fact, I have to get them to care so much for me that they're willing to take on the greatest risk that they will ever take on in their entire lives. That risk is not whipping out a knife and taking on some kid out in the alley. That's day-to-day operation with those kids. The biggest risk is to try to do something in front of their peers that they know they cannot do, like show that they've learned something, read something, write it down. I've got to get them to the point where I can go to them and say, "Hey pal, do it for me, please. I know you can do it."

There's only way I know to get that done. On the very first day of school you will see me out in front of my door, shaking hands with those kids, looking in their eyes, smiling and saying, "I'm glad you're going to be in my room." Right away they suspect something crazy. Nobody's ever said that to them before.

I get them doing something in the room that anybody could do, so they can keep busy while I meet every one of those kids before they come into the room. From that day on I'm out there saying, "Gimme five," giving handshakes and smiles, looking at them and showing them I care. I want to be human with them. I want to show that I care about them as a person far more than I care about them as a student.

Then I start noticing little things about them and asking questions. I say, "Did your sister get back from the hospital yet?" "How's your mom doing with the new baby?" "Did you get to play ball this week?" "Are you driving yet?" I ask about those kinds of personal things so that they start to know that I know them as a person. Largely because of this relationship I have with my kids, I have some special privilege at school. For instance, I am the only person on that staff who can leave the faculty meeting before the principal finishes talking. We have a staff meeting every Wednesday morning and we have a long-winded principal, so he often does not finish on schedule.

The first time he didn't end on time I got up and said, "I have to leave; I have to meet my kids at the door." He looked a bit indignant and said, "This is important, stay here." To that I said, "Look, if I can't meet those kids ahead of time, then somebody else on this staff is going to have to teach them." At that point, all of the teachers said in unison, "Send her, it's okay. We'll share the information with her later." I'm the only person on the staff that can get by with that. I'm also the only person on the staff who doesn't have to worry about my car in the parking lot. Those kids take care of that for me.

The only thing that I have to rely on is the fact that I can build a relationship with them so they want to do for me what they may not even be willing to do for themselves and they don't want to mess up my life by messing around in class.

As I listened to her "presentation," it was a gentle reminder that we can't abandon this whole idea that teaching is building positive relationships with kids so that they want to do what we ask them to do. It's an art.

Introductory Letters

Whenever I have read about behavior strategies, most often the topic is what to do when or after the student is actually engaged in the misbehavior. However, there is much to say for setting an atmosphere prior to problems happening and for addressing what causes most misbehavior in the first place (e.g., inflictions of self-concept and autonomy).

These pre-interventions, as it were, can have significant effect, because information is given when most people are in the thinking state and not just running on emotion. When I first started teaching Love and Logic as a graduate course, we used a manual that had a story from Jim's early experience as a principal. This story taught me a couple of things. First, preparatory activities have a great value in reducing the potential for problems. Second, discipline problems are not always just centered on the kid. Parents who cause trouble also need to be within the loop.

The problem centered around students not bringing lunch money. Before Jim took on the principalship of an elementary school, lending kids money for lunch took hours of valuable secretarial time. One of Jim's first decisions was that children would no longer be lent money for lunch or allowed to use school phones for free. Parents in that upscale community rose up in arms and wanted Jim's head on a platter. Jim learned from this experience that many problems can be avoided if information is given when everyone is relatively calm. His letter went as follows:

Dear Parents:

In the past, we have done a poor job of teaching your children responsibility. We have been lending them money for lunches if they forgot their lunch money or sack lunch. Needless to say, we have a number of chronic forgetters. From now on, we are going to do a better job of teaching responsibility and not lend lunch money. If you feel that your child is one of those few who may not be able to cope with learning the realities of life in this new way, please give me a ring and we'll talk it over personally.

There was not one call from parents. Now, you may ask, what does this have to do with a discipline strategy? This concept can be applied to writing each kid a personal letter before school begins. Putting your picture with the letter adds to familiarity. Better yet, visit your students in their homes. If it is not possible to do this for all of your students, do so on a selective basis or meet with small groups at a time. Of course, this is time consuming, but it is well worth the investment.

Rituals

Getting kids to feel they are accepted as part of a group is not only a worthy goal, it is a practical one as well. When kids feel they are part of the class, it becomes much like their own possession. And unless there is some extreme circumstance, we usually take pretty good care of our own stuff.

A teacher in one of my graduate courses presented this idea as a class project. He always has some introductory activity written on the chalkboard or overhead for kids to start on as the enter the class. Most of these are visual brain-teasers that must be deciphered to identify a common saying. He celebrates success with scripted cheers ("Ahoogah, ahoogah, shish boom bah"), and daily sends a kid on a "mission" to run to another classroom and wish the teacher a good day. The room is completely decorated by the kids (not a bare wall present) and music (selected by the kids, screened by the teacher) plays at appropriate times.

When a classroom is unique and kids are part of that uniqueness, a sense of belonging locks in. This addresses the issue of self-worth and starts the cycle of maintaining a positive learning environment. An extension of this concept of ritual is providing opportunity for student input into the operation of the classroom. Think about the long-term effects reflected in the following concepts:

Have students identify what they want to know about a particular curricular topic as soon as the required content is covered. ("What would you like to learn once we get through chapter 5?")

Guide students into developing rules for the classroom that conform to given parameters. ("What rule could we write to show people we want everyone in class to feel safe?")

Create situations that will develop more effective evaluation procedures. ("We have identified several ways students can show they have learned the content [e.g., tests, reports, presentations, etc.]; however, how can we tell what letter grade a student should get?")

A Word About Intensive Interventions

Whether we have worked in special education for a long time or a short time, we all recognize that there are periodic situations that will take more intensive intervention than any described in this text. These kinds and levels of strategies have been purposely left out of this book because without specific training (and oftentimes certification), liability for both individual staff and the district can increase substantially. Such techniques require specific coaching, practice, and periodic formal review and cannot be learned from reading a book.

In addition, some students require intervention that is therapeutic, not educational. Interventions that use techniques that are invasive, require medication, or utilize psychotherapy are outside the purview of even the most skilled teacher. Legal penalties for actions outside one's certification area are not at all fun to deal with.

We must also recognize that there are some students who are so damaged that the strategies teachers are able to implement are not sufficient. Students who are in the deep throes of reactive attachment disorder (RAD), schizophrenia, or other mental conditions need more than what even the finest public school can provide. Unfortunately for all concerned, the presumption is generally that being educated with peers of one's own age in a regular school is an absolute right. It isn't, and some kids need healing before academics become a priority.

There is recourse in the special education process, but it is far from simple. When an IEP team recognizes that the student's needs go way beyond what schools can provide, there is a legal obligation to determine what services and placement are necessary to meet the student's disability-related educational needs.

If meeting such needs is not simply a matter of mandating additional staff training, obtaining some technology device, or accessing some other available resource, the IEP team has the authority to ensure that necessary provisions are made available. Such decisions can be costly and inconvenient, and not at all fun; however, so is becoming entangled in the legal system when schools are brought to task for not making appropriate decisions.

I realize the hesitancy of IEP teams in such situations. Often, there will be parental resistance, and there is always the "opportunity" to explain such decisions to district administrators. Coupled with this is the fact that some IEP teams will make decisions to avoid the actual responsibility of dealing with kids they simply don't want anymore. But the honest fact is that some kids need more than what even the most sophisticated program with the most highly skilled teachers can provide. In such cases, as my grandmother used to say, we must "take the bull by the horns" and do what is right.

The End

I end this chapter and this book with words from Jim Fay, the person who got me started with Love and Logic, and who became my mentor and eventually a good friend:

My mission is to present Love and Logic in a way that people can decide if it is right for them, not so they will buy it.

My sincere hope is that I have done this as well.

Index